Elementary Mathematics for Teachers

Thomas H. Parker
Professor of Mathematics
Michigan State University

Scott Baldridge
Professor of Mathematics
Louisiana State University

SEFTON-ASH PUBLISHING
Okemos, Michigan

First published 2004
Reprinted 2008 with typographical errors corrected
Reprinted 2015 with typographical errors corrected and minor wording changes

Published by Sefton-Ash Publishing.
Printed and bound by Quebecor World, MI.
Printed in the United States of America.

ISBN 0-9748140-0-8

Distributed by:
SingaporeMath.com Inc.
404 Beavercreek Road # 225
Oregon City, OR 97045.

To buy this textbook, please visit www.singaporemath.com or call (503) 557−8100.

Cover Artwork: Copyright © 1999 Mary Jean Reusch, *Moral Compass: Disappearing Pear,* oil on canvas, dimensions: 30"× 24," Collection of Grand Valley State University.
Cover Design: Justin Reusch.

To our wives,

Judith Fleishman

and

Lisa Baldridge,

to Daniel and Gregory Parker, who learned it all before the book was finished,

and to Autumn Baldridge, who is learning it now:

www.scottbaldridge.net/autumn

Contents

Preface

This course is a *mathematics* course for elementary teachers. We will not be talking about teaching methods per se — methods are left for your teacher education courses. However, understanding elementary school mathematics from a teacher's perspective requires many things not discussed in most mathematics courses. All teachers, of course, must have a solid knowledge of the material they teach. But an elementary school mathematics teacher needs to know much more, including: (i) how to present the material in the simplest, clearest way, (ii) the appropriate sequential order for developing mathematics skills, and (iii) what the students will find difficult and what errors they are likely to make. A teacher also needs a good sense of how each topic helps advance the mathematical level of the students.

Obviously we cannot develop all those skills in one course. Indeed, such teaching knowledge can be mastered only after years in the classroom. But this course will get you started and, we hope, show you a way of thinking about elementary mathematics that will guide you to become a better teacher every year.

Teaching Elementary Mathematics — Overview

Teaching mathematics well requires a firm understanding of its goals and how they can be attained. This requires knowing the overall structure of the elementary mathematics curriculum, and knowing how the unique features of mathematics bear on teaching.

Elementary school mathematics is not a scattering of topics. Rather, it should be viewed as an upward spiral with two major phases:

- Grades K–4 should thoroughly cover the basics: addition, subtraction, multiplication, division, fractions, and a little geometry.

- Grades 5–7 should be preparation for the more abstract mathematics that starts with a grade 8 Algebra course focusing on quadratic equations and polynomials, and a grade 9 course in Euclidean Geometry, with proofs. Most students find these courses hard and discouraging. But these two subjects are not intrinsically difficult. In other countries *all* students take them as a matter of routine and are expected to master the material. They succeed because they spend grades 5–7 moving beyond arithmetic, taking steps toward algebra and geometry with proofs.

In all grades, a well-designed curriculum takes a balanced approach. The idea of balance has been neatly summarized by Richard Askey, a leading expert in mathematics education:

Like a stool which needs three legs to be stable, mathematics education needs three components: good problems, with many of them being multi-step ones, a lot of technical skill, and then a broader view which contains the abstract nature of mathematics and proofs. One does not get all of these at once, but a good mathematics program has them as goals and makes incremental steps toward them at all levels [9].

All three components are important; none should be neglected or underemphasized. The level of instruction spirals upward as the three components reinforce each other: increased skill at calculational procedures leads to more sophisticated word problems, experience with word problems solidifies conceptual understanding, which in turn allows students to move to the next level of calculational skills.

Teachers should keep the vision of the upward spiral in mind, and should ask themselves during every instructional unit "How will this help my students get to Algebra and Geometry?"

Mathematics is a distinct discipline that uses distinctive thought processes. It cannot be taught in the same manner as language arts or social studies. Successful elementary mathematics curricula, and successful teaching, reflect the uniqueness of mathematics by adhering to the following three principles.

Steady incremental development — More then any other subject, mathematics builds on itself. Knowledge of addition is necessary for learning multiplication, multiplication is necessary for division, division is necessary for fractions, and all are needed for algebra. Coherent curricula proceed step-by-step, with each step carefully placed to build on previous knowledge.

Teachers must take care that the steps are in the correct order, that each step moves the class forward, and that the steps are small enough to be easily taken. In this book we call a series of small steps a "teaching sequence." Larger steps that occur across grade levels are called "curriculum sequences.".

Everything in math makes sense — The ideas of elementary mathematics are simple, logical, and intuitive. Furthermore, different topics are completely consistent with one another. For example, once one knows how to add any two whole numbers, it is not difficult to see how to add decimals. Teaching becomes easier when the simplicity, intuition, and consistency of the subject is brought out.

With this in mind, effective teachers present new ideas in a simple, direct way that helps students make sense out of mathematics. They then provide problems, beginning with easy ones, which allow the students to absorb and internalize the new idea. They slow down and review whenever students are not understanding. At the same time, they guard against reducing mathematics to a set of "rules to be learned," and are careful never to make simple mathematics appear complicated.

Practice — The need for practice and repetition has always been obvious to teachers. Here, for example, is E.B. Huey, a well-known educator from 100 years ago:

Repetition progressively frees the mind from attention to details, makes facile the total act, shortens the time, and reduces the extent to which consciousness must concern itself with the processes [38, pg. 104].

For example, a simple second grade word problem that involves finding $6 + 7$ will be very difficult for the student who is not adept at simple addition. That student will have to focus complete attention on finding $6 + 7$ and will have no energy or attention left to focus on the important skill to be learned from the problem, namely how to move back and forth between the real world situation of the word problem and the underlying arithmetic problem.

Cognitive psychology confirms this. Interesting and varied experiments demonstrate that our short-term memory is quite limited: we can simultaneously retain only 6–8 items in our "working memory." Complex situations can be handled only by filling short term memory with *procedures*. Thus students must be able to find $6 + 7$ quickly enough to be able to keep it in memory as a single item. Such abilities come only through practice and repetition.

For these reasons, practice is an integral part of learning mathematics at all levels. The explanation of cognitive psychologist Steven Pinker is a contemporary echo of Huey's words:

> *The [way] to mathematical competence is similar to the way to get to Carnegie Hall: practice. Mathematical concepts come from snapping together old concepts in a useful new arrangement. But those old concepts are assemblies of still older concepts. Each subassembly hangs together by the mental rivets called chunking and automaticity: with copious practice, concepts adhere into larger concepts, and sequences of steps are complied into a single step. Just as ... recipes say how to make sauces, not how to grasp spoons and open jars, mathematics is learned by fitting together overlearned routines [48, pg. 341].*

Finally, because it is a distinct discipline, mathematics requires distinct classroom instructional methods. We briefly mention four daily goals for mathematics lessons. These are among the many aspects of mathematics which are addressed in teaching methods courses.

Focus on the mathematics — Actual classrooms have many distractions and time constraints. Teachers should enter into each lesson knowing exactly what *mathematics* they want the students to learn that day and should keep the class focused on that topic. For example, an effective lesson on ratios can be built around a series of short, directed word problems. In contrast, an extended baking project intended to teach ratios is more likely to shift students' concentration from the mathematics to cookies.

Thorough coverage — Good teachers adopt the motto: *Do it right the first time, and get all students to understand.* Because mathematics builds on itself, it is important that it be learned thoroughly the first time around. Teaching becomes extremely difficult when material covered in previous years has been mastered by only some of the students.

Anticipating, detecting and correcting errors — Uncorrected errors and misconceptions cause frustration and set the stage for future disaster. A student who believes that $3 \times 4 = 7$ will not understand anything done with multiplication. A student who believes that $1/2 + 1/5 = 2/7$ will never learn algebra. Such misconceptions should be detected and corrected immediately.

Many student errors can be anticipated by the teacher. When introducing topics and giving explanations, an experienced teacher is especially clear about those points which have led students astray in previous years. A teacher who notices, classifies, and remembers common errors will be more successful every year.

Building confidence through mastery — Today's schools place considerable value on developing students' self-esteem. This is sometimes interpreted as meaning that students should not be given challenging tasks and errors should not be corrected. In mathematics at least, exactly the opposite is true: confidence is built through challenge and correction. Mathematics is full of skills that seem very hard at first, but can be mastered with a few weeks of effort. Students who initially struggle with such a skill but go on to become proficient get a boost of confidence and are proud of accomplishing something they know is difficult.

Common Core Mathematics Standards — Today's teachers must implement all this in the context of the Common Core Mathematics Standards. The timelines and curriculum development in this textbook are fully compatible with these standards. The fluencies, concepts, and application problems in this textbook are designed to prepare teachers to teach using any mathematics curriculum, including curricula based upon the Common Core Mathematics Standards.

About the Textbook

This text is organized around numbers and arithmetic. The topics are covered roughly in the order they are developed in elementary school. The first three chapters cover most of the arithmetic of grades K-3. Chapters 4 and 5 jump ahead to topics (prealgebra and prime numbers) usually covered in grades 6 and 7; that jump allows us to review ideas about algebra and proofs which are needed for a "teacher's understanding" of the subsequent material. Chapters 6 and 7 return to the original timeline, developing fractions (as is done beginning in grades 3 or 4) and the follow-up topics of ratios, proportions, percentages, and rates. The last two chapters complete the development of elementary arithmetic by discussing negative and real numbers.

The textbook is divided into short sections, each on a single topic, and each followed by a homework set focused on that topic. The homework sets were designed with the intention that all or most of the exercises will be assigned. Many of the homework exercises involve solving problems in actual elementary school textbooks (the 'Primary Mathematics' books described below). Others involve "studying the textbook" — carefully reading a section of the book and answering questions about the mathematics being presented, with attention to the prerequisites, the ordering, and the variety of problems on that topic. Both types of exercises will help you develop a teacher's understanding of elementary mathematics.

Supplementary Texts

This textbook is designed to be used in conjunction with the following five Primary Mathematics books (all are U.S. Edition):

- Primary Mathematics 3A Textbook (ISBN 981–01–8502–2)

- Primary Mathematics 4A Textbook (ISBN 981–01–8506–5)

- Primary Mathematics 5A Textbook (ISBN 981–01–8510–3)

- Primary Mathematics 5A Workbook (ISBN 981–01–8512–X)

- Primary Mathematics 6A Textbook (ISBN 981–01–8514–6)

All five are part of an elementary mathematics curriculum developed by Singapore's Ministry of Education. While initially created for Singapore students, they have been adapted for use in other countries, including the United States. We will refer to them as "Primary Math 3A," "Workbook 5A," and so on. They can be purchased from the distributor in the U.S. at the website www.singaporemath.com.

The Primary Mathematics series is printed as one course book per semester, each with an accompanying workbooks. The semesters are labeled 'A' and 'B', so '5A' refers to the first semester of grade 5. In each grade, the first semester focuses mainly on numbers and arithmetic, while the second semester focuses more on measurement and geometry.

Why the Primary Mathematics books?

The aim of this course is to develop an understanding of elementary mathematics *at the level needed for teaching*. The best way to do that is to study actual elementary school textbooks and to do many, many actual elementary school mathematics problems. The Primary Mathematics books were chosen for that purpose.

We will read and study these books with two goals in mind: understanding the mathematics and understanding the curriculum development. The Primary Mathematics books give an extraordinarily clear presentation of what elementary mathematics is and how it is organized and developed. They lay out the subject in depth, and they include a rich supply of exercises and word problems. The mathematics is always clean and correct, and topics are repeatedly covered from different approaches. Viewed from a broader perspective, these books provide much useful guidance about curriculum issues. They exhibit the principles of a well-designed curriculum better, it seems, than any textbook series currently available in English.

It is not surprising, then, that the Primary Mathematics books are also successful with children! It is also not surprising that writers of the Common Core Mathematics Standards turned to the textbooks of Singapore, along with those of Hong Kong and Korea, as models of highly coherent curricula (see the introduction to the standards). These beautifully designed books are a major factor in student success.

As you read and do problems from these books, notice the following:

1. The absence of clutter and distraction. These books contain mathematics and nothing but mathematics. The presentation is very clean and clear, and is done using simple, concise explanations.

2. The coherent development. Each topic is introduced by a very simple example. It is then incrementally developed until, quite soon, difficult problems are being done. Topics are revisited for 'review' and the level of the mathematics is constantly ratcheted upward.

3. The short, precise definitions.   The children pictured in the margins give the precise definitions and key ideas in very few words. These 'student helpers' often clearly convey an idea that might otherwise take an entire paragraph!

4. The "concrete ⇒ pictorial ⇒ abstract" approach. This approach produces very clear introductions to topics.

5. The books serve as teacher guides. The books make the mathematical content of each lesson clear to the teacher and help teachers plan lessons. They also provide examples and activities to be done in class and allow teachers flexibility in designing lessons.

The first of the above points should be stressed. The Primary Mathematics books are deliberately focused. They contain no distracting extras such as long introductions and summaries, biographical stories, explorations, or discussions of non-mathematical topics. Homework is relegated to workbooks, and group projects and explorations are put in separate teacher guides. The pictures effectively convey meaning; they are not stylistic extras. The judicious use of white space makes the books easy and enjoyable to read. These short textbooks keep young students focused on learning mathematics.

If you compare the Primary Mathematics books to other elementary textbooks, you will appreciate these points. Many textbooks feature distracting side-bar messages, unnecessary drawings, showy photographs and highlighted boxes, and frequent font changes. The mathematics is obscured and perhaps lost altogether.

Study and enjoy these books — and keep them! When you become a teacher, these books will be a valuable resource, helping with explanations, providing extra problems, and giving guidance in how to present mathematics.

Reading this Textbook

Students reading the Primary Mathematics books interact with the books at the places indicated by colored boxes. As explained in the preface of each book, the colored 'patches' are prompts for student participation and class discussions. The prompts occur in relatively easy exercises, where they encourage active learning and allow students to check their understanding.

Similarly, this textbook includes "learning exercises" embedded in the text, many with blanks or boxes □ of various sizes prompting you to answer. Some of these exercises will be discussed in class, but you will usually encounter them while reading on your own. Do these exercises as you read! Most only take a minute or two. Write your answers next to the boxes (the boxes themselves are usually not large enough to hold answers). These exercises are designed to clarify the text. Some mathematical ideas are difficult to communicate in words, but quickly become clear by *doing problems*.

That same principle — that mathematics is best learned by solving problems — applies to the course as a whole. Read each section of the textbook, but leave plenty of time for doing the homework sets. They are the most important part of the course.

The Homework Sets

This course is built around homework problems from the Primary Mathematics books. As you do homework, bear in mind that your goal is not merely to *do* the problems as a child would. Rather, your goal is to study the problems from the perspective of a teacher. Teachers must be able to identify the key steps in solving a problem so they can guide and prompt students. They must also be able to give clear, grade-appropriate presentations of solutions. Try to bring out these teaching aspects of problems in your homework solutions. In general,

> Make your answers clear, concise, legible, and simple. They should look like an answer key to be handed out to an elementary school class.

This idea — clear, concise solutions — is one of the main themes of this course. You will learn many tricks and teaching devices which will help you craft such solutions, including models (introduced in §1.1), number bonds (§1.4), bar diagrams (§2.2), and "Teacher's Solutions" (§2.3). These devices convey mathematical ideas without words, making short explanations possible. In mathematics, longer explanations are often *more confusing*. Consequently, you should avoid writing out paragraph-long explanations — short solutions are less work for you and are clearer to students (and to your instructor!). If you practice brevity in your homework solutions you will find yourself becoming increasingly comfortable giving teacher-quality mathematical explanations.

Solutions to selected homework problems are available at: www.sefton-ash.com

Mathematics not covered

In addition to the arithmetic topics covered in this book, elementary mathematics includes a second main set of topics centered on measurement and geometry. The authors' textbook *Elementary Geometry for Teachers* (ISBN 978-0-9748140-5-6) presents the topics below in the same style and format as this book. The two textbooks are designed to be used together for a one-year college mathematics course for elementary teachers.

Measurement and the metric system	Pythagorean theorem
Figures and unknown angle problems	Congruence and similarity
Deductive geometry	Volume and surface area
Area	Basic probability and statistics

Acknowledgments

We wish to express sincere appreciation to the many mathematicians, math educators, and teachers who read the preliminary version of this book and made valuable suggestions. Particular thanks are due to Richard Askey, Hyman Bass, Solomon Fleishman, Thomas Fortmann, Madge Goldman, Roger Howe, Steffen Lempp, Fred Reusch, Ralph Raimi, Robert Seeley, Sharon Senk, Joan Stamm, Andre Toom, and Hung-Hsi Wu.

We also benefited from lively discussions and correspondences with Deborah Ball, Sybilla Beckmann, Wayne Bishop, Richard Bisk, Herb Gross, Richard Hill, Gary Jenson, Glenda Lappan, Frank Lester, Liping Ma, Joan Ferrini-Mundy, Stanley Ocken, Patsy Wang-Iverson, and David Wright.

We are especially appreciative of the efforts of Madge Goldman, whose constant encouragement and practical advice played a key role in creating this book. We also thank the Gabriella and Paul Rosenbaum Foundation for help in the early stages of distributing this textbook.

Finally, we thank Mary J. Reusch for the use of her painting on the cover and Justin Reusch for the cover design.

CHAPTER 1

Place Value and Models for Arithmetic

Young children love to count! Teachers should get them started immediately by having them count, measure, add, and subtract at every opportunity. Mathematics is a language and a way of thinking. Early exposure is enormously beneficial.

Teaching beginning arithmetic might appear to be straightforward, but it requires a surprising amount of 'teacher knowledge.' Specialized teacher knowledge is needed because numbers are so deeply ingrained in our adult minds that it is not easy to anticipate where children may run into difficulties. Beginning arithmetic is difficult to teach precisely because it is so familiar!

This chapter focuses on the foundational topics of arithmetic covered in grades K–2. The main challenge of that material is the difficulty associated with the idea *place value*. Place value is described in Section 1.2. The chapter continues with a first look at addition, subtraction, multiplication, and division. Along the way we introduce models, teaching sequences, and thinking strategies which clarify the mathematics.

Teacher education builds on such subject-matter knowledge. An addendum at the end of this chapter comments on the classroom methodology pertaining to mathematics that you will learn in the Teacher Education courses.

1.1 Counting

Mathematics begins with counting. The numbers we use to count are called the *whole numbers*. Because the number of objects is sometimes zero ("how many elephants are in this room?"), the whole numbers begin with zero.

> **DEFINITION 1.1.** *The numbers*
> $$0, 1, 2, 3, \ldots$$
> *(beginning with zero!) are called **whole numbers**.*

cardinal numbers
ordinal numbers

Whole numbers are used for two distinct purposes. When whole numbers are used to count objects they are called *cardinal numbers*. When they are used to put items in order their names are modified slightly ("first, second, third, . . .") and they are called *ordinal numbers*.

A number is an abstract idea. We can speak of '3 apples' or '3 people,' but when we say simply '3' or '3 + 3 = 6' we mean something more abstract. Fortunately, that abstraction is innate — it is built into our brains. In fact, it has been shown that apes, dolphins, and even parrots understand small numbers [47]. As for humans, three-year-olds easily learn to count, and 94% of all entering kindergarten children can count to 10 and read one-digit numbers [72]. Thus teachers need never worry whether students are "developmentally ready" for numbers — they are. What is required is daily exposure and practice. Furthermore, children learn quickly; three-year-olds are capable of learning 10–15 new words a day. This is remarkably effortless; children do not 'memorize' new words and new concepts, they simply assimilate them. Young children can easily be taught to count into the hundreds.

Numbers are initially taught by

- counting chants, including "skip counting" by twos, fives, and tens, and

- counting exercises with objects and pictures.

counting chants

Learning to count up to and beyond 100 by twos, fives, and tens is an important step in developing number sense and solidifying understanding of the place value concepts discussed in the next section. Skip counting skills also provide a springboard for learning multiplication and division.

Numbers arise in one of two broad settings, usually called the set model and the measurement model.

Set Model — Here one counts discrete objects. The answer must be a whole number.

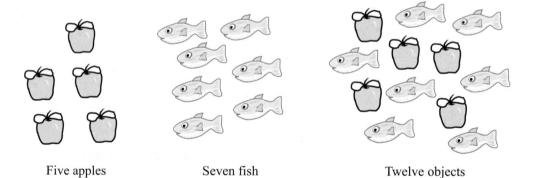

| Five apples | Seven fish | Twelve objects |

Measurement Model — Here one thinks of a scale along which one measures a quantity such as distance, time, or weight. The answer often is not a whole number.

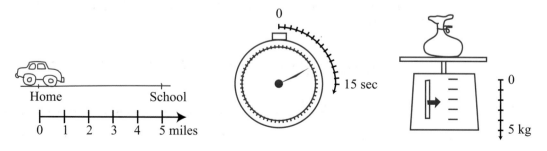

Thus the question "How many people are in this class?" asks us to use a set model, while the question "How high is the ceiling?" asks us to use a measurement model. Sometimes both models can be used.

Below is the first of many "reading exercises" you will encounter in this textbook. Answer these as you read. They are designed to help you understand the text.

EXERCISE 1.2. *Identify whether the following questions are most naturally illustrated using a set model or a measurement model.*

    (a)   How many eggs are in a one-dozen carton?   _____

    (b)   How many feet tall is the Sears Tower?   _____

    (c)   How many people are there on earth?   _____

    (d)   How many months have passed so far in the new millennium?   _____

    (e)   How many red shirts do you own? _____

These examples show that there is an underlying model even when the answer is unknown or unknowable, as in (c), and when the question needs clarification, as in (e) (do you count pink shirts?). Also notice that some questions can fit both models depending on the point of view one takes: in (d) one can think of a timeline or of calendar pages. Later we will see useful combinations and variations of these two models.

Using the set model, students can also count *groups* of objects. This is a prelude to multiplication.

4 groups of 10 eggs

The set model can be formalized by "Set Theory," a mathematical subject where words such as union, intersection, and inclusion are defined. But that level of rigor is not useful in elementary schools. Thus for us the word 'set' will have its common English meaning: a group of objects.

The simplest version of a measurement model is the *number line*.

number line

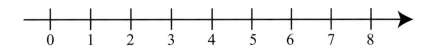

The number line is the most useful model in all of mathematics! This single picture shows the whole numbers in order. It illustrates their relative magnitude (how far to 100? 1000?). It also leads naturally to fractions (what is between two whole numbers?) and negative numbers ("what is to the left of zero?"). In fact, the number line is the only model that continues to work as elementary school mathematics progresses through whole numbers, fractions, and on to negative, rational, and irrational numbers.

We will use both the set and measurement models throughout this textbook — they will soon be very familiar! The models complement each other; in topic after topic, conceptual understanding depends on seeing problems using both models. Familiarity with the models will enable you, as a teacher, to ensure that your students see the needed breadth of problems.

Numerals

While the idea of numbers is natural, there are many ways of writing them. We write numbers using symbols called *numerals*. Throughout history, dozens of numeration systems have been devised. For teaching purposes it is important to understand the logic that led to our present system. That can be done by looking at three systems, beginning with the simplest and most ancient.

Tallies. The simplest and most intuitive way to record numbers is by tallies: |, ||, |||, ||||, ... But this very quickly becomes cumbersome — try writing 73.

Egyptian Numerals. The ancient Egyptians used tally marks for the numbers up to 9, but then introduced new symbols

∩ ("heel") for 10 tallies,

Ꮀ ("scroll") for 100 tallies, and

𝒮 ("lotus") for 1000 tallies.

Thus, for example, 'one thousand three hundred thirty four' could be written as

$$\text{𝒮 Ꮀ Ꮀ Ꮀ ∩ ∩ ∩ | | | |}$$

This is shorter and clearer than tallies, but is still cumbersome for some numbers — try writing 989.

Decimal Numerals. These are the numerals we use. With just ten symbols — the digits $0, 1, 2 \ldots 9$ — any number, no matter how large or small in magnitude, can be represented. The trick for this is seen in the conversion from Egyptian numerals.

$$\text{Ꮀ Ꮀ Ꮀ} \quad \text{∩∩∩∩∩} \quad \text{| | | |}$$
$$\downarrow \qquad\qquad \downarrow \qquad\qquad \downarrow$$
$$3 \qquad\qquad 5 \qquad\qquad 4$$

Each digit records the number of units of a certain value and that value (ones, tens, hundreds...) is recorded by the *position* of the digit. This use of position is called the *place value* system. Position indicates values without any additional marks on the page. Each position within the number has an assigned value: beginning on the right there is the ones place, the tens place, the hundreds place, etc. Notice that this scheme requires the use of zero as a place holder digit to distinguish, for example, 2030 from 23.

> **DEFINITION 1.3.** *Place value refers to the fact that in our numeration system the value of a digit is specified by its position within the number. (For example, the first 3 in 3437 has a value of three thousand while the second 3 in 3437 has a value of thirty.)*

The decimal numeral system has important advantages.

millions
billions
trillions
quadrillions

1. It easily records very large numbers, such as

$$\underbrace{23}_{quadrillions} , \underbrace{456}_{trillions} , \underbrace{789}_{billions} , \underbrace{123}_{millions} , \underbrace{456}_{thousands} , \underbrace{789}_{ones}$$

To make large numbers easier to read, commas are inserted every third digit as shown.

2. It extends to a way of recording numbers to any desired accuracy, as in 126.3807.

3. There are easy methods of adding and subtracting decimal numerals, and multiplication and division are *much* easier than with other numeral systems (in the ancient world multiplication was an art practiced only by highly trained scribes).

4. It is used throughout the world.

There is a price to pay for this convenience: decimal numerals are more abstract than Egyptian numbers. Place value is tricky to learn and causes many problems in the early grades. We will discuss this further in the next section.

Finally, Roman numerals are a useful topic in elementary school. The book of Adler [1] gives a clear and entertaining explanation for students; other expositions can be found on the internet. Here is a short explanation.

Roman numerals parallel Egyptian numerals using four basic symbols

I	for 1,
X	for 10,
C	(as in 'century') for 100,
M	(as in 'millenium') for 1000.

Thus "one thousand two hundred thirty-four" is written as $MCCXXXIIII$. To shorten the notation, the Romans added new symbols for intermediate values:

V for 5,   L for 50,   D for 500.

Using this shortcut, we can write 'seven' as VII instead of IIIIIII, and "one thousand six hundred eighty-six" as

$$MDCLXXXVI.$$

The numerals are written in order, beginning with the one with the largest value. Around 100 A.D. the numerals were further shortened through the use of the "subtractive principle," in which symbols that appear before their expected position count negatively. Specifically, IIII was shortened to IV, VIIII shortened to IX, and 40, 90, 400 and 900 were written as XL, XC, CD and CM respectively. "One thousand nine hundred and ninety-seven" was thought of as $M + CM + XC + VII$, so written as $MCMXCVII$. To read such numerals, move from left to right, forming pairs whenever the value of the symbol increases.

Homework Set 1

Solutions to selected homework problems are available at: www.sefton-ash.com

1. Make the indicated conversions.

   a) To decimal: ∩∩∩||||||||, 𝔛𝔛𝔛℮℮∩|||, 𝔛𝔛∩||, 𝔛𝔛∩∩∩

   b) To Egyptian: 8, 37, 648, 1348

   c) To decimal: MMMDCCXXXIII, MCMLXX, MMLIX, CDXLIV

   d) To Roman: 86, 149, 284, 3942

2. Write the number 8247 as an Egyptian numeral. How many fewer symbols are used when this number is written as a decimal numeral?

3. a) Do column addition for the Egyptian numerals below. Then check your answer by converting to decimal numerals (fill in and do the addition on the right).

   ℮∩∩∩|||||
   + ℮℮℮∩∩∩∩∩∩| ↔ +   135

   Write a similar pair of column additions for

   b) $273 + 125$ and

   c) $328 + 134$.

   d) Write a sentence explaining what you did with the 12 tallies that appeared in the sum c) in Egyptian numerals.

4. Make up a first-grade word problem for the addition $7 + 5$ using a) the set model and another b) using the measurement model.

5. Open Primary Math 3A to page 12 and read Problems 1 and 2. Then write the following as decimal numerals.

   a) 6 billion 3 thousand 4 hundred and 8

   b) 2 quadrillion 3 billion 9 thousand 5 hundred 6

   c) 230 hundreds 32 tens and 6 ones

   d) 54 thousands and 26 ones

   e) 132 hundreds and 5 ones.

6. Write the following numerals in words.

   a) 1347   b) 5900
   c) 7058   d) 7,000,000,000
   e) 67,345,892,868,736

7. Multiply the following Egyptian numerals by ten *without converting or even thinking about decimal numbers*.

   a) | b) ∩   c) ℮

   d) ℮∩| e) ∩∩||| f) ℮℮∩|||

8. a) Fill in the missing two corners of this chart.

   ℮∩∩∩|| ⟷ 132
   ↓×10   ↓×10
   _____   _____

   b) Fill in the blanks: to multiply an Egyptian numeral by 10 one shifts symbols according to the rule

   | → ___ → ___ → ___.

   c) To multiply a decimal numeral by 10 one shifts each digit to the _____, making the shift apparent by inserting a _____ in the ones place.

1.2 The Place Value Process

Our decimal system of recording numbers is ingenious. Once learned, it is a simple, versatile, and efficient way of writing numbers. The system first came into use in the Middle East around 500-800 A.D. (decimal numerals are also called Hindu-Arabic numerals). The system's advantages were so clear that it spread throughout the world and played a decisive role in the development of commerce and science. The decimal system is now used by all modern societies. It is one of the most significant intellectual advances in human history.

But the system is not obvious nor easily learned. The use of place value is subtle, and mastering it is the single most challenging aspect of elementary school mathematics. Ironically, those challenges are largely invisible to untrained parents and teachers — place value is so ingrained in adults' minds that it is difficult to appreciate how important it is and how hard it is to learn. This section describes the structure and pitfalls of the place value system and alerts you to the hurdles it presents to elementary school children. The points made here, and variations on them, occur repeatedly in later sections.

Decimal notation suggests a specific process for counting. Suppose you are given a large pile of sticks and asked to count them and write the total as a decimal numeral. One way is to make bundles of 10 sticks ("tens bundles"), tying them together with a ribbon and making as many such bundles as possible. Next, tie tens bundles together into bundles of 100 sticks each ("hundreds bundles"), making as many hundreds bundles as possible. Continue, making "thousands bundles," etc., until no new bundles can be created. In the end, you have bundles consisting of 1, 10, 100, etc. sticks; we call these bundle sizes *denominations*. The decimal numeral is formed by counting the number of bundles of each denomination as shown in the picture below.

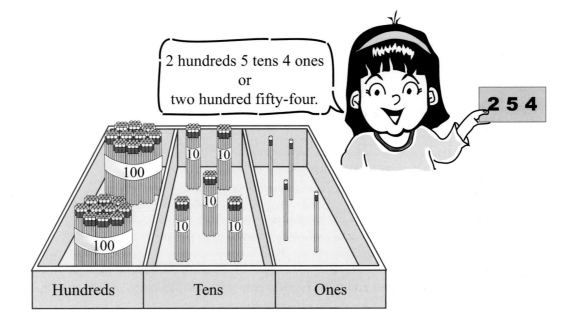

Addition of decimal numerals involves a similar process. Suppose you are given two piles of sticks, already tied into ones, tens, and hundreds bundles, and are again asked to write the total as a decimal numeral. One way is to push the piles together and *rebundle*. For example, if there are 13 tens bundles, you can tie 10 of them together to make a new hundreds bundle. You can continue rebundling until there are at most 9 bundles of each denomination. With that done, you need only count the number of bundles of each denomination and record the decimal numeral.

Both of the situations above are examples of the following three-step "Place Value Process."

The Place Value Process

(i) Form bundles of 1, 10, 100, 1000, etc.

(ii) If necessary *rebundle* to ensure that there are at most 9 bundles of each denomination.

(iii) Count the number of bundles of each denomination and record that number in the appropriate position.

Step (i), forming bundles of different sizes and naming the bundles, is something that the human brain is good at. For example, children have little trouble understanding that a dime is worth 10 pennies, and a dollar is worth 10 dimes. The interaction between Steps (ii) and (iii) is more difficult. The thinking involved in Steps (ii) and (iii) is more than just counting and naming — it is a specific mental procedure for organizing our counting. This procedure underlies nearly everything in arithmetic. It must be learned and mastered.

EXAMPLE 2.1. *Here are three types of problems that help develop place value skills in grades K–3.*

(a) Counting by tens: "10, 20, 30, ..." Counting by tens is far easier than counting by nines! We need only count bundles of tens just as we count ones and record the answer as in Step (iii).

(b) Switching decades: what comes after 39? 89? The number after 39 is not "thirty-ten," we must rebundle (Step (ii) of the place value process).

(c) What number is 20 more than 532? To answer we add 2 bundles of ten and record the answer as in Step (iii). This can be done by skip-counting by tens:

The place value process can be demonstrated using number chips and illustrated by pictures of number chips arranged in columns (number chips are disks with clearly displayed values of 1, 10, 100, and 1000). Notice the use of zero as a placeholder in the following example.

Hundreds	Tens	Ones
(100) (100) (100) (100)		(1) (1) (1) (1) (1)

$$4 \qquad 0 \qquad 5$$

"Chip Model"

Such 'chip model' pictures make clear that underlying every numeral are place value 'columns' which carry the values ones, tens, hundreds, etc. (denominations).

Another good way of clarifying place value concepts is to expand numbers as sums which explicitly show the value associated with each digit. Thus 3784 can be written as follows.

3 thousands + 7 hundreds + 8 tens + 4 ones

$$3000 \; + \; 700 \; + \; 80 \; + \; 4$$

"Expanded Form"

Many elementary textbooks (including Primary Mathematics) illustrate expanded form using overlapping cards. Such cards are useful in the classroom.

Coins or expanded form show that decimal numerals add by the simple principle: *add the hundreds, tens and ones separately.* For example,

$$(2\,\text{hundreds}+4\,\text{tens}+2\,\text{ones}) + (3\,\text{hundreds}+2\,\text{tens}+1\,\text{ones}) = (5\,\text{hundreds}+6\,\text{tens}+3\,\text{ones}).$$

Chip model pictures organize this into column addition in a way that parallels what you did with Egyptian numbers in the homework for the previous section.

EXAMPLE 2.2. *Add* $242 + 314$.

Hundreds	Tens	Ones
(100) (100)	(10) (10) (10) (10)	(1) (1)
(100) (100) (100)	(10)	(1) (1) (1) (1)

$$\begin{array}{r} 200 + 40 + 2 \\ + \quad 300 + 10 + 4 \\ \hline \end{array} \qquad \begin{array}{r} 242 \\ + \quad 314 \\ \hline \end{array}$$

Notice that in this particular example there is no logical reason to add the ones first — the columns can be added in any order. That is true because this example does not involve Step (ii) of the place value process — it avoids the complications of "rebundling" or "carrying."

The place value process is particularly important in multiplication. We can multiply any number by 10 by appending a zero, and we can multiply by 100 by appending two zeros. This important idea is not obvious to children. It is not a mathematical fact about multiplication. Rather, it is a feature of the special role of the number 10 in our numerals, namely that the place value units, ones, tens, hundreds,..., are each 10 times as large as the previous unit. This principle can be explained and used in a variety of ways.

- Multiplying by 10 and 100:

$$
\begin{aligned}
4 \times 10 &= 4 \text{ tens} = 40, \\
13 \times 10 &= 13 \text{ tens} = 130, \\
7 \times 100 &= 7 \text{ hundreds} = 700, \\
578 \times 10 &= (5 \text{ hundreds} + 7 \text{ tens} + 8 \text{ ones}) \times 10 \\
&= (5 \text{ thousands} + 7 \text{ hundreds} + 8 \text{ tens}) = 5780.
\end{aligned}
$$

- Multiplying by multiples of 10:

$$
60 \times 7 = (6 \text{ tens}) \times 7 = (6 \times 7) \text{ tens} = 42 \text{ tens} = 420.
$$

Such problems provide useful methods for quick calculations and build familiarity with the place value process.

You can see the place value skills being developed in Primary Math 3A pages $6 - 17$, extended to larger numbers in Primary Math 4A pages $6 - 11$ and further extended in Primary Math 5A pages $6 - 10$ (you will study those sections in the homework). Many of the problems in those sections quite clearly focus on the place value process, but there are also problems whose connection with place value is more subtle, most notably those which ask the student to order numbers.

EXAMPLE 2.3. *(a) Which is larger, 75 or 57?*

(b) Put the numbers 543, 453, and 345 in order, beginning with the smallest.

To answer such ordering questions one must reverse the place value process, in effect writing the number in expanded form and thinking about the relative sizes of the units (ones, tens, hundreds, ...). This is nicely illustrated in Primary Math 3A, page 10, Problem 7 — have a look. The problems on pages 10 and 11 lead students to discover the principle that to compare two numbers one should look first at the digits with the highest unit value. Generally, problems asking about comparing and ordering numbers force students to think hard about the place value process. They are also a useful assessment tool as we will point out at the end of this section.

More difficult place value skills involve Step (ii) of the place value process: rebundling (the term *regrouping* is also commonly used). Rebundling works in two directions. These can be explained by referring to the coin model pictures.

1. **(Composing a ten)** When there are more than 9 coins in a column we *compose a ten* by bundling 10 together and moving them to the next column. Thus to find $17 + 15$ we add the tens and the ones to get 2 tens + 12, then regroup to get 3 tens + 2 = 32.

2. **(Decomposing a ten)** In subtraction, when we have fewer coins of some denomination than we require, we are free to *decompose a ten* by taking a coin from the column with the next higher value and converting it to 10 coins of the required denomination. Thus to find $43 - 15$ we first regroup to think of 43 as (3 tens + 13), and 15 as (1 ten + 5), then subtract the tens and the ones to get 2 tens + 8 = 28.

These two ways of regrouping are the mathematical underpinnings of "carrying" in column addition and "borrowing" in column subtraction. They also occur in some of the Mental Math strategies we will discuss in Section 2.1.

One can also decompose 10 as the sum of two smaller numbers. There are five such *tens combinations*, shown below as "number bonds" (see page 21). In this form, there are only 5 facts to learn, but each encodes many arithmetic facts: knowing the first one allows children to find $1 + 9$, $9+1$, $10 - 1$ and $10 - 9$.

tens combinations

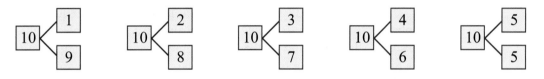

"Tens Combinations"

Tens combinations can be combined with regrouping. For example, one can find $74 + 6$ by recognizing that $4 + 6$ is a tens combination. Students can solve this problem mentally, and teachers can depict the thinking steps this way:

$$74 + 6 = 74 + 6 = 70 + 10 = 80.$$
$$70 \quad 4$$

EXERCISE 2.4. *What is $80 - 7$? Write your solution in several steps which, as above, show how to use regrouping and a tens combination.*

The Primary Mathematics textbooks also develop and use "hundreds combinations" with multiples of 5, such as $35 + 65$. Like tens combinations, these are surprisingly useful. For example, if you buy a carton of milk for \$1.85 and give the cashier \$5, your change will be

$$\$5 - \$1.85 = 4 \text{ dollars} - 85 \text{ cents} = 3 \text{ dollars} + (100 - 85) \text{ cents} = \$3.15.$$

When done mentally, such problems promote understanding of place value.

Looking back over this section, you will see that there are distinct levels of applications of the place value process. The simplest problems use only Steps (i) and (iii). The hardest problems require using all three steps in the course of a larger calculation. In between are problems that combine regrouping with one other skill. Thus the three steps of the place value process are not equally difficult — Step (ii) is mathematically more sophisticated and harder to learn.

Using the principle of "steady incremental development" described in the preface, teaching proceeds from easiest, to intermediate difficulty, and then to hardest. In this way, students face only one conceptual difficulty at a time. At each stage they learn a new skill and integrate it with their previous skills. The following problems represent three levels of place value problems for subtraction beginning with the simplest and first taught (*do these*).

$$746 - 400 = \underline{\hspace{1.5cm}} \qquad 400 - 99 = \underline{\hspace{1.5cm}} \qquad 413 - 157 = \underline{\hspace{1.5cm}}$$

$$300 \quad 100$$

| No regrouping | Simple regrouping | Complex regrouping |

Notice that the levels of difficulty are determined by the underlying mathematics: *the mathematics determines the teaching sequence*. In later sections we will see many instances where the mathematical aspects of a topic determine the teaching order. For those topics, we will examine the conceptual difficulties and discuss how the mathematics can be systematically organized as a 'teaching sequence' that breaks the topic into a series of incremental steps leading to mastery.

In the teaching profession, the term 'place value' is frequently used in a broad sense. The phrases 'place value concepts,' 'place value issues,' and 'place value difficulties' refer to those aspects of a particular mathematical topic which require attention to the position of digits, or which stem from the special role that the powers of 10 play in our numerals.

A simple example of a teaching issue involving place value is transposition of digits. When students begin to write numbers in kindergarten and grade 1, they will sometimes say '17' as they write '71.' This may be due to carelessness, to confusion about place value, or to the fact that left-to-right writing is not yet deeply ingrained. In your teaching methods courses you will learn that the last difficulty generally disappears as the student becomes more proficient at reading and writing. You will also learn tricks teachers can use to assess student understanding. For example, in this case the teacher can very easily determine whether the student can distinguish '17' from '71' by pointing to the '71' and asking, "what is the number after this one?" or, "is this number greater than 20?" Such on-the-spot assessments are a quick and effective method for assessing a student's understanding of place value concepts.

Homework Set 2

Study the Textbook!   In many countries teachers study the student textbooks, using them to gain insight into how mathematics is developed in the classroom. We will be doing this daily with the Primary Mathematics textbooks. The problems below will help you study the beginning pages of Primary Math 3A, 4A and 5A.

1. Primary Math 3A begins with 11 pages (pages 6 − 17) on place value. This is a review. Place value ideas were covered in grades 1 and 2 for numbers up to 1000; here those ideas are extended to 4–digit numbers. Many different ways of thinking about place value appear in this section.

   a) Read pages 6 − 9 carefully. These help establish place value concepts, including chip models and the _____ form of 4–digit numbers.

   b) The problems on page 10 use chip models and expanded form to explain some ideas about putting numbers in order. The picture at the top of page 10 helps students see that to compare 316 and 264 one should focus on the digit in the ____ place.

   c) The illustrations comparing 325 and 352 show that when the first digits are the same, the ordering is determined by what? Why did the authors choose numbers with the same digits in different orders?

   d) Parts (a) and (b) of Problem 7 ask students to compare 4–digit numbers. What place value must be compared for each of these four pairs of numbers?

   e) What digit appears for the first time in Problem 8a?

   f) Solve Problems 9, 11, and 12 on pages 10 and 11.

   g) On the same two pages, list the two numbers which answer Problem 10, then the two numbers which answer Problem 13.

2. a) Continuing in Primary Math 3A, explain the strategy for solving Problem 14a on page 11.

   b) What is the smallest 4-digit number you can make using all of the digits 0, 7, 2, 8?

   c) Do Problem 5 on page 12. This is a magnificent assortment of place-value problems! Write the answers as a list: 1736, 7504, . . ., omitting the labels (a), (b), (c), etc. We will refer to this way of writing answers as *list format*.

   d) Do Practice 1B on page 13, answering the five problems in list format. Note that Problems 3 and 4 again use numbers with the same digits in different orders, forcing students to think about place value.

   e) Read pages 14 − 16, answering the problems mentally as you read. These show students that it is easy to add 10, 100, or 1000 to a number. On page 15, the top chip model shows that to add 100 one needs only to think about the digit in the hundreds place. The bottom chip model shows that to _____ one need only think about the _____ digit.

3. Read pages 6 − 11 in Primary Math 4A, doing the problems mentally as you read.

   a) Do Problem 3 on page 9 in your Primary Math book (do not copy the problem into your homework). The problem is self-checking, which gives the student feedback and saves work for _____.

   b) Do Problems 4 and 5 on page 9. These extend place value cards and chip models to 5–digit numbers. Fourth-graders are ready for large numbers!

   c) Do Problem 7 on page 10. Part (a) asks for a chip model as in Problem 6. This problem shows one 'real life' use of large numbers.

   d) Answer Problem 8a on page 11 in list format. This asks students to identify *unmarked* points on the number line.

   e) Do Problem 10 mentally. The thinking used to solve part (a) can be displayed by writing: $6000 + 8000 = (6+8)$ thousands $= 14,000$. Write similar solutions for parts (c), (e) and (g).

4. Read pages 6 − 9 of Primary Math 5A, answering the problems mentally as you go. Write solutions to Problems 1ach, 2e, 3e, 4cf, 5ce, and 6c on page 10 in list format.

5. a) Study page 15 of Primary Math 5A. Write the answers to Problems 1, 3, and 5 on page 16 in list format.

   b) Study page 17 and Problem 2 on page 18. Write the answers to Problems 1 and 3 on page 18 in list format.

6. In decimal numerals the place values correspond to powers of ten (1, 10, 100, 1000...). If one instead uses the powers of five (1, 5, 25, 125, ...) one gets what are called "base 5 numerals." The base 5 numeral with digits 2 4 3, which we write as $(243)_5$ for clarity, represents 2 twenty-fives + 4 fives +3 ones=73. To express numbers as base 5 numerals, think of making change with pennies, nickels, quarters, and 125¢ coins; for example 47 cents = 1 quarter+4 nickels+2 pennies, so $47 = (142)_5$.

   a) Convert $(324)_5$ and $(1440)_5$ to decimal numerals.

   b) Convert 86 and 293 to base 5 numerals.

   c) Find $(423)_5 + (123)_5$ by adding in base 5. (Think of separately adding pennies, nickels, etc., rebundling whenever a digit exceeds 4. Do not convert to decimal numerals).

1.3 Addition

sum
addend
summand

Addition is an operation that combines two numbers, called the *addends* or *summands*, to form a third, called the *sum*. Addition arises in the set model when we combine two sets, and in the measurement model when we combine objects and measure their total length, weight, etc.

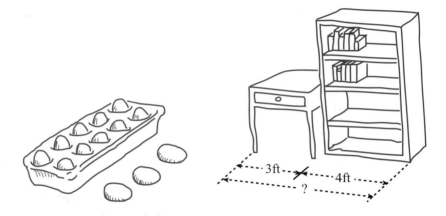

One can also model addition as "steps on the number line." In this number line model the two summands play different roles: the first specifies our starting point and the second specifies how many steps to take.

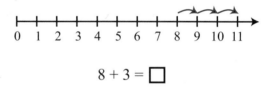

$$8 + 3 = \square$$

Addition and subtraction are taught together, with subtraction lagging addition. It is helpful to think of three main stages: a short introductory stage, a long development stage, and a short concluding stage focusing on the algorithms (see Chapter 3). The timeline below is the one followed by both the Primary Mathematics Curriculum and by the Common Core Mathematics Standards. We will discuss the first two stages in this section, and the third in Section 3.1.

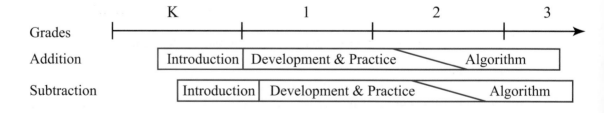

In the introductory stage children learn the *meaning* of addition by doing problems based on all three models: set, measurement, and number line. This involves some activity with manipulatives: counting coins and measuring with a carpenter's tape measure are two excellent activities. But mostly it involves picture problems asking for sums in a great variety of contexts.

At this stage it is the variety of models and contexts, not the difficulty of the problems, that builds understanding.

from objects to numbers

The goal at this stage is to get students to manipulate numbers, not objects, and to move beyond counting to arithmetic. Thus as students move through this introductory stage they are weaned off manipulatives and pictures and begin increasingly to do straight arithmetic problems such as $8 + 4 = $ ___ , and simple word problems such as the following.

EXAMPLE 3.1. *Sara had 8 books. Her mother gave her 3 more. How many did she then have?*

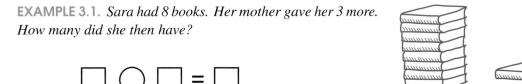

$$\square \; \bigcirc \; \square \; = \; \square$$

Sara then had ___ books.

Children initially learn to add by "counting-on." To find $6 + 2$ the child starts with 6 and silently counts 2 numbers forward ("... 7, 8"). Already at this stage one sees the benefits of having all the models. The number line model clearly illustrates counting-on and can be used to clarify confusion. In contrast, when presented with an addition problem illustrated with a set model, children tend to simply count the objects starting with $1, 2, \ldots$. With that approach they are simply counting, and are not thinking about addition at all!

Counting-on is an excellent strategy for adding 1, 2, or 3 to a number; with practice, children quickly become adept at such additions. However, counting-on is difficult and frustrating for problems, such as $9 + 5 = $ ___ , where the second summand is greater than 3. The burden on short-term memory is too great to ensure consistently correct answers. Other strategies are needed.

The goal of the second stage (labeled 'Development & Practice' in the timeline above) is to develop a robust understanding of addition with numbers up to 100 or so. This involves three areas which we discuss next: the properties of addition, thinking strategies for the 'addition within 20' facts, and further work on place value. All three are developed using a mix of Mental Math problems, worksheets, and short word problems.

Properties of Addition. By definition, addition combines numbers two at a time. What, then, do we do when faced with a sum of many numbers:

$$8 + 9 + 10 + 11 = \underline{\hspace{1cm}} ?$$

In the set model for this problem we push together piles of $8, 9, 10$ and 11 objects; it is clear that the piles can be pushed together in any order.

Any-order Property for Addition: A list of whole numbers can be added in any order. Thus $3 + 6 + 2$ can be computed as $(3 + 6) + 2$ or $(2 + 3) + 6$, etc.

Notice that in expressions like $(3 + 6) + 2$ the order of addition is indicated by the convention that *operations inside parentheses are done first*. This convention is followed in all mathematical writing.

The Any-order property is one of the first basic principles of addition that children learn. It is immediately useful. For example, it is extremely difficult to find $2 + 7$ by starting at 2 and counting-on, but when it is pointed out that this is the same as $7 + 2$ the counting is easy! Similarly, finding $19 + 14 + 1$ is made easy by adding $19 + 1$ first.

Along with the Any-order property, children encounter a second principle at this stage when they see problems like

$$8 + 0 = \underline{\quad}.$$

The idea that "adding zero does nothing" is obvious *after it is explained*. An explanation is necessary because this principle is part of the meaning of what zero is. And the principle itself is important, in fact essential, for later place value applications. For example, to find $20 + 18$ by separately adding the tens digit and ones digit, one needs understand that $8 + 0 = 8$.

The words "adding zero does nothing" can be rephrased as "when 0 is added to a number, the result is *identical* to the original number." For this reason, the number zero is sometimes called the *additive identity*.

In mathematics textbooks the above principles are usually stated as three formal *arithmetic*
properties. The properties are:

arithmetic properties of addition

- Additive identity property: e.g. $5 + 0 = 5$,
- Commutative property: e.g. $7 + 5 = 5 + 7$, and
- Associative property: e.g. $(3 + 7) + 5 = 3 + (7 + 5)$.

The commutative and associative properties emphasize two separate aspects of the Any-order property. The commutative property states that, whenever we add two numbers, the order of the *summands* does not matter. In contrast, the associative property is a statement about the order of *operations*; it states whenever we do two successive additions it does not matter which is done first. A general reordering requires doing both.

EXERCISE 3.2. *Fill in the blanks to explain why each line follows from the previous.*

$$
\begin{aligned}
(3 + 7) + 5 &= 3 + (7 + 5) &&\text{by the associative property} \\
&= 3 + (5 + 7) &&\text{by the \underline{\hspace{3cm}} property} \\
&= (3 + 5) + 7 &&\text{by the \underline{\hspace{3cm}} property.}
\end{aligned}
$$

Similarly, by repeatedly applying the commutative and associativity properties one can show that all of the different ways of adding $4 + 2 + 5 + 7$ give the same result. This is tedious and has little value for elementary school students. But teachers should understand the point: *together, the commutative and associative properties imply the Any-order property.*

Thinking Strategies.   *Thinking strategies* are easy methods for solving a problem. One thinking strategy was mentioned above: to calculate $2 + 7$, find $7 + 2$ by counting-on. This stage also includes the learning the *addition with* 20 — all sums from $0 + 0$ up to $10 + 10$.

addition within 20

"Addition within 20" is sometimes presented as 121 separate facts ($0 + 0$ to $10 + 10$) to be memorized using drill and flashcards. This sounds daunting! But in fact, when taught efficiently, students easily master these facts. The trick is to systematically develop thinking strategies and to capitalize on childrens' sense of fun and their amazing ability to learn through exposure. The blue boxes below outline one such approach; each line names a skill, gives an example, and a comment on how it is learned. The first three skills are the ones mentioned above.

Adding +1, +2	$7 + 2 = 9$	easy by counting-on
Adding +0	$5 + 0 = 5$	trivial, once taught
Commutativity	$3 + 9 = 9 + 3$	pointed out and used.

Commutativity is not immediately obvious to children. In the beginning they often attempt to find $3 + 9$ by counting-on from 3; the advantages of reversing the order must be explicitly pointed out. It can also be "discovered" and reinforced by practice sets which include pairs such as $7 + 2 =$ ___ and $2 + 7 =$ ___ as consecutive problems.

Children become familiar with doubles as they do addition problems.

Doubles	$3 + 3, 4 + 4, \ldots, 9 + 9$	learned through practice

These sums are the even numbers $2, 4, 6, 8\ldots$. Learning is faster when these facts are given "personalities" and illustrated with props: $5 + 5 = 10$ is the 'fingers fact,' $6 + 6 = 12$ is the "egg-carton trick," and by a play on words, $8 + 8 = 16$ is the "8-carton trick."

Next come two place-value skills. These are steps toward learning addition of multi-digit numbers.

Tens Combinations	$5 + 5, 6 + 4, 7 + 3, 8 + 2, 9 + 1$	learned with practice
Adding 10	$7 + 10 = 17$	pointed out and used

Again, the easy way of adding 10 is not obvious to children — why should adding 10 be any easier than adding 9? *Like other place value issues this is surprisingly subtle.* Fortunately, it can be easily taught using mental math exercises.

Last come two thinking strategies:

Relating to Doubles	$6 + 7 = (6 + 6) + 1 = 13$	practiced as Mental Math
Compensation	$9 + 6 = 10 + 5$	practiced as Mental Math

In words, the "relating to doubles" strategy is simply the observation that $3 + 4$ is 1 more than $3 + 3$, $4 + 5$ is 1 more than $4 + 4$, etc. (In Homework Problem 4 you will learn another "relating to doubles" strategy.)

In the compensation method one adjusts one summand up and the other down to compensate. Thus $6 + 9$ is found by "letting the 6 give one to the 9" and then finding the easier sum $5 + 10$.

These thinking strategies can be applied in many different ways.

EXERCISE 3.3. *Use compensation to find the following sums. In the first the arrow indicates that "the 22 gives 2 to the 58." Draw similar arrows for the remaining problems and write the answer.*

a) $58 \overset{\frown 2}{+} 22 = $ ___

b) $71 + 49 = $ ___

c) $342 + 96 = $ ___

d) $45 + 47 = $ ___

e) $45 + 47 = $ ___ (another way)

f) $893 + 328 = $ ___

From a teaching perspective, this approach of focusing on strategies rather than 'the basic facts' is systematic but not rigid. It serves to minimize memory load, allows children to proceed quickly to larger numbers and more interesting problems, and simultaneously teaches skills that will be useful later. It is flexible because these strategies can be learned *in any order*. All children will begin addition by counting-on. But beyond that, each child will have favorite strategies and will be ahead on some methods and behind on others. Assessments will reveal these strengths and weaknesses, allowing the teacher to adjust lessons accordingly. In the end, memorization will be necessary for a small number of the addition within 20 facts (see Homework Problem 6).

This list of thinking strategies is a system: all children learn to use these strategies; with practice they rely more on memory for 1-digit additions and reserve the strategies for use with larger numbers.

Equality. The equal sign is usually introduced at the same time as addition, but it is seldom explicitly defined. In fact, the equal sign has a very specific meaning: *the symbol = means that the number to its left is the same as the number to its right*. When students are left to figure out that meaning by themselves, they often erroneously conclude that the symbol = means "now I will do something." That interpretation applies for most problems in grades 1 and 2, but *it is wrong*. This misimpression often endures. It can cause confusion all the way through high school.

meaning of =

misuse of =

Common Student Error: *To find* $3 + 5 + 9 + 2$*, Vince writes* $3 + 5 = 8 + 9 = 17 + 2 = 19$*.*

Vince is writing as if he were entering the problem into a calculator. His teacher can help by pointing to each of his equal signs and asking whether the number to its right is equal to the number to its left.

Homework Set 3

1. Illustrate the equality $3 + 7 = 7 + 3$ using (a) a set model, and (b) a bar diagram.

2. Which thinking strategy or arithmetic property (or properties) is being used?

    a) $86 + 34 = 100 + 20$

    b) $13,345 + 17,304 = 17,304 + 13,345$

    c) $0 + 0 = 0$

    d) $34 + (82 + 66) = 100 + 82$

    e) 2 thousands and 2 ones is equal to 2 ones and 2 thousands.

3. *(Mental Math)* Find the sum mentally by looking for pairs which add to a multiple of 10 or 100, such as $91 + 9 = 100$ in Problem a).

    a) $91 + 15 + 9$

    b) $4 + 17 + 32 + 23 + 36 + 20$

    c) $75 + 13 + 4 + 25$

    d) $11 + 45 + 34 + 55.$ e) $34 + 17 + 6 + 23$

    f) $28 + 32 + 35 + 7.$

4. One can add numbers which differ by 2 by a "relate to doubles" strategy: take the average and double. For ex-

ample, $6 + 8$ by twice 7. Use that strategy to find the following sums.

a) $7 + 9$ b) $19 + 21$

c) $24 + 26$ d) $6 + 4$.

5. *(Mental Math)* Do Problems 1 and 2 on page 22 of Primary Math 3A using compensation.

6. *(Thinking Strategies)* Only a few of the 121 "Addition within 20" facts need to be memorized through practice. Learning to add 1 and 2 by counting-on leaves 99 sums to learn. Adding 0 or 10 is easy, and using compensation to add 9 reduces the list further. After learning to use commutativity, students are left with only 21 facts:

$$
\begin{array}{cccccc}
3{+}3 & 3{+}4 & 3{+}5 & 3{+}6 & 3{+}7 & 3{+}8 \\
& 4{+}4 & 4{+}5 & 4{+}6 & 4{+}7 & 4{+}8 \\
& & 5{+}5 & 5{+}6 & 5{+}7 & 5{+}8 \\
& & & 6{+}6 & 6{+}7 & 6{+}8 \\
& & & & 7{+}7 & 7{+}8 \\
& & & & & 8{+}8
\end{array}
$$

Make a copy of this table and answer the following questions.

a) In your table, circle the doubles and tens combinations (which students must learn). How many did you circle?

b) Once they know doubles, students can add numbers which differ by 1 (such as $3 + 4$) by relating to doubles — no memorization required. Cross out all such pairs in your table. How many did you cross out?

c) Which addition facts are left? Thus how many addition-within-20 facts require memorization?

7. Match the symbols $=, \approx, \leq, \neq, \geq$ to the corresponding phrase. Answer in list format.

a) is less than or equal to

b) is equal to

c) is greater than or equal to

d) is approximately equal to

e) is not equal to

8. Here are some common examples of inappropriate or incorrect uses of the symbol "=."

a) A student writes "Ryan= \$2." What should he have written?

b) A student answers the question "Write 4.8203 correct to one decimal place" by writing $4.8203 = 4.8$. What should she have written?

c) A student answers the question "Simplify $(3 + 15) \div 2 + 6$" by writing $3 + 15 = 18 \div 2 = 9 + 6 = 15$. What should he have written?

1.4 Subtraction

When adding, we combine two addends to get a sum. For subtraction we are given the sum and one addend and must find the "missing addend."

> **DEFINITION 4.1.** *Subtraction is defined by missing addends:* $13 - 5$ *is the number that fits in the blank*
> $$5 + \underline{\quad} = 13.$$

The three numbers in a subtraction problem play different roles. To distinguish them teacher's manuals use the terms, *subtrahend*, and *difference*:

$$\underbrace{133}_{\text{minuend}} - \underbrace{45}_{\text{subtrahend}} = \underbrace{88}_{\text{difference.}}$$

These terms may seem unwieldy at first, but they are needed for clear professional discussions.

In the classroom, subtraction is more complicated than addition because it has three interpretations, each of which can be illustrated by set models or measurement models. *Understanding subtraction means understanding all cases.*

part-whole

- In the **part-whole interpretation** a part of a set or quantity is specified and we want to know how much is needed to make it whole. Thus we must find a missing part.

The class has 26 students. 11 are boys. How many are girls?	Abby's family drives to a lake 92 miles away. They stop for lunch after going 60 miles. How much further is it to the lake?
Set Model	Measurement Model

take-away

- In the **take-away interpretation** we remove objects from a set or decrease a measurement by a specified amount.

Sarah had a dozen eggs. She used 5 to make a cake. How many were left?	Jenny had \$23. She spent \$8 for a book. How much did she have left?
Set Model	Measurement Model

comparison

- In the **comparison interpretation** we compare *two different* sets or measurements; subtraction is interpreted as the *difference*.

Lilly has 11 dolls. Megan has 8 dolls. How many more dolls does Lilly have?	Sam weighs 56 pounds. Beth weighs 48 pounds. How much heavier is Sam?
Set Model	Measurement Model

In number line pictures, the part-whole interpretation is illustrated by an unknown gap, the take-away interpretation is illustrated by steps backwards, and the comparison interpretation is illustrated by *two bars along a number line* or, perhaps better, by 'bar diagrams' as shown below.

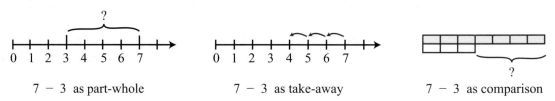

$7 - 3$ as part-whole $7 - 3$ as take-away $7 - 3$ as comparison

The part-whole, take-away and comparison interpretations are not mutually exclusive; some problems can be interpreted in two ways.

The Primary Mathematics books have a wonderful method of displaying whole-part-part combinations called *number bonds*. Each number bond shows a way of decomposing a number into two parts.

number bonds

"Number Bond"

Number bonds are extremely useful! They are simple, clear and efficient, and can be used by both teachers and students to clarify mathematical thinking in many contexts. If you look back at Section 1.2, you will see that we have already used number bonds for two purposes: to display "tens combinations," and to show examples of regrouping.

To adults, these interpretations and models are all aspects of the single idea of subtraction. But to children, they initially appear unrelated. Children must *learn* that all of these reduce to a single arithmetic operation — subtraction. That learning comes naturally in the course of doing a wide variety of word and picture problems, including many examples of each of the interpretation/model combinations described above.

As children learn the interpretations and uses of subtraction, they also practice computational skills. As with addition, computational work starts with 1–digit subtractions, proceeds to 'subtraction within 20' (subtraction up to $19 - 9$) and place value skills, and on to multi-digit subtraction. Again, children practice thinking strategies, and use them for subtractions not yet known. Here are four such thinking strategies for subtraction.

Counting down. Simple subtractions, such as $8 - 2$, are easily done by counting down; for this purpose, children learn the count down chant "10, 9, 8, ..., 0," and later practice counting down from any number, "32, 31, 30, 29, 28, ..." More sophisticated count-downs make an intermediate stop at a multiple of 10. For example, to find $13 - 6$ one can start at 13, count-down 3, then count down 3 more. This two-step method is sometimes called *splitting the subtrahend*. It can be illustrated with number bonds:

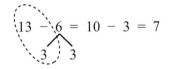

$$13 - 6 = 10 - 3 = 7$$

Counting up. One can also compute differences by *counting up*. For example, to find $15 - 12$ we can start at 12 and count up to 15 to conclude that $15 - 12 = 3$. For numbers in different decades we can count in two steps: to find $15 - 8$, we start at 8, go up 2 to 10, then 5 more to 15, so the answer is $2 + 5 = 7$. This strategy is useful but not obvious; students must be carefully guided to it.

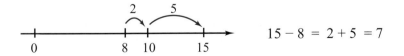

$$15 - 8 = 2 + 5 = 7$$

EXERCISE 4.2. *Find $234 - 188$ by counting up from 188. How far to 200? How much more to 234? Illustrate your thinking with a "hops on the number line" picture like the one above.*

Four-fact families.   A key step in teaching subtraction is to get students to relate subtraction facts to already-known addition facts. One common method is to introduce "four-fact families." These are sets of four facts that correspond to one whole-part decomposition, for example,

$$\begin{cases} 3+4 \;=\; 7 \\ 4+3 \;=\; 7 \end{cases} \qquad \begin{aligned} 7-3 \;=\; 4 \\ 7-4 \;=\; 3 \end{aligned}$$

A much better method is to use number bonds, which display *all four facts in a single picture.*

Four-fact families are sometimes misconstrued as lists of facts to be memorized. Actually, their role is the opposite — to *reduce* memorization by pointing out that what seems to be four different problems is actually a single already-known fact. Thus the four fact families are not themselves important; their role is simply to help get children mentally moving back and forth between addition and subtraction.

Compensation.   For addition, compensation was a way of adjusting the summands to make the problem easier. Compensation for subtraction has the same goal, but this time we adjust the problem by adding or subtracting *the same amount* to both the minuend and the subtrahend, thereby leaving the difference unchanged. For example, $26 - 9$ is the same as adding 1 to both the minuend and the subtrahend, getting the simpler problem $27 - 10 = 17$.

add or subtract the same amount from both

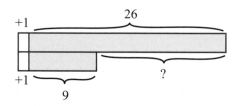

This method works well when the subtrahend — the amount subtracted — is converted to a multiple of 10 or 100. To see why, consider the problem of finding $86 - 19$. Note that 19 is an awkward number to subtract, 20 would be easier. We can arrange that by compensation:

$$86 - 19 \quad \xrightarrow[\text{to both}]{\text{add 1}} \quad 87 - 20 \qquad \text{now easy!}$$

The alternative — using compensation to replace the 86 by 90 — gives

$$86 - 19 \quad \xrightarrow[\text{to both}]{\text{add 4}} \quad 90 - 23$$

but does not make the problem much easier! Thus it is generally easiest to use compensation to "simplify the amount subtracted."

EXERCISE 4.3. *Use compensation to find the following differences. Write your answer in two steps as shown in part (a).*

(a) $35 - 18 = 37 - 20 = $ ____

(c) $93 - 25$

(b) $71 - 33$

(d) $124 - 57$

Place value considerations. Children become bored with the numbers $0 - 20$! One of the goals for the end of first grade is to begin addition and subtraction with larger numbers, up to 100 and beyond. The new ideas and difficulties that arise are not due to the intrinsic size of the numbers. Rather, they stem from place value issues. Children must learn how addition and subtraction play out in decimal place-value notation. That can be done by introducing place value thinking strategies in two stages.

The first stage is a sequence of thinking strategies which lead to the idea that *one adds (and subtracts) the tens and ones separately*. The sequence moves step-by-step beginning with the simplest cases. As shown in the chart below, the first step is adding two multiples of 10, the second is adding a multiple of 10 to a general 2–digit number, and the third is adding two 2–digit numbers which do not involve "carrying," "borrowing," or "rebundling." All cases can be nicely illustrated with dimes and pennies. Coins also show how to extend the principle to 3–digit numbers ("add the hundreds, tens, and ones separately"). At this stage the ones and tens can be added in either order; there is no logical reason or advantage to adding the ones first.

Place value thinking strategies I

$30 + 40$	$3 \text{ tens} + 4 \text{ tens} = 7 \text{ tens}$
$34 + 10, \; 52 + 40,$	add tens
$22 + 13$	add tens and ones separately

The second stage of place value thinking strategies develop the idea of rebundling. For addition that means recognizing that $50 + 12$ is the same as 62. For subtraction it means learning to go the other way, to think of 82 as $70 + 12$. These rebundling strategies are preparation for learning the standard methods of column addition and subtraction.

Place value thinking strategies II

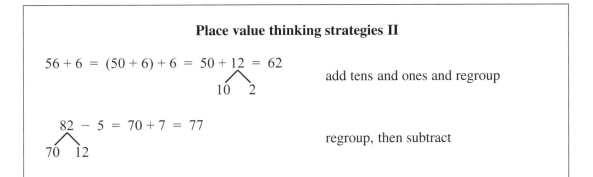

$56 + 6 = (50 + 6) + 6 = 50 + 12 = 62$
$\qquad\qquad\qquad\quad\, \overset{\displaystyle \frown}{10 \quad 2}$

add tens and ones and regroup

$82 - 5 = 70 + 7 = 77$
$\overset{\displaystyle \frown}{70 \quad 12}$

regroup, then subtract

We will return to these place value strategies in the context of Mental Math in Section 2.1, and will see how they are applied to algorithms in Section 3.1.

Homework Set 4

1. a) Illustrate $13 - 8$ by crossing out objects in a set model.
   b) Illustrate $16 - 7$ as hops on a number line.

2. (*Study the Textbook!*)   Study pages $18 - 23$ of Primary Math 3A and answer the following questions.

   a) How does the pictured "student helper" define the difference of two numbers? What is the difference between 9 and 3? The difference between 3 and 9? Do you see how this definition avoids negative numbers?

   b) State which interpretation is used in the following subtraction problems: (i) Pages $20 - 21$, Problems 4, 6, and 7   (ii) Page 23, Problems 6, 8b, and 9a.

3. (*Mental Math*) Do the indicated calculations mentally by looking for pairs whose difference is a multiple of 10.
   a) $34 + 17 - 24 - 27$ b) $28 - 16 + 36 - 4$.

4. (*Mental Math*) Do the indicated subtractions mentally by "counting up."
   a) $14 - 8$ b) $178 - 96$ c) $425 - 292$.

5. (*Mental Math*)   Do the indicated calculations mentally using compensation.
   a) $57 - 19$ b) $86 - 18$
   c) $95 - 47$ d) $173 - 129$.

6. a) Illustrate the take-away interpretation for $54 - 28$ using a set model. (Draw pennies and dimes and cross some out, but be careful!)

   b) Illustrate the counting-up method for finding $54 - 28$ by showing two hops on the number line.

   c) Illustrate the comparison interpretation for $54 - 28$ using a set model (use pennies and dimes again and ask a question).

   d) Illustrate the comparison interpretation for $54 - 28$ using a measurement model. (Before you start, examine *all* the diagrams in this section).

7. Make up first grade word problems of the following types:

   a) The take-away interpretation for finding $15 - 7$.

   b) The part-whole interpretation for $26 - 4$.

   c) The comparison interpretation for $17 - 5$.

8. Answer the following questions about this section:

   a) In which grade should teaching of subtraction facts begin?

   b) What is "subtraction within 20?"

1.5 Multiplication

Multiplication of whole numbers is often introduced as repeated addition:

$$3 \times 5 = \underbrace{5 + 5 + 5}_{3 \; times}.$$

factors
product

In the multiplication $3 \times 5 = 15$, the numbers 3 and 5 are called *factors* and 15 is the *product*.

The notation 3×5 is used exclusively through most of elementary school. The common alternative notations $3 \cdot 5$ and $3(5)$ are introduced only in grade 6, after the students have a firm understanding of multiplication, including multiplication of fractions. These alternative notations are shorter and avoid confusion between $\times$ and the letter x used in algebra. On the other hand, the very idea of having three different notations for multiplication is confusing. Thus it is best to consistently use the $\times$ notation until students are very comfortable with multiplication.

Multiplication is taught and explained using three models. Again, it is important for understanding that students see all three models early and often, and learn to use them when solving word problems.

Set model: 3×5 is interpreted as "3 groups of 5 objects."

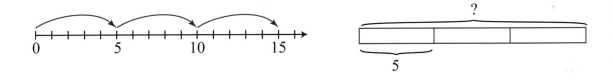

Measurement model: 3×5 is illustrated as '3 hops on the number line, each of length 5' or by a bar diagram showing 3 sections of length 5.

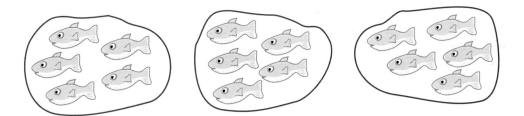

Rectangular array model: 3×5 is illustrated as 3 rows of 5 objects.

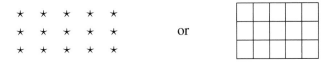

Caution — The picture on the right is frequently called the 'area model,' but that term is misleading in this context. It is important to draw in the grid in the above diagram and explain that the product 3×5 is the total number of squares in the array. One cannot explain 3×5 as the "area of a 3 by 5 rectangle" because *area is not introduced until grade 3 or 4*. In fact, area is taught starting from the rectangular array model of multiplication.

commutative
associative
distributive

Properties of Multiplication.   The operation of multiplication of whole numbers has arithmetic properties' similar to those of addition:

- Multiplicative Identity: $5 \times 1 = 5$,
- Commutative property: $6 \times 7 = 7 \times 6$, and
- Associative property: $3 \times (4 \times 8) = (3 \times 4) \times 8$.

There is also an arithmetic property describing how addition and multiplication interact:

- Distributive property: $3 \times (5 + 8) = (3 \times 5) + (3 \times 8)$.

The identity property is obvious to children *after it is explained*. The explanation is simple: 1×5 is 1 group of 5, which is 5. This property, learned as the principle that "multiplying by 1 doesn't change a number," describes the special role of the number 1 in multiplication.

Commutativity is clear from rectangular arrays: the array

can be thought of as 3 (horizontal) groups of 5, or 5 (vertical) groups of 3, but the total number of squares is the same, namely 15. (Note that commutativity is definitely not clear because the first and second factors play different roles in the set model, the measurement model, and in the definition of multiplication!) Associativity can be illustrated by problems like counting the flowers in the picture below.

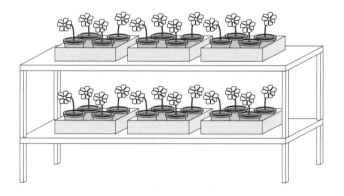

$$(2 \times 3) \text{ boxes of 4 flowers} = 2 \text{ shelves of } (3 \times 4) \text{ flowers,}$$
$$(2 \times 3) \times 4 = 2 \times (3 \times 4).$$

The commutative and associative properties are special cases of a single, much more intuitive property:

> **Any-order Property for Multiplication:** A list of whole numbers can be multiplied in any order, always with the same result. Thus $3 \times 4 \times 2$ can be computed as $(3 \times 4) \times 2$, or $(2 \times 3) \times 4$, or $4 \times (2 \times 3)$, etc.

As in the previous section, the Any-order property can be verified by repeatedly applying the commutative and associative properties. But it is the Any-order property, not the more formal commutative and associative properties, that students learn to use.

The distributive property can be illustrated using rectangular arrays:

$$\underbrace{3(2 + 5)}_{\text{total}} = \underbrace{(3 \times 2)}_{\text{shaded}} + \underbrace{(3 \times 5)}_{\text{unshaded}}.$$

The distributive and Any-order properties are central ideas in elementary school mathematics. They explain and justify Mental Math strategies, computational procedures such as column multiplication, and the rules for adding and multiplying fractions and negative numbers. The arithmetic properties for addition and multiplication are the most fundamental properties that are true for all numbers; for that reason they form the backbone of algebra. Fluency with arithmetic is impossible without a clear intuitive understanding of the arithmetic properties.

The arithmetic properties are taught *as principles* about the ways that whole numbers behave; they are illustrated with models using specific numbers and are practiced with Mental Math and word problems. They are not 'rules' to be memorized. As you will see, the Primary Mathematics textbooks never mention the terms commutative, associative, or distributive, yet they instill a deep understanding of those properties!

Thinking Strategies for Multiplication

Multiplication is commonly taught in three overlapping stages. As with the three stages for teaching addition, the ordering and timing of these stages is largely determined by the difficulty of the mathematics. Before starting multiplication, students should be proficient at three skills:

- counting to one hundred,
- addition doubles from $1 + 1$ up to $10 + 10$, and
- skip counting by 2, 3, 5, and 10.

Stage I. The introductory stage, usually begun at the end of grade 1, develops the meaning and interpretations of multiplication. Multiplication is introduced using repeated addition, groups, and rectangular arrays. Children work out picture and word problems interspersed with straight numerical questions (3×5). The emphasis is on recognizing multiplication as a new operation, separate from addition. To that end, children are taught the following simple thinking strategies.

Multiplying by 2	doubles known from addition
Multiplying by 3 and 4	skip counting
Multiplying by 0 and 1	easy, once explained
Multiplying by 10	$3 \times 10 = 3$ tens $= 30$

Practice problems also lead students to realize that remembering basic multiplication facts (such as $3 \times 4 = 12$) saves much effort, and that known facts can be used to construct new ones (e.g. 4×4 is 4 more than 3×4).

Stage II. The long middle stage of teaching multiplication lasts through grades 2 and into grade 3 and has two goals: increasing calculational proficiency and deepening conceptual understanding. This is done in Primary Math 2A, 2B, and 3A. During this stage students see plenty of word problems, Mental Math, and 'worksheet' problems and begin committing 1–digit multiplication facts to memory.

The word problems are initially simple, but evolve into two-step problems like the following.

EXERCISE 5.2. *Mrs. Larson bought 2 boxes of cakes. Each box contained 18 cakes. If each cake cost $5, what was the total cost?*

Why is this a two-step problem? How can you use the Any-order property to find the answer easily?

Mental Math builds up to applications of the distributive rule such as the quick ways of multiplying by 9 and 11 described in this section's homework, and the following examples.

EXAMPLE 5.3. *(a) We can find 6×20 mentally by*

$$6 \times 20 = 6 \times (2 \times 10) = (6 \times 2) \times 10 = 12 \text{ tens} = 120.$$

This 'teacher's solution' displays in writing the intermediate thinking steps that are done mentally. Notice that this solution involves a place value notion, the Any-order property, and a known 1–digit multiplication.

(b) We can find 7×9 mentally by using the distributive property:

$$7 \times 9 = 7 \times (10 - 1) = (7 \times 10) - 7 = 70 - 7 = 63.$$

By grade 3, Mental Math involves multiplication of 2–digit numbers, for example

$$7 \times 14 = 7 \times (10 + 4) = (7 \times 10) + (7 \times 4) = 70 + 28 = 98.$$

The goal here is not to teach the fact that $7 \times 14 = 98$, but rather to have students understand the distributive property and begin to appreciate its power. In fact, understanding this method for finding 7×14 is an essential first step toward developing the standard paper and pencil procedure for multiplication.

During this second stage students also learn to make use of the following thinking strategies:

Multiplying by 5	from skip counting
Commutative property	clear from rectangular arrays
Multiplying by 9	$6 \times 9 = 6$ tens $- 6$
$3 \times 40, 20 \times 30$	place value
Any-order and distributive properties	Mental Math practice

Stage III. The third stage is a relatively brief time spent closing the topic of 1–digit multiplication and obtaining fluency. This is done in Primary Math 3A pages 68–90, and is a third grade Common Core standard. The goal is simple: *all students should have memorized the multiplications up to* 9×9 *by the end of third grade.*

Why? Ironically, the ability to immediately recall these 'basic facts' is essential for the *conceptual* understanding of multiplication. It enables children to regard one-digit multiplication as trivial, which it is. This frees up short-term memory, allowing them to turn their attention to the overall structure of the problem. Conversely, children who have not memorized the basic facts will continue to think of multiplication as a *procedure* requiring time and attention. This can exhaust limited short-term memory. Children who do not know the basic facts are not merely slower at calculating, they have conceptual difficulties solving multi-step problems — see Problem 9 in Homework Set 5 below.

Finally, fluency with the basic multiplication facts gives children confidence, confidence that they have mastered elementary multiplication and are ready to tackle harder problems. Confidence is a major factor in learning and enjoying mathematics and mastery instills confidence.

The thinking strategies developed in Stages I and II greatly reduce the effort needed to learn the 121 facts from 0×0 to 10×10. Commutativity reduces this number almost in half to 66. Multiplication by 0, 1, and 10 are trivial, and multiplication by 2 is already known from doubles in addition. That leaves only 28 facts. Standard tricks help in learning multiplication by 5 and 9 (see the homework problems below), leaving only 15 facts. Five of these ($3 \times 3, 3 \times 4, 4 \times 4,$ $3 \times 6, 4 \times 6$) involve small numbers and are usually learned early. Thus only about 10 facts remain as students enter the closing stage of basic multiplication. Those remaining facts can be systematically taught in three steps:

Remaining squares $6 \times 6, \ldots, 9 \times 9$	learned
$6 \times 7, 7 \times 8, 8 \times 9$	learned via distributive property
Remaining 1–digit multiplications	memorized!

For the multiplications listed in the middle row, the thinking strategy is to use known squares and the distributive property; thus $6 \times 7 = (6 \times 6) + 6 = 36 + 6 = 42$.

Talk about "memorizing math facts" may be misleading. Multiplication is learned by doing problems — hundreds and hundreds of problems involving a balanced mix of Mental Math problems, worksheet arithmetic problems, and word problems. As students do those practice problems, they see the advantages of memorizing the 1–digit multiplication facts. Simultaneously, practice makes those facts very familiar, and many are learned. This learning is natural in the context of solving problems — children learn by doing!

Only at the very end are the students asked to consciously memorize whatever facts they remain unsure about (research has shown that the most troublesome facts are 6×7, 6×8, 6×9, 7×8, 7×9, and 8×9). When those are learned the whole class has mastered 1-digit multiplication and the topic is closed.

Homework Set 5

1. (*Study the Textbook!*)   The following questions will help you study Primary Math 3A.

   a) Problem 1 on page 40 shows multiplication as a rectangular array and as repeated addition, in order to illustrate the _____ property of multiplication.

   b) (i) Problems $3 - 5$ on pages 41 and 42 all use the _____ model for multiplication.
   (ii) Problems 3 and 4 on page 46 describe set model situations, but illustrate them using _____.
   (iii) The word problems on page 47 use a variety of models. Which is used in Problem 6? In Problem 9?
   (iv) Which model is used in the three illustrated problems on page 49?

   c) The purpose of Problem 2 on page 40 is to link multiplication with _____.

2. Continuing in Primary Math 3A,

   a) What are students asked to make on pages $68 - 69$? What will they be used for?

   b) On page 71, what model is used in Problem 1? What property is being illustrated in 1b?

   c) Problem 2 on pages $71 - 72$ shows how one can use a known fact, such as $6 \times 5 = 30$, to find related facts, such as 6×6 and 6×7. What arithmetic property is being used?

   d) Draw a rectangular array illustrating how the fact $6 \times 6 = 36$ can be used to find 6×12.

   e) Problem 3 on page 73 shows that if you know the multiplication facts obtained from skip counting by 6 then you know ten additional facts by the _____ property.

3. Illustrate the following multiplication statements using a set or rectangular array model:

   a) $5 \times 3 = 3 \times 5$
   b) $2 \times (3 \times 4) = 6 \times 4$
   c) $3(4 + 5) = (3 \times 4) + (3 \times 5)$.
   d) $6 \times 1 = 6$.

4. Identify the arithmetic property being used.

   a) $7 \times 5 = 5 \times 7$
   b) $6 + 0 = 6$
   c) $3 + (5 + 2) = (3 + 5) + 2$
   d) $1 \times \text{ꓵꓵ} = \text{ꓵꓵ}$
   e) $3 + 4 = 1(3 + 4)$
   f) $3(8 \times 6) = (3 \times 8)6$
   g) $(7 \times 5) + (2 \times 5) = (7 + 2) \times 5$

5. (*Mental Math*)   Multiplying a number by 5 is easy: take half the number and multiply by 10. (For an odd number like 17 one can find 16×5 and add 5.) Use that method to mentally multiply the following numbers by 5: 6, 8, 7, 12, 23, 84, 321. Write down your answer in the manner described in the box at the end of Section 2.1.

6. (*Mental Math*)   Compute 24×15 in your head by thinking of 15 as $10 + 5$.

7. *(Mental Math)* Multiplying a number by 9 is easy: take 10 times the number and subtract the number. For example, $6 \times 9 = 60 - 6$ ("6 tens minus 6"). This method is neatly illustrated at the bottom of page 72 in Primary Math 3A.

   a) Draw a similar rectangular array that illustrates this method for finding 9×4.

   b) Use this method to mentally multiply the following numbers by 9: 5, 7, 8, 9, 21, 33, and 89.

   c) By this method 7×9 is $70 - 7$. That is less than 70 and more than $70 - 10 = 60$, so its tens digit must be 6. In fact, whenever a 1-digit number is multiplied by 9, the tens digit of the product is _____ less than the given number. Furthermore, the ones digit of $7 \times 9 = 70 - 7$ is $10 - 7 = 3$, the tens complement of 7. When a 1-digit number is multiplied by 9, is the ones digit of the product always the tens complement of the number?

   d) Use the facts of part c) to explain why the "fingers method" (Primary Math 3A page 87) works.

   e) These mental math methods can be used in the course of solving word problems. Answer Problems 5 and 6 on page 89 of Primary Math 3A.

8. *(Mental Math)* Explain how to compute the following mentally by writing down the intermediate step(s) as in Example 5.3.

(a) $5 \times 87 \times 2$
(b) $4 \times 13 \times 25$
(c) 16×11
(d) 17×30.

9. Try to solve the following multi-step word problems in your head.

   • After giving 157¢ to each of 3 boys and 54¢ to a fourth boy, Mr. Green had 15¢ left. How much did he have to start with?

   • After giving 7 candies to each of 3 boys and 4 candies to a fourth boy, Mr. Green had 15 candies left. How many candies did he have at first?

These two problems are solved by the same strategy, but the first is much harder because the first step overloads working memory — while doing the multiplication one forgets the rest of the problem.

   a) How would the second problem appear to a student who does not know what 7×3 is? Is there an advantage to instantly knowing $7 \times 3 = 21$, or is it enough for the student to know a way of finding 7×3?

   b) If one first observes that $150 \times 3 = (15 \times 3)$ tens $= 450$, what must be added to 450 to solve the first problem? Write down the intermediate steps horizontally like in Example 5.3.

1.6 Division

Division of whole numbers is defined in terms of multiplication using the idea of a "missing factor."

> **DEFINITION 6.1.** *Division is defined by missing factors: the number* $56 \div 8$ *is the missing factor in* _____ $\times\, 8 = 56$.

dividend
divisor
quotient

The numbers in a division problem are called the *dividend*, *divisor*, and *quotient*:

$$\underbrace{56}_{\text{dividend}} \div \underbrace{8}_{\text{divisor}} = \underbrace{7}_{\text{quotient.}}$$

By this definition $(56 \div 8) \times 8 = 56$, so if we divide by 8 and then multiply by 8 we get our original number back. Thus multiplication and division are "opposite operations" in exactly the same way that addition and subtraction are.

As with multiplication, division word problems can use either a set or a measurement model. But division is more interesting because there are *two distinct interpretations of division*. For example, we can explain $20 \div 4$ using the "missing factor" approach: $20 \div 4$ is the solution to either

$$20 = 4 \times \text{\_\_\_\_} \qquad\qquad \text{or} \qquad\qquad 20 = \text{\_\_\_\_} \times 4.$$

Because multiplication is commutative, these two equations have the same numerical answer, namely 5. But they have different interpretations. The first asks "20 is 4 groups of what size?" while the second asks "20 is how many groups of 4 units?" These two interpretations of division have names, and each can be neatly visualized as bar diagrams.

partitive
division

measurement
division

Interpretation	Interpretive question	Diagram
Partitive division:	20 is 4 groups of what size?	20 ?
Measurement division:	20 is how many groups of 4?	20 ... ? ... 4

When we know the original amount and the *number of parts*, we use partitive division to find the size of each part. On the other hand, when we know the original amount and the *size or measure of one part*, we use measurement division to find the number of parts. These two interpretations are easily distinguished in word problems. Primary Mathematics 2A uses simple word problems and illustrations to describe both interpretations and show why they are different.

EXAMPLE 6.2. *5 packets of coffee beans weigh 750 g. How much does each packet weigh?*

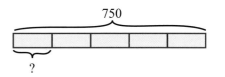

This problem asks "750 g is 5 packets of what size packet?" This is partitive division — the number of groups (packets) is specified and we must find the size of each. One can also think of distributing the 750 grams equally among 5 packets (or 5 people), and for that reason partitive division is sometimes called *sharing division*.

sharing division

We use divison to find the number in each group.

750 ÷ 5

EXAMPLE 6.3. *Sarah made 210 cupcakes. She put them into boxes of 10 each. How many boxes of cupcakes were there?*

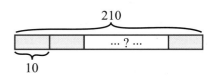

This question asks "210 is how many boxes of 10 cupcakes?" This is measurement division — the unit (10 cupcakes) is specified and we must find the number of units.

We also use divison to find the number of groups.

210 ÷ 10

Division word problems use one or the other of these interpretations. To identify which, draw the bar diagram, or note whether we are asked for the size of each part (partitive) or the number of parts (measurement). On the other hand, straight numerical problems, such as $35 \div 5$, have no built-in interpretation. In order to create a word problem illustrating $35 \div 5$ *one of the interpretations has to be chosen.*

Creating a division word problem for $a \div b$ involves three steps:

1. Make a choice: partitive or measurement division.

2. Think of the corresponding diagram or question ("X is Y groups of what size?" or "X is how many groups of Y?"). This provides a 'skeleton' of a word problem.

3. Flesh this out into a real-world problem.

EXAMPLE 6.4. *Here are two ways to create a word problem for $35 \div 5$ following the steps above.*

a) Choosing partitive division, the question is "35 is 5 groups of what size?" Thinking of weight and food leads to the word problem "If 5 candy bars weigh 35 ounces, how much does each one weigh?"

b) Choosing measurement division, the question is "35 is how many 5s?" Thinking of money and clothes leads to the word problem "T-shirts cost $5 each. How many can you buy for $35?"

Making up word problems is a skill acquired through practice. It is discussed in Chapter 2.

A Teaching Sequence for Division

The Primary Mathematics textbooks introduce division in second grade, first as partitive division and then as measurement division. Pictures are very important in the beginning. Shortly after division is introduced, four-fact families with the associated pictures are presented.

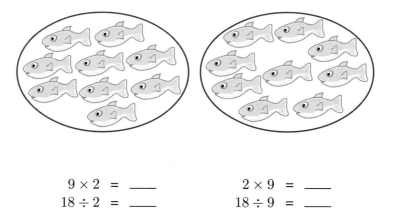

$$9 \times 2 = \underline{\qquad} \qquad 2 \times 9 = \underline{\qquad}$$
$$18 \div 2 = \underline{\qquad} \qquad 18 \div 9 = \underline{\qquad}$$

This encourages students to do division by recalling known multiplication facts. From that point on, multiplication and division are taught in tandem. For instance, students learn the multiples of 2 and 3, then in the next section learn how to divide by 2 and 3.

In any curriculum, it is important that students see many examples of both partitive and measurement division — both are needed for 'real-life' applications and for understanding later concepts (for example, division of fractions). Students who see a balanced mix of the two types of division problems will more quickly learn to recognize division in its different guises and to view division as a single, simple, mathematical operation.

Why distinguish partitive and measurement division? This distinction is not something students need to know, but it is something that can make you a better teacher. A key point of this section is that students must come to associate the operation of division with completely two different types of word problems. That difference is not apparent to adults, who long ago learned to instantly associate both with division; it requires effort to become conscious of that automatic association. But teachers who learn to distinguish partitive and measurement division are better able to understand their students' thinking. They are in a better position to insure that their students see an appropriate mix of division problems, and are better prepared for making up word problems for division.

Thus far in this section, as in the Primary Mathematics textbooks through the middle of grade 3, all division problems have had whole number answers — there have been no remainders. The introduction of remainders is the next stage in teaching division. Remainders appear naturally in both set and measurement models as the two examples below show.

40 eggs is how many dozen?	How many feet in 40 inches?

3 dozen, with 4 eggs remaining.	Three feet, with 4 inches remaining.

Underlying all divisions-with-remainder problems is a single mathematical fact, called the Quotient–Remainder Theorem. The theorem generalizes the missing factor definition of division. For the example $40 \div 12$, it says that there are unique whole numbers which fill in the blanks

$$40 = (12 \times \underbrace{\boxed{}}_{\text{quotient}}) + \underbrace{\boxed{}}_{\text{remainder}}$$

in such a way that the remainder is less than 12. The proof is exactly as in the pictures above: starting at 40 we can repeatedly subtract 12 until we reach a whole number less than 12. Of course, there is nothing special about the numbers 40 and 12. The theorem holds if we replace the number 40 by an arbitrary whole number called 'A' and similarly replace 12 by a whole number 'k.' If A is a multiple of k then the quotient $A \div k$ is the number q which satisfies $A = k \times q$. In general, there is a remainder r and that remainder is less than k. Thus

THEOREM 6.5 (Quotient–Remainder Theorem). *For any two whole numbers A and k with $k \neq 0$ there are unique whole numbers q (the quotient) and r (the remainder) such that*

$$A = (k \times q) + r$$

and $0 \leq r < k$.

EXAMPLE 6.6. *The Quotient–Remainder Theorem for* $23 \div 4$ *can be illustrated by a "rectangular array with remainder"*

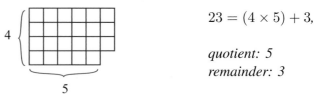

$$23 = (4 \times 5) + 3,$$

quotient: 5
remainder: 3

Finally, there is one point that inevitably comes up in discussions of division: division by 0. Most textbooks state that division by 0 is "undefined." That statement does not mean that dividing by zero is against some rule or law. Rather, it means that *there is no answer that makes sense*. Understanding that point requires considering two separate cases.

dividing by 0

Case 1: If $10 \div 0$ were equal to some number, it would be the missing factor in ____ $\times\, 0 = 10$. ("How many groups of size 0 make 10?") There is no such number! Thus $10 \div 0$ does not specify a number.

Case 2: $0 \div 0$ is also undefined, but for a different reason. Solving $0 \div 0 =$ ____ is the same as solving $0 = 0 \times$ ____. But *any* number fits in this blank! Thus the division expression $0 \div 0$ does not represent one particular number, as all other division expressions do.

In the first case division by zero does not specify *any* number, while in the second case it specifies *every* number. The phrase "division by 0 is undefined" is the standard way of expressing both these cases at once.

Homework Set 6

1. Identify whether the following problems are using measurement (MD) or partitive division (PD) (if in doubt, try drawing a bar diagram).

   a) Jim tied 30 sticks into 3 equal bundles. How many sticks were in each bundle?

   b) 24 balls are packed into boxes of 6. How many boxes are there?

   c) Mr. Lin tied 195 books into bundles of 5 each. How many bundles were there?

   d) 6 children shared 84 balloons equally. How many balloons did each child get?

   e) Jill bought 8 m of cloth for $96. Find the cost of 1 m of cloth.

   f) We drove 1280 miles from Michigan to Florida in 4 days. What was our average distance per day?

2. To understand the different uses of division, students must see a mix of partitive and measurement division word problems. This problem shows how that is done in the Primary Math books, first in grade 3, then again (with larger numbers) in grade 4.

   Identify whether the following problems use measurement or partitive division by writing MD or PD for each, separated by commas.

   a) Problems 10 and 11 on page 43 of Primary Math 3A.

   b) Problems 6 − 10 on page 65 of Primary Math 3A.

   c) Problems 7 − 9 on page 35 of Primary Math 4A.

3. Illustrate with a bar diagram.

   a) measurement division for $56 \div 8$.
   b) partitive division for $132 \div 4$.
   c) measurement division for $2000 \div 250$.
   d) partitive division for $256 \div 8$.
   e) measurement division for $140 \div 20$.
   f) measurement division for $143 \div 21$.

4. Make up a word problem for the following using the procedure of Example 6.4.

   a) measurement division for $84 \div 21$.

b) partitive division for $91 \div 5$.

c) measurement division for $143 \div 21$.

5. Illustrate the Quotient–Remainder Theorem as specified.

a) A number line picture for $59 \div 10$ (show jumps of 10).

b) A set model for $14 \div 4$.

c) A bar diagram, using measurement division, for $71 \div 16$.

d) A rectangular array for $28 \div 6$.

6. One might guess that the properties of multiplication also hold for division, in which case we would have:

a) Commutative: $a \div b = b \div a$.

b) Associativity: $(a \div b) \div c = a \div (b \div c)$.

c) Distributivity: $a \div (b + c) = (a \div b) + (a \div c)$.

whenever a, b, and c are whole numbers. By choosing specific values of the numbers a, b, and c, give examples (other than dividing by zero) showing that each of these three "properties" is *false*.

1.7 Addendum on Classroom Practice

This course focuses on mathematics. But in addition to knowing subject matter, teachers must also know what works and does not work in the classroom. Thus this course is only a first step toward becoming an effective mathematics teacher. Your education courses will build on this course, giving you the knowledge and classroom skills needed to teach mathematics effectively, topic by topic.

The distinction between what is mathematics and what is teaching methodology can be confusing. This course contains many discussions (of models, component skills, teaching sequences, potential student errors, etc.) which might at first seem to be pedagogy, not mathematics. But those topics are instances where *the logic of the mathematics dictates the order and manner in which mathematics is developed in the classroom.* Understanding such topics is essentially a matter of understanding the mathematics.

This supplementary section gives some ideas about what lies beyond this course. It mentions some aspects of classroom practice that will be covered in your teacher education courses. Of course, classroom practice varies from grade to grade, subject to subject, and topic to topic. The teaching techniques that work best for teaching division to second-graders are different from those best for teaching fractions to fourth-graders. To keep the discussion concrete we will give examples related only to teaching counting, leaving it to you to see how the same themes apply to other topics in mathematics.

Lesson Planning. As a teacher, you will plan and prepare lessons every day. The quality of that preparation will be a major factor in your success as a teacher. Yet there will be no one in the classroom to help you and the time available for preparation will be limited. You will get essentially no guidance or support from your school administrators. Your teacher's manual is likely to be woefully inadequate. You will be continually scrambling to produce, from somewhere, supplementary material for the best students, for the weakest students, and for the class as a whole. There will be whole weeks when you will have to prepare mathematics lessons with no materials at all to work from. How will you manage?

Well, teaching mathematics will seem much more manageable at the end of this course, when you have a clear vision of what elementary mathematics *is* and a solid understanding of its details. You will then appreciate how teaching mathematics differs from teaching other subjects. For example, one important principle is:

- Mathematics is learned through practice. Practice means doing problems — hundreds and hundreds of problems each year. In elementary school, one hour per day should be devoted to mathematics.

In your mathematics education methods course you will learn how to use your knowledge of mathematics to select and organize problems and prepare interesting lessons around them. You will also learn how to initiate lessons, provide encouragement, anticipate student difficulties, and how to keep the class focused on the mathematics.

Assessment. Good teaching requires that the teacher know, at all times, where the students stand: what they know and don't know, what is easy and hard, what is new and what is familiar. Gifted teachers acquire a feel for this. But even the best teachers must regularly confirm their beliefs about student knowledge through assessments.

The word 'assessment' refers to any kind of test, written or oral, formal or informal, planned or spontaneous — anything used to gauge what students know and what they have learned. This includes tests and quizzes, but it also includes one-on-one conversations with students, and listening to students' responses when called on. It does not include students' *volunteered* responses to teachers' questions; the volunteers are, of course, the students who know the answers and their responses can mislead the teacher into thinking that other students know as much.

There are several types of assessment, distinguished by their purposes. *Prognostic* tests measure students background skills; they are used to predict achievement of individuals and of entire classes and to gauge where to begin instruction. The very first assessment of elementary school is a prognostic test:

EXAMPLE 7.1. *Before beginning instruction in counting, a kindergarten teacher should determine (a) to what number each child can already count, and (b) whether each child understands what the numbers represent.*

Of course, similar prognostic assessments are necessary at the beginning of each grade and each new mathematics topic.

Diagnostic tests are intended to reveal the strengths and weaknesses of students on a specific topic or skill. The evaluation serves two purposes: it shows the student how well he is accomplishing the tasks set for him, and it gives the teacher feedback about teaching effectiveness.

Diagnostic tests

Instructional tests are intended to promote and consolidate learning. An example is a weekly spelling quiz. Students learn both while preparing for the quiz and, as research indicates, during the quiz itself [21, 51]. Mathematics, more than any other subject, builds on itself. Thus instructional tests which are cumulative, that is, which contain items from topics covered earlier, are particularly appropriate for mathematics teaching. Cumulative testing keeps earlier material fresh and helps make it familiar and comfortable, which in turn makes learning new material easier. In that way, repeated cumulative assessment keeps instruction spiraling upward.

Instructional tests

All teachers must know how to construct assessments and how to use the results to guide lesson planning. Making up mathematics assessments requires a solid knowledge of the subject, careful judgements about the capabilities of the students, and familiarity with some pedagogical theory (for example, knowing the several reasons why one should begin each test with an easy question). You will learn these things in your teaching methods classes.

Cognitive Issues. The literatures of mathematics education and cognitive psychology contain interesting studies about how children respond to specific conceptual difficulties and teaching approaches. The quality of those studies varies considerably; some studies contain errors [7] and omit important variables (such as how much teaching parents are doing). Nevertheless, those studies point out pitfalls teachers should watch for. Here are two examples related to counting.

(1) The teen numbers 13, 14, ..., 19 can cause trouble because in English they are read starting at the right ("fourteen"), while all higher numbers are read left to right (23 is "twenty three"). This leads to confusion between numbers like 15 and 51. It may help to pass quickly on to the regular numbers $20 - 100$.

(2) The counting chart (below) used in many elementary school programs can confuse children. Because the numbered boxes have width it is not clear where to start and stop counting. Some children attempt to find '4+3' by pointing to '4' and counting three steps ("4 ... 5 ... 6"), concluding that $4 + 3 = 6$. Worse, when a teacher explains the correct procedure both methods seem equally valid, further confusing the child. These issues are completely avoided by using the number line, where the numbers label *points*.

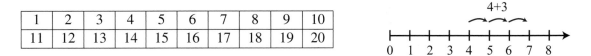

1	2	3	4	5	6	7	8	9	10
11	12	13	14	15	16	17	18	19	20

Developmental Issues. Elementary school children are developing and maturing. With each passing year they increase their attention span, fine motor skills, and reading and writing abilities. Their social skills develop and their attitude toward school and their place in it evolves. Consequently, some aspects of teaching vary from grade to grade. Here are three such considerations that affect teaching mathematics in grades K–2.

(1) Young children have short attention spans. Mathematics is best learned in the mornings when the students are better able to concentrate.

(2) Many five and six year olds, especially boys, do not yet have the fine motor skills needed for writing numbers and letters less than, say, a half inch tall. This is acquired with practice. In the meanwhile, teachers should be on guard for worksheets requiring tiny writing.

(3) Similar considerations hold for reading. Some children may be unable to *read* a word problem or the directions on a worksheet, yet still be fully capable of doing the exercise. It often helps for the teacher to read the problems and directions aloud.

In the early grades mathematics ability is generally ahead of reading and writing skills. There exist elementary school programs that place a heavy burden on reading and writing, effectively postponing beginning arithmetic until second grade. But as the Primary Mathematics textbooks in grades 1 and 2 illustrate, one can do a substantial amount of mathematics with only a minimal amount of reading and writing. *Do not postpone mathematics until reading and writing skills develop.*

Manipulatives, computers and calculators. These classroom aids should be used judiciously.

manipulatives

1. *Manipulatives* are physical objects given to children and used as teaching aids. School districts often supply teachers with collections of plastic knick-knacks specially designed for teaching mathematics. Manipulatives can be helpful to initiate a new concept, but frequent use runs the risk that students will focus on the manipulatives rather than the arithmetic. In your education courses you will learn that manipulatives are useful for a limited number of topics, such as teaching about place value in grades K–2.

EXAMPLE 7.2. *a)* *The best manipulatives are ones used in everyday life, such as coins and tape measures.*

b) Pictures of objects, rather than actual physical objects, are the most useful because they are more abstract and can depict a great variety of situations.

c) *Teaching place value using Dienes Blocks (pictured below) requires care; the thousands block and the tens block look very different, while the two ones in the numeral 1813 look the same. The very point that has to be made — that it is the position that carries the information — is not true of the Dienes Blocks.*

Dienes blocks

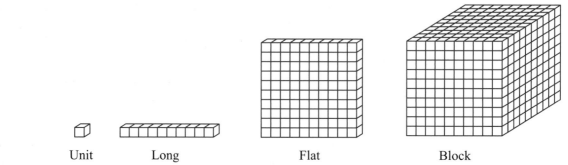

Unit   Long   Flat   Block

The goal of elementary school mathematics is getting students to manipulate numbers, not objects, and to regard numbers as concrete things, not abstractions. Consequently, *paper and pencil are by far the most useful and important manipulatives* and are ones the students will be using for the rest of their lives.

computer programs

2. *Computer programs* for teaching mathematics are usually loaded with distractions and poor exercises. Approach such programs with caution and a healthy skepticism about their claimed value. The better ones provide useful supplementary practice, but none can take the place of classroom instruction.

Here is one especially effective computer exercise for preschool or kindergarten students. It uses the computer simply to bypass the process of writing numbers by hand, which is laborious for children at this age.

Open up a word processor. Set the font size large (24 point). Have the child start typing, preferably at the numeric end of the keyboard,

1 (space, space) 2 (space, space) 3 (space, space) ...

with a parent or teacher saying the number aloud as the child types it, correcting errors, and giving hints. The child should keep going, a few minutes a day, day after day (yes, children will want to do this!). By the time 1000 is reached the child will have a good understanding of the decimal numeral system.

---

calculators

3. *Calculators* enable people to do arithmetic quickly without thinking about the actual numbers involved. There are times when this aids understanding. For example, high school

chemistry involves many calculational problems ("divide the measured mass 462.83 grams by the volume 0.367 liters to get the density"). Using a calculator is fast and keeps the focus on the chemistry. In that setting laborious hand calculations have no educational value because *chemistry students already know arithmetic*.

Elementary school students, on the other hand, are still learning arithmetic. Calculators also enable them to do arithmetic quickly without thinking about the numbers involved. But thinking about numbers is the main point of elementary school mathematics! Calculators allow students to bypass the very exercises which enable them to acquire an intuitive understanding for numbers and arithmetic, exercises in which the numbers are chosen to illustrate specific aspects of arithmetic with decimal numbers. In contrast, pencil and paper calculations force students to focus on such specifics and learn from them.

Calculator use also has psychological repercussions. Some students come to depend on them, and even begin to think of arithmetic as an activity which involves coaxing answers out of a little black box. Such students are missing one of the main benefits of mathematics education: confidence that they can solve problems *by themselves*.

For these reasons, most European and Asian countries minimize the use of calculators until grade 6, that is, until the students have mastered arithmetic.

Finally, many important aspects of teaching have little to do with either the mathematics or psychology. Children are remarkably quick to learn and have imaginations which enable them to handle abstractions well. They are enthusiastic about seeing new things, and they want to make a game of everything. Skillful teachers use those characteristics to make learning easy and natural. But that is possible only for teachers who have a very solid understanding of the mathematics they are teaching — teachers whose familiarity with the material enables them to focus their energy and attention on the children, rather than the mathematics. The goal of this course is to bring your understanding of elementary mathematics to that level.

CHAPTER 2

Mental Math and Word Problems

"Mental Math" means just that: doing calculations in your head. Solving problems mentally is a remarkably effective way to learn place value skills and the use of the distributive property. As students practice mental math they develop quick and flexible ways of doing simple arithmetic, and their understanding of arithmetic deepens. Mental Math is particularly appropriate for young children because it does not require reading or writing skills. For these reasons, Mental Math problems are incorporated into nearly all elementary school mathematics programs.

Word problems are another essential part of teaching mathematics. They show how mathematics is used in the real world and they develop skills at organizing and abstracting information, skills important for many things beyond mathematics. Teachers must be able to select, explain, and make up word problems. That requires learning to recognize the model and the arithmetic underlying a word problem. In Sections 2.2 and 2.3 we will discuss the use of models, one versus two-step problems, and pictorial methods of solving word problems.

2.1 Mental Math

Mental Math has several roles in elementary school. It can be an entertaining way for students to practice arithmetic facts. More importantly it

- solidifies understanding of place value, as in the problem $52 \times 10 = \_$,

- teaches how numbers can be rearranged and manipulated according to the Any-order and distributive properties, and

- demonstrates how the same answer can often be reached in different ways, some dramatically easier than others.

These skills are important aspects of understanding arithmetic. They are prerequisites for the arithmetic of fractions and decimals, and they help bridge the gap between arithmetic and algebra.

Being able to do complicated computations in your head is *not* one of the goals of Mental Math — that's what calculators are for. But with calculators there is no need to pay attention to place value, no need to simplify calculations by rearranging numbers, and no incentive to search for easier ways to do the arithmetic. Those important skills are not developed if all computations are done with a calculator.

Mental Math versus calculators

Why teachers need mental math →

Teachers must be adept at Mental Math, most obviously because they will be teaching it, but also to help their spontaneous interactions with students. Teachers need mental calculational skills to recognize student errors. They must be able to verify answers quickly while looking over a student's shoulder, and must be able to quickly judge the correctness of students' answers in conversations and in whole-class sessions.

This course will give you practice with Mental Math. You will do Mental Math problems in class and in many homework exercises. These will often involve numbers larger than the numbers used in elementary school Mental Math. This is not a form of punishment — there is a good reason for working with larger numbers. To understand Mental Math strategies, one must practice on problems where the answer is not immediately clear. When asked to find 9×8, for example, most adults simply remember the answer. No thinking is needed. But a similar problem with larger numbers, such as 9×28, forces adults to use Mental Math techniques. Those techniques are the same ones that elementary school students can be taught to use to find 9×8.

Facility at Mental Math can be developed by building on a few basic techniques and tricks. With practice, you can learn to apply these flexibly, alone and in combination, and to spot several different ways of doing the same problem. Below is a table summarizing some basic Mental Math methods. More detailed explanations and examples are given after the table.

Method	Example
Rearranging.	$40 + 37 + 60 = 100 + 37 = 137$
Split numbers as sums or products.	$4 \times 107 = (4 \times 100) + (4 \times 7)$ $8 \times 400 = 8 \times 4 \times 100 = 3200$
Compatible numbers: find pairs of numbers which are easily combined.	$25 \times 17 \times 4 = (25 \times 4) \times 17 = 1700$
Compensation: convert the problem to an easier one with the same answer.	see below
Left-to-right calculations may be easier.	$309 + 607 = 900 + (9 + 7) = 916$ $3 \times 706 = (3 \times 700) + (3 \times 6) = 2118$
Methods for multiplying and dividing by 4, 5, 8, 9, 10, 25, and 100.	see below

compatible numbers

compensation

left-to-right calculations

These methods can be applied in combination, and are especially useful when combined with estimation. This section focuses on Mental Math with whole numbers. We will later use the same methods with fractions, decimals, and real numbers. Estimation is covered in Section 3.5.

Rearranging. This means using the Any-order and distributive properties to simplify or to "split off an easier problem."

EXAMPLE 1.1.

    a) $2 \times 178 \times 5$ is $(2 \times 5) \times 178 = 1780$.

    b) 256×4 is $(250 \times 4) + (6 \times 4) = 1000 + 24 = 1024$.

    c) $84 \div 7$ is $(70 + 14) \div 7 = 10 + 2 = 12$.

    Rearranging is especially useful if one can spot *compatible numbers* — pairs or groups of numbers which are advantageously combined. In the problem $2 \times 178 \times 5$ above, the 2 and the 5 are compatible numbers.

EXAMPLE 1.2. *Here are three examples of rearrangements using compatible numbers.*

$$\overbrace{83 + 124 + 17} = 100 + 124 = 224.$$

$$\overbrace{4 \times 3 \times 23 \times 25} = 3 \times 23 \times 100 = 6,900.$$

$$40 + 25 + 60 + 5 + 35 + 70 = 100 + 100 + 35 = 235.$$

Can be done with 3 numbers (handwritten annotation)

Compensation. This technique comes in four varieties, one for each operation. In all cases the goal is to convert the problem to an easier one with the same answer.

Adding & Subtracting from numbers to be more managable (handwritten annotation in margin)

For $+$, one addend gives to the other.	$99 + 34$	"34 gives 1 to 99"	$= 100 + 33$
For $-$, change minuend and subtrahend by the same amount (simplify the amount subtracted).	$97 - 29$	increase both by 1	$= 98 - 30$
For $\times$, one factor gives to the other.	50×12	double 50, halve 12	$= 100 \times 6$
For $\div$, multiply (or divide) dividend and divisor by the same number.	$1600 \div 50$	double both	$= 3200 \div 100$

Thus for addition and multiplication "one number gives to the other," while for subtraction and division you do the same thing to both numbers. Generally, one tries to convert to a problem which involves a multiple of 10 or 100. For subtraction and division it should be the *second* number (the subtrahend or divisor) that is a multiple of 10 or 100.

EXERCISE 1.3. *Use compensation to find $82 - 43$, 35×18, and $420 \div 20$:*

$$82 - 43 = \Box - 40 = \Box.$$
$$35 \times 18 = \Box \times 9 = \Box.$$
$$420 \div 20 = \Box \div 10 = \Box.$$

Multiplying and dividing by 4, 5, 8, 9, 10, 25 and 100. It is easy to multiply by 10 or 100: just append one or two zeros to the end of the given number. In previous homework problems you have also seen some of the following shortcuts.

Goal	Strategy	Example
Multiply by 4	double twice.	$22 \times 4 = 44 \times 2 = 88$
Divide by 4	halve twice.	$168 \div 4 = 84 \div 2 = 42$
Multiply by 5	halve and multiply by 10.	$24 \times 5 = 12 \times 10 = 120$
Divide by 5	divide by 10 and double.	$130 \div 5 = 13 \times 2 = 26$
Multiply by 9	use $9x = 10x - x$ (append a zero and subtract the original number).	$46 \times 9 = 460 - 46 = 414$

The strategies for 4 can also be used for 8: to multiply by 8, double 3 times. To divide by 8, halve 3 times.

Multiplying and dividing by 25 is especially intuitive if one thinks about changing dollars and cents into quarters. For example, to find 36×25 ask yourself "How many dollars is 36 quarters?" and convert to cents. Similarly, to find $800 \div 25$ ask yourself "$8 is how many quarters?" That strategy can be tabulated as follows.

Multiply by 25	four 25s make 100	$36 \times 25 = (9 \times 4) \times 25 = 900$
Divide by 25	each 100 is four 25's	$800 \div 25 = 8 \times 4 = 32$

These methods are easier than they look in written form. Do not try to memorize them, just start practicing! Pick a method and try it, starting with small numbers: What is 12×5? 18×5? 26×5? 54×5? 242×5? Once you are adept at one method, move on to another. You will get practice in class and in homework problems, but to learn these methods you must also practice on your own and with classmates.

You will be surprised at how quickly you can learn to do seemingly difficult problems. Try accepting challenges and showing off ("I can multiply any two digit number by 9 in my head!") Like simple magic tricks, these Mental Math methods, once honed by practice, can be used to impress your friends — and yourself. Practicing Mental Math will also make you a more confident and more flexible teacher.

For the test →

Writing Mental Math

Mental Math is done in your head. But on homework, quizzes, and exams you will be asked to write down your solutions to Mental Math problems. The examples in this section show how that should be done: write down the intermediate steps in a way that makes your thinking clear. Include parenthesis to indicate the order in which you did the operations. For example,

$$
\begin{aligned}
99 \times 19 &= (100 - 1) \times 19 \\
&= 1900 - 19 \\
&= 1881.
\end{aligned}
$$

Homework Set 7

Solve the following Mental Math problems, writing your solution as described in the box above. Problems 1-5 are Mental Math for grown-ups; Problem 6 refers to Mental Math for children.

1. Calculate mentally by rearranging, using compatible numbers, etc. Show your intermediate steps.
   a) $(26 + 83) + 54$ b) $(4 \times 34) \times 25$
   c) 256×6 d) $288 \div 24$
   e) $(44 \times 56) + 56^2$ f) 402×12

2. Calculate mentally using compatible numbers.
   a) $123 + 326 + 4 + 77$ b) $2 \times 6 \times 7 \times 5$
   c) $3200 \times 34 \div 16$

3. Calculate mentally using compensation.
   a) $197 + 568$ b) $62 - 39$
   c) 48×25 d) $500 \div 25$
   e) $71 - 42$ f) $180 \div 15$ (*Hint:* double both.)

4. Calculate mentally using left-to-right method.
   a) $124 + 522$ b) $821 + 134$
   c) $7855 - 723$ d) $840 - 60$
   e) $845 - 62$ (think: $84 - 6$ tens)

5. Calculate mentally using your own method.

   a) 78×9 b) 37×4
   c) $136 \div 8$ d) $1500 \div 25$
   e) $1575 \div 25$ f) $325 \div 5$

6. Not all arithmetic problems are appropriate for elementary school Mental Math. Classify each of the following problems as either PV (Mental Math developing Place Value), DP (Mental Math developing the Distributive Property), or X (not easily done mentally by PV or DV).
   a) $37 + 99$ b) 20×40
   c) 7×102 d) 13×28
   e) $326 - 98$ f) $337 + 879$
   g) $119 \div 7$ h) 3×32.

2.2 Word Problems

In the real world, mathematics problems seldom come as straightforward arithmetic problems; people do not run up to you in the street gasping "Quick! What is $346 - 287$?" Instead, mathematics occurs in forms much more like word problems. It is by doing word problems that students realize the importance and applicability of mathematics. Word problems also reinforce concepts understanding and fluency skills. Consequently, word problems are an essential part of any mathematics curriculum — one of the legs of a balanced mathematics education (see the Preface).

Can first-graders learn to do word problems? Yes, they do in the Primary Mathematics curriculum! Early word problems are pictures-puzzles. The boy-with-balloons picture below is such a "wordless word problem." These evolve into short word problems that use simple words that can be read aloud by the teacher and the students together. Answers require a minimal amount of writing. The simple format actually helps develop reading skills.

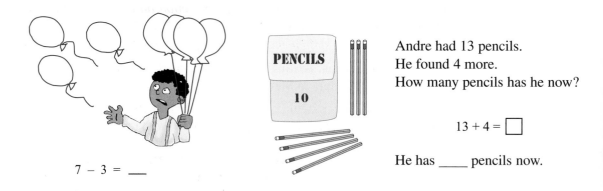

$7 - 3 = \underline{\quad}$

Andre had 13 pencils.
He found 4 more.
How many pencils has he now?

$13 + 4 = \boxed{}$

He has ____ pencils now.

A balanced program integrates word problems into the curriculum *starting in grade 1*. Word problems are included in almost every topic covered and grow in difficulty along with the rest of the material. Students come to see word problems as a natural part of mathematics rather than a type of extra-hard problem.

Word problems have another advantage: they are a rich source of interesting challenging problems which teachers can use to keep the more mathematically skilled students engaged with work *on the same topic that the rest of the class is working on*. Without this, the teacher's only options for these students are to have them i) sit in boredom, ii) do dozens of routine problems they find trivial, or iii) move on to the next section. Option iii) puts a greater distance between the higher performing students and the rest of the class, and only postpones the day when they will have to go into a "holding pattern" while the rest of the class catches up.

Teaching Sequence

Word problems necessarily involve three steps:

- converting the word problem to an arithmetic or algebra problem,
- solving that arithmetic or algebra problem, and
- interpreting the solution.

The first is the hard step. If the second is also difficult there is a real risk of frustrating the students. It is therefore crucial to integrate word problems into instruction in a carefully designed teaching sequence. Examples of such teaching sequences occur repeatedly in the Primary Mathematics texts. It is helpful to think of these sequences as organized into two levels: a "Primary Level" that solidifies understanding of a new idea, and a "Secondary Level" that integrates the new idea with previous knowledge.

Primary Level.   A Primary Level teaching sequence introduces a new idea and develops it in small steps. Typically, the sequence proceeds as follows.

a) A specific concept or type of problem is introduced.

b) Simple calculational problems are done.

c) Students do word problems which reduce to calculations like those done in b).

d) Steps b) and c) are repeated with larger numbers and with a greater variety of word problem situations.

EXAMPLE 2.1. *In Primary Math 3A, the section on multiplication and division begins with a review (pages 39 through 42). Next, on page 43, students are given twelve calculations (4 × 3, 16 ÷ 2, etc.). Then, only then, come word problems. Here is one example.*

Devi saved $5 a week for 8 weeks. How much did she save altogether?

The language in this word problem is simple and direct, and the students have been prepared for the calculation involved. They are ready to do this problem!

Secondary Level. After completing the primary level, students have moved back and forth between calculations and applications several times. They are now ready for applications which integrate their new skill with previously learned mathematics. Here again, it is helpful to distinguish between two types of word problems:

two-step problems

a) *Two-step problems*, in which the student must combine the skill just learned with a previous skill.

multi-step problems

b) *Multi-step problems*, in which the new skill is one of several steps in the solution.

As before, students move to the next level of difficulty only when they are ready.

Multi-step word problems have particular advantages for teaching. They involve conceptual complications not found in other types of problems, they help students solidify their knowledge, and they show that mathematics is useful and relevant in many contexts. Try this one:

EXERCISE 2.2. *A shopkeeper bought 20 watches for $900. He sold all of them for $56 each. Find his profit.*

This problem combines multiplication with subtraction (do you see how to do it without division?) The wording is again simple and direct, and it is clear that this is a practical problem. Just reading this problem shows students the value of learning mathematics!

Solving word problems

The key to successfully solving word problems is to follow the general strategy

word problem ⇒ diagram ⇒ arithmetic.

It is much easier to convert words to a diagram, and then the diagram into arithmetic, than it is to go directly from the words to the arithmetic. The best diagrams are abstract representations, not literal pictures. Detailed pictures of people, houses, etc. are unnecessary and confusing. A well-constructed diagram is often extremely helpful. It displays the entire problem and makes clear the reasoning needed to complete the solution.

The standard advice on solving word problems goes like this: First, read the entire problem and identify the key unknown (which is usually announced in the last sentence of the problem). Then draw a diagram and record the given information from the word problem, including a '?' to show the unknown. At this point you can often see what calculations are needed to find the unknown. Do the required arithmetic, and finish by stating your answer clearly. If you get stuck, *reread the problem*, checking that you have considered all the given information.

Of course, there is no universal recipe for solving word problems — that is one of the reasons for teaching word problems. The above steps are merely guidelines to keep students focused on the problem without getting sidetracked. They boil down to a few words of advice:

> Make a complete diagram, then do the arithmetic, rereading the problem as you go.

bar diagrams

The Primary Mathematics textbooks show how to convert word problems into *bar diagrams*. This is a powerful and flexible way to solve *and to teach* word problems. Learning to use bar diagrams is one of the main goals of this course. The best way to get started is to open the Primary Mathematics textbooks and start doing problems. Many sections in these books begin with partially worked-out problems which show how to make bar diagrams.

Below are two examples to get you started. Your homework solutions should look like these. Like most of the problems in Primary Math 3A these the word problems are simple — simple enough that adults can immediately see the underlying arithmetic question. Nevertheless, it is important to draw and label the diagrams. A labeled diagram is an excellent way of explaining a solution to a class. Bear in mind that most students will not immediately see through to the underlying arithmetic. The purpose of the diagrams is to help them follow the route

$$\text{Words} \Rightarrow \text{diagram} \Rightarrow \text{arithmetic}.$$

Learning to draw complete bar diagrams is also preparation for the more difficult word problems of grades 5 and 6. For those, diagrams are enormously helpful, as you will see later.

EXAMPLE 2.3. *There were 27 desks to clean. 3 boys shared the work equally. How many desks did each boy clean?*

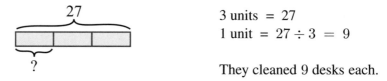

3 units = 27
1 unit = 27 ÷ 3 = 9

They cleaned 9 desks each.

Notice that the diagram completely summarizes the problem. All the given information is included and the unknown (the quantity to be determined) is labeled with a question mark. The answer on the right is a complete solution — it makes the reasoning perfectly clear with a minimal number of words, and it includes a summary sentence stating the answer.

EXAMPLE 2.4. *Kelly has $16. She has twice as much as her brother. How much money do Kelly and her brother have together?*

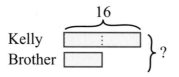

2 units = $ 16
1 unit = $ 8
3 units = 8 × 3 = $24

They have $24 altogether.

This is a two-step problem. After reading the question it is not immediately clear how to proceed. But the diagram makes it obvious! Note that the solution is presented in exactly the same format as the previous example.

Tips:

- Generally, draw diagrams unless it is immediately clear what arithmetic to do (multistep word problems usually require a single diagram only for the hardest step). Drawing diagrams is good practice for when you will be teaching. Furthermore, as this course progresses, the word problems will get harder, so it is important to become adept at diagram drawing now.

- It is important to label the unknown with a question mark *(you may be marked off on your homework for omitting this!)*. That label focuses attention on what must be found and provides guidance about how to proceed.

The next section includes further tips for constructing bar diagrams and a discussion of their use in teaching.

Homework Set 8

1. (*Study the Textbook!*) In Primary Math 3A, read pages 36 and 37, noting the illustrations and filling in the answers in the book (but not on your homework sheet). Then read some of the problems in Practice 2E on page 38. All of these problems require a two-step solution. For example, Problem 1 is solved, and the steps made clear, as follows.

   Step 1: There are $1930 - 859 = 1071$ duck eggs,

   and therefore,

   Step 2: $1930 + 1071 = 3001$ eggs altogether.

   a) Give similar two-step solutions to Problems 4, 5, and 6.

   b) Draw a bar diagram and give a similar two-step solution to Problem 8.

2. (*Study the Textbook!*) On page 43 of Primary Math 3A, read Problems 8 − 11 and solve each mentally (no need to write your answers). Carefully read the problems on pages 44 − 46, paying careful attention to how the bar diagrams are drawn.

For each problem listed below, draw a bar diagram and then solve. Your solutions should look like those on page 45 and 46.

   a) Problems 8, 10 and 12 of Practice 3B.

   b) Problems 9 − 12 of Practice 3C.

   c) Problem 11 of Practice 3E.

3. Continuing in Primary Math 3A,

   a) Give a two-step solution, as you did in Problem 1 above, to Problems 10 and 11 on page 56.

   b) Which of the word problems on page 67 are two-step problems? Notice how in Problem 8 the text helps students by asking two separate questions.

4. Draw a bar diagram and solve the following two-step multiplication problems.

   a) Pierre's weight is 90 kg. He is 5 times as heavy as his daughter. Find the total weight of Pierre and his daughter.

   b) Heather weighs 32 kg. Alexi is twice as heavy as Heather. Olga weighs 21 kg less than Alexi. What is Olga's weight?

2.3 Selecting Word Problems

A large part of a teacher's job is keeping the students interested and motivated. A rich supply of word problems is an excellent resource for that. Word problems engage the students, build understanding and confidence, and demonstrate the uses of mathematics. Elementary school teachers regularly spend time selecting appropriate word problems, and skilled teachers are able to make up effective word problems.

There are good word problems and there are bad word problems. This section discusses the features of good word problems and offers guidance for arranging them. This is just the start; in this course you will be solving many, many word problems, and you will occasionally be asked to make up word problems. By the end of the course you will have developed a sense for what constitutes a good word problem.

What makes a good word problem? Well-written word problems can be recognized by the following characteristics.

• **Short, Clear, and Succinct** — Word problems should be short and easy to understand, but not trivial.

• **Interesting** — The best word problems lay out an interesting problem in very few words. Anyone can make a word problem *seem* more interesting by surrounding it with a long, colorful story. But embellishment distracts students and makes problems less useful for teaching.

• **Realistic or Whimsical** — Realistic problems ask questions that you would *want to know* in a situation that could plausibly occur. For example,

"A carpenter is using 3-inch nails. How long are 267 nails laid end-to-end?"

is a perfectly good arithmetic problem (3×267). But it is not realistic — carpenters don't lay nails end-to-end. Students will realize this right away, and it will reinforce their suspicions that mathematics is only good in unrealistic, artificial situations, exactly the opposite of the teacher's intentions.

Realistic does not mean mundane! Word problems can be whimsical or based upon fantasy, capturing children's imaginations and attention. For example:

"Mrs. Rex gave 7 tin cans of Stego Stew to Tiny T, who piled them on top of each other. If each can is 4 inches high, how tall is Tiny T's tin tower?"

The question is realistic within the fantasy — it is plausible that Tiny T might like to know the height of his tower.

• **Self-contained with a single answer** — Each problem should have a definite answer that can be determined from the information provided. To avoid frustrating students, word problems should include all required facts. For example, if a problem uses the fact that water freezes at $32°F$, this fact should be explicitly stated for the benefit of those students who do not know it.

Furthermore, each problem should have a single definite answer, even when there are many methods of arriving at the answer. (The single answer need not be one number; it may, for example, be a list of numbers.) Problems with definite answers provide feedback to both teachers and students. Correct solutions build confidence while incorrect solutions signal that more work is necessary.

Here are three problems that violate this criterion.

- Emmy ran 1/4 of the way down the football field. How far did she go?

- I am a multiple of 12. I am greater than 40. What number am I?

- Find a button. Write down as many words as you can which describe your button.

Many third-graders do not know the length of a football field, and there are infinitely many multiples of 12 greater than 40. Notice that Problem 2 can be fixed by changing the middle sentence to "I am between 40 and 50" (the single answer is then 48) or to "I am between 40 and 100" (the single answer is then the list 48, 60, 72, 84, 96). Problem 3, which is an actual first grade mathematics problem, has no wrong answers and no mathematical content.

EXERCISE 3.1. *What is wrong with the following word problem?*

At the Cinemaplex All-You-Can-Watch movie theater, Juan is trying to decide whether to buy one large chocolate bar or two small chocolate bars. Both size bars are rectangular. Juan thinks that the heights and widths are about the same, but that the smaller chocolate bar is about half the length of the larger chocolate bar. A large chocolate bar costs $3.00, and a small chocolate bar costs $1.49. To get the most chocolate for his $3.00, should Juan buy one large chocolate bar or two small chocolate bars? Explain your answer.

EXERCISE 3.2. *Open Primary Math 5A to any page with word problems. Read five problems. Do they meet the above criteria? Can you find some that don't?*

As you learn to make up word problems of your own, you will come to appreciate just how demanding these criteria are. Constructing word problems is an art!

sequencing of
word problems

Even well-written word problems can be trivial, frustrating, or simply irrelevant if served up at the wrong time. Thus the *sequencing of word problems* is important. That sequencing should be varied, integrated, and coherent.

Varied. If a page of word problems are identical except for the numbers being changed, then they are really just a repetitive list of arithmetic problems. But if the context varies (e.g. some involve area, others involve volume or weight) while the mathematical structure is the same, then the students can begin to see through the particulars of the problem and recognize the underlying mathematics.

Integrated. Sets of word problems should fit with the surrounding material. Word problems should build on material recently introduced, reinforcing the concepts and skills, showing how that topic is applied, and combining it with previously learned material.

Coherent. This refers to the consistency and general upward spiral of the curriculum. The vocabulary, mathematical content, and the difficulty of the problems should be appropriate for the level of the students. Sets of word problems should move from single-step to two-step and multi-step problems. The underlying concepts and calculations systematically become more difficult. The problems build on previous material and prepare students for future material.

EXERCISE 3.3. *Read the section "Multiplying and Dividing by 7" on pages* 76 − 79 *of Primary Math 3A. Then do word Problems* 5 − 11 *on page 80. Notice how multiplication and division are integrated with addition and subtraction, and how the level of problems moves upward.*

By now you are familiar with bar diagrams. We conclude this section by describing the use of bar diagrams in the classroom.

Bar diagrams are not just for students, they are marvelous, powerful *teaching* devices. They can be used to display the reasoning leading to a solution of a word problem — the diagram is far clearer than a verbal explanation. Teachers can also use them to assist and guide students by providing partial or complete diagrams. Communication between students is facilitated when students begin problems by constructing diagrams.

Teacher's
Solution

To make bar diagrams work in the classroom, teachers must be able to construct appropriate diagrams quickly, correctly, and confidently. As you work toward that goal use the following example as a model. It displays the features that make a bar diagram solution useful for teaching. We will refer to solutions with these features as *Teacher's Solutions*.

EXAMPLE 3.4. *Four children bought a present for $28. They shared the costs equally. How much did each child pay?*

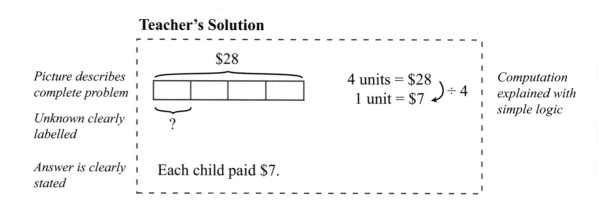

Teacher's Solution

Picture describes complete problem

Unknown clearly labelled

$28

?

4 units = $28
1 unit = $7 ⎞÷ 4

Computation explained with simple logic

Answer is clearly stated

Each child paid $7.

Features of a Teacher's Solution

1. All given information is labeled on the picture and the unknown labeled with a '?' symbol. The problem is clear from the picture alone.

2. The computations are shown in a way that makes clear the reasoning and the steps involved.

3. The answer is clearly stated in a complete sentence.

Getting all this right requires practice; it is a learned art. Sometimes your first approach will not work. Even when your approach works there may be a clearer and simpler way to solve the problem. These tips may help.

1. A single picture is usually better than several.

2. You may need to try different pictures and settle on the best.

3. Verify your picture by rereading the problem.

4. Include a few written words explaining your arithmetic *as you solve it*. The fewer the better. Usually $5 - 10$ words are enough to make the reasoning clear. Longer explanations actually make the solution *less* clear.

EXAMPLE 3.5. *A table and chair cost $168 together. The table costs $110 more than the chair. What is the price of the table?*

Students came up with three different solutions.

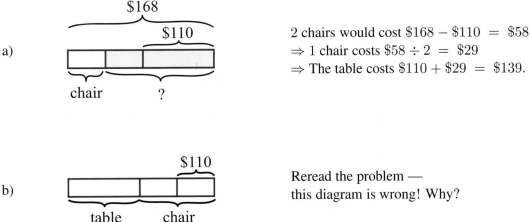

a)

2 chairs would cost $168 - $110 = $58
$\Rightarrow$ 1 chair costs $58 \div 2 = $29
$\Rightarrow$ The table costs $110 + $29 = $139.

b)

Reread the problem —
this diagram is wrong! Why?

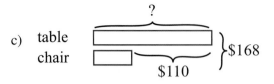

c) table / chair

2 tables cost $168 + $110 = $278

$\Rightarrow$ one table costs $278 \div 2 = \$139$.

Notice that solution c) uses the comparison model for the subtraction, and solves directly for the cost of the table without finding the cost of the chair, which was not asked for. While a) and c) are both correct, c) is a clearer and more efficient solution.

Homework Set 9

(*Study the Textbook!*)   Below are some tasks to help you study word problems in Primary Math 5A and Workbook 5A.

1. In the Primary Mathematics curriculum students get a textbook and a workbook for each semester. The material in the textbook is covered in class, and the workbook problems are done as homework. The students own the workbooks and write in them. Leaf through Primary Math Workbook 5A.

   a) How many pages of math homework do fifth grade students do in the first semester (semester 5A)?

   b) If the school year is 180 days long, that is an average of roughly _____ pages of homework per day.

2. a) In Primary Math 5A, read pages 22 – 24. Notice the arrows at the bottom of the page that direct students (and teachers!) to Workbook exercises. Students do those exercises for homework to consolidate the day's lesson.

   b) Try that homework: in Primary Math **Workbook** 5A, give Teacher's Solutions for Exercises 9 and 10.

3. Returning to Primary Math 5A, give Teacher's Solutions for all problems in Practice 1D.

4. In Primary Math 5A, give Teacher's Solutions for Problems 28 – 32 on pages 63 – 64.

5. In Primary Math 5A, give Teacher's Solutions for Problems 9, 16 – 18 on pages 89 – 90.

CHAPTER 3

Algorithms

When most people think of arithmetic they think of the familiar procedures for adding, subtracting, and multiplying in column form, and dividing by "long division."

$$
\begin{array}{r}
1 \\
27 \\
+\quad 85 \\
\hline
112
\end{array}
\qquad
\begin{array}{r}
5\ \ 15 \\
\not{6}\ \ \not{5} \\
-\quad 1\ \ 9 \\
\hline
4\ \ 6
\end{array}
\qquad
\begin{array}{r}
2 \\
27 \\
\times\quad 3 \\
\hline
81
\end{array}
\qquad
\begin{array}{r}
6 \\
7\,\overline{)4\ \ 8} \\
4\ \ 2 \\
\hline
6
\end{array}
$$

These four procedures are examples of *algorithms*.

> An *algorithm* is a systematic step-by-step procedure to solve a class of problems. A *mathematical algorithm* is a cyclic computational algorithm which solves problems in a finite number of steps.

Cooking recipes are algorithms, and so are all computer programs. We have already seen one important mathematical algorithm: the method for writing decimal numerals using the three steps listed at the beginning of Section 1.2. This chapter focuses on the four *standard algorithms* of arithmetic illustrated above.

In elementary school the four standard algorithms are the final step of learning whole number arithmetic. They bring the class together on common ground and serve to mark the end of whole number arithmetic. They serve the following purposes as well.

• *The standard algorithms always work.* Mental Math works nicely for some problems but not for others. The standard algorithms provide a fallback method that always works. As a result, knowing the algorithms gives students *confidence* that they can solve any addition, subtraction, multiplication or division problem without too much thought.

There are, of course, many ways of obtaining an answer — from a friend, from the teacher, from the back of the book, or from a calculator. But true confidence flows from the knowledge that you can do something completely on your own.

• Ironically, the ability to do the four arithmetic operations in a routine manner enables students to think more conceptually. As the standard algorithms become increasingly automatic, students come to view expressions like $6347 - 2581$ as a single number that can easily be found, rather than thinking of it as a complicated problem to work out. That frees up working memory, allowing them to concentrate on other aspects of a problem, including new concepts.

• Algorithms of all types are used in mathematics, science, and engineering, and we are surrounded by machines which work because of the algorithms built into them. To understand the modern world one should understand the concept of an algorithm. That understanding develops from seeing examples, beginning with simple ones. The standard algorithms of arithmetic are an excellent introduction to the idea of an algorithm.

• The long division algorithm is especially important because it is the only place in elementary math where one sees the idea of repeatedly correcting estimates to get better and better approximations. That process is a central concept of higher mathematics with many engineering applications.

Notice that the availability of calculators affects none of these points. When the goal is to answer a numerical problem, say 3975×4875, use a calculator. But when the goals are to solidify understanding of mathematics, build confidence, and prepare students for more advanced ideas, teach the standard algorithms.

The basic form of each of the four algorithms is determined by the mathematics — by place value and the commutative, associative, and distributive properties. The only possible variations are minor, involving the order in which partial steps are performed and recorded on paper.

As you study the Primary Mathematics textbooks you will be struck by how little time and attention seems to be needed for students to master the algorithms. That is possible because the Primary Mathematics curriculum carefully develops the prerequisite skills before starting algorithms. The students practice the place value ideas we covered in Section 1.2, and they do many exercises, including many Mental Math exercises, which expose the role of place value in arithmetic. Mental Math exercises are particularly valuable because, as we will see, *the standard algorithms are the same methods used in Mental Math, systematically organized and reduced to a very succinct form.*

3.1 The Addition Algorithm

Think about how you might teach the "column addition" algorithm. What would you teach first? One systematic approach would be to begin by adding single digit numbers, move on to numbers in the teens, then twenties, etc., moving to ever larger numbers. But the mathematics points to a different teaching sequence.

The addition algorithm is built around a central mathematical fact: *place value allows us to find the sum of any two numbers, however large, by doing a series of one-digit additions, rebundling (carrying) when necessary.* Thus for students who can already add one-digit numbers, learning the addition algorithm is a matter of understanding place value processes.

This basic mathematical fact organizes the development of the algorithm in the classroom. It determines the prerequisite skills needed before starting the algorithm, and it identifies two levels of difficulty: addition without rebundling and addition with rebundling. These become the main steps of teaching the algorithm. The logic and the two steps can be seen in the following example.

EXAMPLE 1.1. Consider the problem $324 + 643$. Using expanded form, we must find

$$(300 + 20 + 4) + (600 + 40 + 3) = \underline{\hspace{3cm}}.$$

We can add these six numbers in any order. Which order is best? The answer is dictated by place value considerations. We want the sum to be in expanded form. Clearly, we should add hundreds, tens, and ones separately, getting $900 + 60 + 7$. Writing those three sums in column form and pushing them together gives the standard method of column addition.

$$
\begin{array}{r} 300 \\ + \ 600 \\ \hline 900 \end{array}
\qquad
\begin{array}{r} 20 \\ + \ 40 \\ \hline 60 \end{array}
\qquad
\begin{array}{r} 4 \\ + \ 3 \\ \hline 7 \end{array}
\qquad \Longrightarrow \qquad
\begin{array}{r} 324 \\ + \ 643 \\ \hline 967 \end{array}
$$

A second level of difficulty appears when we consider additions involving rebundling. Such additions require all three steps of the place value process described on page 8. For example, to find $754 + 172$ we again use expanded form and separately add hundreds, tens, and ones, getting

$$(700 + 50 + 4) + (100 + 70 + 2) = 800 + 120 + 6.$$

To finish we must apply Steps (ii) and (iii) of the place value process, writing 120 as $100 + 20$, then adding hundreds, tens, and ones. When written in column form this translates into the addition algorithm. But notice that the additions of hundreds, tens, and ones are no longer interchangeable — when regrouping is necessary there are clear advantages to starting at the right with the ones place. Mastering these complications is the second main step in learning the addition algorithm.

Incidentally, notice that the level of difficulty is determined not by the size of the summands, but rather by the amount of regrouping that is necessary. For example, finding $3241 + 6453$ requires no regrouping, so is easier than finding $87 + 34$, which requires regrouping in two columns.

Before looking in detail at the specific skills involved in the two steps of the addition algorithm, we discuss the prerequisites. Bear in mind that the algorithm is the *final* step in teaching addition.

Prerequisites. The nature of the algorithm points to two main prerequisite skills. Before attempting the algorithm, students should (i) know most of the 1–digit addition facts, and (ii) should be well-practiced and comfortable with the place value concepts described in Section 1.2. Both of these prerequisite skills can be developed through Mental Math. In particular, the algorithm becomes easier and more transparent when the following component skills are known before instruction on the algorithm begins.

  1. Expanded form: $300 + 40 + 5 = \underline{\hspace{1cm}}$ and $600 + \underline{\hspace{1cm}} + 3 = 673$.

2. The idea of adding ones, tens, and hundreds separately, including the Mental Math skills

    a) adding multiples of 10 and 100 to one another: finding $5+3$, $50+30$, and $500+300$,

    b) adding multiples of 10 and 100 to other numbers: finding $37+40$ or

What number is 30 more than 123?

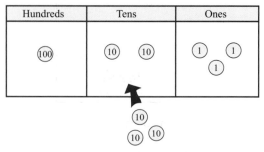

3. Rebundling, that is, "cashing in" 10 units of one denomination for 1 unit of the next larger denomination. Students can practice rebundling with Mental Math problems like "what number is 4 more than 88?" and by money problems.

13 dimes can be changed for one dollar and _____ dimes.

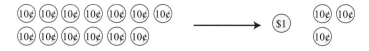

Step 1 — Addition without rebundling. Students' first column-addition problems involve only separately adding the hundreds, tens, and ones columns. At this step the columns can be added in any order; there is no logical reason for adding the ones column first. To well-prepared students, chip model pictures like the one below make the reasoning immediately clear. Primary Math 2A has students do about 10 problems with chip models, and then practice with numbers.

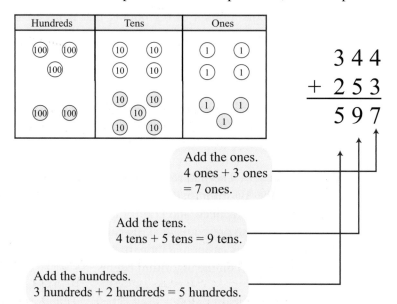

Add the ones.
4 ones + 3 ones = 7 ones.

Add the tens.
4 tens + 5 tens = 9 tens.

Add the hundreds.
3 hundreds + 2 hundreds = 5 hundreds.

Step 2— Addition with rebundling. The conceptual difficulty of rebundling already occurs for 2–digit numbers, so that case should be understood thoroughly before proceeding to larger numbers. Chip models again work nicely.

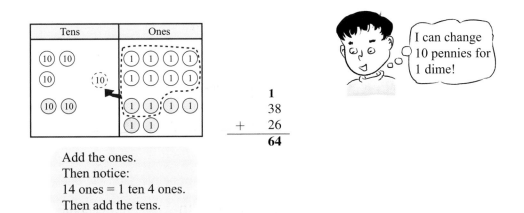

Add the ones.
Then notice:
14 ones = 1 ten 4 ones.
Then add the tens.

$$\begin{array}{r} 1 \\ 38 \\ + \ 26 \\ \hline 64 \end{array}$$

This step is commonly called "carrying." That word is misleading because it suggests that we are sliding digits from one column to the next, rather than rebundling. In the last decade or so textbook authors have made an effort to replace the word "carrying" by terms or phrases which directly refer to the rebundling process, such as "exchanging 10 ones for 1 ten," "composing a 10," or "bundle 10 ones to get 1 ten." Similarly, for subtraction, the misleading phrase "borrowing" (when does it get paid back?) is being replaced by more suggestive phrases such as "splitting up a bundle of 10."

When one moves to 3–digit numbers there are several possibilities for rebundling. In order of increasing complication they are

1. 3–digit plus a 2–digit with bundling ones,

2. two 3–digit numbers with bundling ones,

3. two 3–digit with bundling tens (students can 'discover' this themselves), and

4. double rebundling.

This order provides a natural route leading quickly to the most difficult cases, as you will see when you do Homework Problem 4a. There is a similar sequence for 4–digit numbers, but that involves no new conceptual difficulties.

EXERCISE 1.2. *Among addition problems with two 3–digit numbers, the most complicated examples occur when bundling ones increases the number of tens enough to require bundling tens. Make up such a problem.*

The Primary Math books introduce the addition algorithm early in second grade, developing it in the teaching sequence described above. By third grade students are using the algorithm to add numbers in the thousands. They are also using it to solve word problems, as on pages 34, 35 and 38 in Primary Math 3A. Word problems provide both practice and motivation for mastering the algorithm.

Other addition algorithms. There are other addition algorithms such as *lattice addition*.

lattice addition

$$
\begin{array}{ccc}
8 & 5 & 7 \\
+ \quad 9 & 8 & 5 \\
\end{array}
$$

Add columns first. Then add down the diagonals.

Do you see how this also uses the principle "add the ones, tens, and hundreds separately" to reduce the addition of large numbers to a series of 1–digit additions, rebundling when necessary?

Homework Set 10

1. Compute using the lattice method: a) $315 + 672$
   b) $483 + 832$ c) $356 + 285 + 261$.

2. Order these computations from easiest to hardest:

$$
\begin{array}{ccc}
\quad 39 & \quad 39 & \quad 30 \\
+ \quad 70 & + \quad 71 & + \quad 69 \\
\hline
\end{array}
$$

3. Reread pages $18 - 23$ in Primary Math 3A. Solve Problems $5 - 9$ in Practice 2B by giving a Teacher's Solution using bar diagrams like those on pages $20 - 21$ (use algorithms — not chip models — for the arithmetic!).

4. (*Study the Textbook!*)   Complete the following tasks involving Primary Math 3A.

   a) Page 24 shows an addition that involves rebundling hundreds. For Problems $2-9$ on pages $25-27$, write down in list format which place values are rebundled (ones, tens, or hundreds). Begin with: 2) ones, 3) tens, 4) hundreds, 5) ones, ones, tens, etc. These include examples of every possibility, and build up to the most complicated case after only three pages!

   b) Illustrate Problems 5bd on page 26 using chip models, making your illustrations similar to the one on

page 24. *Include the worked-out arithmetic next to your illustration.*

   c) Similarly illustrate Problems 7bdf on page 26.

   d) Similarly illustrate the arithmetic in Problem 9b on page 27. Explain the steps by drawing a "box with arrows" as shown at the bottom of page 27.

5. Sam, Julie, and Frank each added incorrectly. Explain their mistakes.

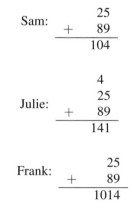

$$
\text{Sam:} \quad
\begin{array}{r}
25 \\
+ \quad 89 \\
\hline
104
\end{array}
$$

$$
\text{Julie:} \quad
\begin{array}{r}
4 \\
25 \\
+ \quad 89 \\
\hline
141
\end{array}
$$

$$
\text{Frank:} \quad
\begin{array}{r}
25 \\
+ \quad 89 \\
\hline
1014
\end{array}
$$

3.2 The Subtraction Algorithm

The teaching sequence for the subtraction algorithm is roughly the same as the addition algorithm. Again, the steps are largely determined by the mathematics and by place value. We continue to use chip models, where we subtract by crossing out chips. The first step involves subtracting the ones, tens, and hundreds separately, without rebundling.

EXAMPLE 2.1. *Subtract* 58 − 23.

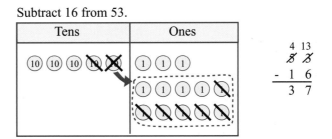

The second step introduces the new idea of unbundling or "decomposing a 10."

EXAMPLE 2.2. *Subtract* 53 − 16.

Subtract 16 from 53.

Just as we did for the addition algorithm, we can arrange 3–digit subtractions in order of increasing complication (you will see the specific order in Homework Problem 6). The most complicated case requires "regrouping across a 0"; that is done by decomposing one of the hundreds into 10 tens, then decomposing one of those tens into 10 ones, and finishing as before.

$$
\begin{array}{r}
\overset{3}{}\ \overset{9}{}\ 16 \\
\cancel{4}\ \cancel{0}\ \cancel{6} \\
-\ \ 1\ \ 3\ \ 9 \\
\hline
2\ \ 6\ \ 7
\end{array}
$$

Chip models help clarify this — see pages 32−33 of Primary Math 3A. But "regrouping across a 0" is conceptually more difficult than anything seen in the addition algorithm, and consequently the second step of the subtraction algorithm is taught after the addition algorithm is completed.

Some teacher's manuals suggest having children "invent their own algorithms." This is asking for trouble. Many students will develop incorrect algorithms. Some will be incorrect in very subtle ways. The teacher will then have to find the errors in 10 or 15 different "algorithms" and explain to each student what is wrong and how to fix it. This is an inefficient and frustrating way to teach.

More importantly, such recommendations miss the point that *learning an algorithm is the structured conclusion of months of creative Mental Math.* It gives students confidence that they can correctly solve complicated problems and brings the class to a common ground from which they can proceed to the next level of mathematics.

Word problems.   Algorithms reduce arithmetic to straightforward tasks, allowing students to concentrate on the rest of the problem.

EXAMPLE 2.3. *There are 4608 members in a club. 2745 are men, 855 are women, and the rest are children. How many children are there?*

Teacher's Solution:

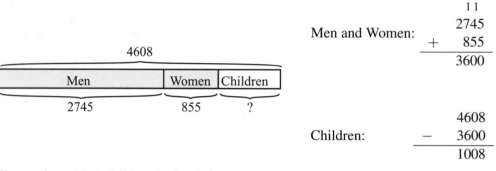

There where 1008 children in the club.

Other subtraction algorithms.   The "Subtract from 10" algorithm illustrated below requires fewer subtraction facts than the standard algorithm.

Add 5 to the tens complement of 7.

EXERCISE 2.4. *Subtract using the "Subtract from 10" algorithm.*

$$
\begin{array}{r} 61 \\ - \ 37 \\ \hline \end{array}
\qquad
\begin{array}{r} 92 \\ - \ 57 \\ \hline \end{array}
\qquad
\begin{array}{r} 272 \\ - \ 138 \\ \hline \end{array}
\qquad
\begin{array}{r} 406 \\ - \ 139 \\ \hline \end{array}
$$

This version of the subtraction algorithm has the same mathematical structure as the standard algorithm: subtract the hundreds, tens, and ones separately, unbundling when necessary. The standard algorithm requires a "subtraction within 20" in each column, while the "subtract from 10" algorithm requires knowing only the tens complements facts. On the other hand, it requires two steps (find the tens complement and add) rather than one (remember a subtraction fact), making it slower for those who do know the subtraction within 20 facts.

Homework Set 11

1. The number 832 in expanded form is 8 hundreds, 3 tens, and 2 ones. To find $832 - 578$, however, it is convenient to think of 832 as _____ hundreds, _____ tens, and _____ ones.

2. To find $1221 - 888$, one regroups 1221 as _____ hundreds, _____ tens, and _____ ones.

3. Use the fact that 1000 is "9 hundred ninety ten" to explain a quick way of finding $1000 - 318$.

4. Order the following computations from easiest to hardest. (*Hint:* Do all three calculations before deciding.)

$$\begin{array}{r} 8256 \\ - \quad 6589 \\ \hline \end{array} \qquad \begin{array}{r} 8003 \\ - \quad 6007 \\ \hline \end{array} \qquad \begin{array}{r} 8256 \\ - \quad 7145 \\ \hline \end{array}$$

5. (*Study the Textbook!*) Carefully read and work out the problem on page 28 of Primary Math 3A. Then work out similar solutions to the following problems.

   a) Illustrate Problem 5b on page 30 using chip models, making your illustrations similar to the one on page 28. *Include the worked-out arithmetic next to your illustration.*

   b) Similarly illustrate Problem 7b on page 30.

   c) Similarly illustrate Problem 12d on page 32. Explain the steps of Problem 12d by drawing a "box with arrows" as shown in the middle of page 32.

6. (*Study the Textbook!*) Page 28 of Primary Math 3A shows a subtraction that involves rebundling thousands.

For Problems $1 - 14$ on pages $29 - 33$, write down in list format, without explanations, which place values are rebundled (ones, tens, hundreds, or thousands) and which required bundling across a zero. This teaching sequence includes examples of almost every possibility, and builds up to the most complicated case in only 40 problems!

7. Solve Problems $5 - 10$ in Practice 2C and 2D of Primary Math 3A by giving a Teacher's Solution for each. Your solutions should look like those on pages 20 and 21.

8. Sam, Julie, and Frank each subtracted incorrectly. Explain each mistake.

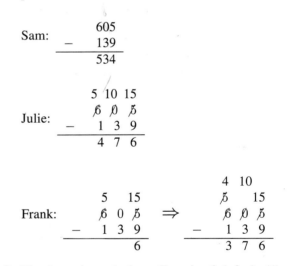

9. The boy pictured above Exercise 2.4 finds $15 - 7$ by adding 5 to the tens complement. Explain how that method is equivalent to finding $15 - 7$ by "counting on."

3.3 The Multiplication Algorithm

The algorithm for column multiplication accomplishes much the same thing as the addition algorithm: it enables us to multiply two numbers, however large, by doing a series of 1–digit multiplications. However, the multiplication algorithm is more complicated and involves some seemingly mysterious "carrying" and column shifting. In this section we will see how the multiplication algorithm, and the stages involved in teaching it, are determined naturally by the mathematics.

In elementary school, the multiplication algorithm emerges from Mental Math. We can find 9×12 by observing that $9 \times 10 = 90$, and then adding $9 \times 2 = 18$, for a total of 108. This computation involves four mathematical ideas. The first is breaking the calculation into two easier multiplications, using the distributive property to think of $9 \times (10 + 2)$ as $(9 \times 10) + (9 \times 2)$. Next comes the place value concept that $9 \times 10 = 9$ tens $= 90$. Clearly, multiplying 9×2 involves knowing 1–digit multiplication facts and the last step, adding $90 + 18$, requires the rebundling process used in multi-digit addition. These four ideas are the mathematical ingredients from which the multiplication algorithm is constructed. Here they are restated:

- the distributive property,
- shifting place values when multiplying by 10,
- 1–digit multiplication facts, and
- rebundling as used in the addition algorithm.

The multiplication algorithm can be developed in more than one way, but any approach must incorporate all four ideas above. We will give a detailed account of how it is developed in the Primary Mathematics curriculum and briefly mention another approach at the end of the section.

A Curriculum Sequence

Multiplication facts in the Primary Mathematics curriculum are introduced in the beginning of second grade (see the three stages in Section 1.5). The development of the multiplication algorithm starts after students can multiply by 1, 2, 3, 4, 5 and 10, but before they have memorized the entire multiplication table. The algorithm is introduced in third grade and is done in two stages, each taking approximately a year.

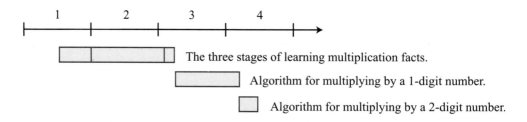

The three stages of learning multiplication facts.

Algorithm for multiplying by a 1-digit number.

Algorithm for multiplying by a 2-digit number.

In the Common Core Mathematics Standards, work with algorithms begins a bit later and extends over a longer period, ending in grade 5.

The reason for breaking the development into two stages is simply because the full multiplication algorithm reduces to a series of multiplications by 1–digit numbers providing a natural progression from easy to more difficult problems.

The two main ideas of the multiplication algorithm are the distributive property, which is nicely illustrated by rectangular arrays, and place value, which is nicely illustrated using chip models. The Primary Math textbooks cleverly combine chip models and rectangular arrays by arranging the chips into a rectangular array (see illustrations below). That one model can be used to illustrate all aspects of the multiplication algorithm.

Stage 1 — Multiply by a 1–digit number. Switching from "$7 \times 6 = \underline{\quad}$" notation to column notation can be motivated using the mathematical idea of "shifting place values when multiplying by 10."

EXERCISE 3.1. *Study page 49 of Primary Math 3A. That page clearly shows the advantages of using columns to keep track of place value. It also shows teachers how to initiate a topic!*

Multiplication without rebundling. The multiplication algorithm can be introduced using chips arranged in rectangular arrays.

Multiply 21 by 4.

Study this illustration — it has many interesting features! The student helper is performing a Mental Math calculation using the distributive property ("21 fours is 20 fours plus 1 more four."). Note how the diagram shows the repeated addition interpretation $21 + 21 + 21 + 21$. The picture has even more features.

EXERCISE 3.2. *Identify the place in the above illustration where the three key mathematical ideas — place value, the distributive property, and 1-digit multiplication facts — are used.*

Multiplication with rebundling. Like the addition algorithm, the difficulty is not the size of the numbers multiplied but whether the multiplication requires rebundling. Models can help explain the process.

Multiply 48 by 2.

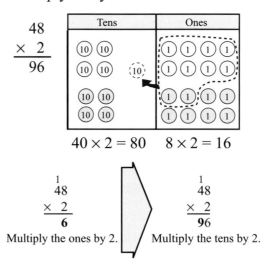

$$40 \times 2 = 80 \qquad 8 \times 2 = 16$$

$$
\begin{array}{r}
\overset{1}{4}8 \\
\times\ \ 2 \\
\hline
6
\end{array}
\qquad
\begin{array}{r}
\overset{1}{4}8 \\
\times\ \ 2 \\
\hline
96
\end{array}
$$

Multiply the ones by 2.   Multiply the tens by 2.

The model shows that 10 of the 16 ones are exchanged for 1 ten; this illustrates *why* a "1" is put in the tens column. Counting the number of tens is equivalent to multiplying 4×2 tens and adding the extra bundled ten — illustrating why the "1" is *added* to the calculation 4×2 to get 9 tens.

With rebundling in the ones place understood, the class can go on to multiplications with rebundling in both the tens and hundreds place. It is important to give plenty of practice problems and correct all errors immediately. This is because erroneous algorithms are like bad habits — they are hard to break.

Stage 2 — The full algorithm. Once students have a firm understanding of the 1–digit algorithm, the extension to multi-digit multiplications is relatively easy. In the Primary Mathematics curriculum this extension is done by building upon the 1–digit algorithm — there is no need to return to pictures and chip models.

There are two new ingredients. The first is the place value fact that in column form multiplication by 20, 30, 40, etc. is the same as multiplication by 2, 3, 4, etc. with a column shift. The second ingredient is the distributive property.

Multiplying by multiples of 10. Mental Math exercises shows that multiplication by 10 is easy: $17 \times 10 = 170$. Multiplication by 20, 30, 40, etc. is not much harder. For example,

$$12 \times 30 \ = \ 12 \times 3 \text{ tens} \ = \ 36 \text{ tens} \ = \ 360.$$

The key point is that if you know what 12×3 is, then you know what 12×30 is. Thus 12×30 can be thought of as a "multiplication by 1–digit number." In column format, "tens" means shift the work to the left one place value.

$$
\begin{array}{r}
12 \\
\times\ \ 30 \\
\hline
\mathbf{360}
\end{array}
$$

Notice that this introductory example is simple enough to be done both by mental math and in column format, so one sees that it is the same computation written in a different manner.

Multiplying by a 2–digit number. The second ingredient is the distributive property, which reduces a 2–digit multiplication to multiplication by a multiple of 10 plus a 1–digit multiplication. For instance, 64×27 is $64 \times (20 + 7) = (64 \times 20) + (64 \times 7)$, so

$$
\begin{aligned}
64 \times 20 &= 1280 \\
64 \times 7 &= 448 \\
\text{total} &= 1728.
\end{aligned}
$$

This is neatly recorded in two column format (where the use of the distributive property is implicit in the format)

$$
\begin{array}{r}
64 \\
\times \quad 27 \\
\hline
448 \quad \longleftarrow \quad 64 \times 7 \\
1280 \quad \longleftarrow \quad 64 \times 20 \\
\hline
1728 \quad \longleftarrow \quad \text{total}
\end{array}
$$

In practice, we concentrate on the bottom factor and perform a series of 1–digit multiplications by moving from its ones digit to its tens digit and so on. This "right to left" procedure helps keep track of place value in an organized way (for each new digit in the bottom factor, we move down and to the left one position to record the results of its 1–digit algorithm calculation).

At this point practice helps solidify the process. This algorithm is more complicated than the addition algorithm, and it requires repeated recollections of 1-digit multiplication facts. Errors will occur frequently at first. It is obviously important that those errors be detected and corrected. That can be done with help from parents, and with the teacher grading problems, going over common mistakes with the entire class, and correcting unusual mistakes individually.

Multiplying by any number. Students can discover in small groups or in a whole class discussion the algorithm for multiplying by a 3–digit number. This discovery is a good test. If the students correctly generalize the algorithm, then the students understand the mathematical ideas described at the beginning of this section. Otherwise review and more practice will be necessary.

Another way to develop the algorithm. There are other routes to developing the standard multiplication algorithm. Another way is by drawing boxes to represent the rectangular arrays and filling them in with the number of rectangles they represent. The example below briefly describes the main models used in developing the multiplication algorithm in this way.

EXAMPLE 3.3. *Compute 34×4 and 23×16.*

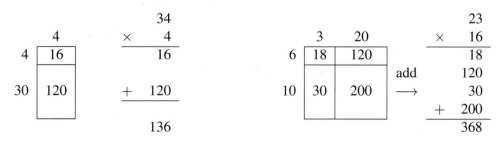

Note the simplification in these pictures — the box labeled 200 in the second diagram should be visualized as a 10×20 rectangular array. The first picture is a rectangular array for $4 \times (4+30)$ and the second picture shows how to draw a rectangular array for $(3+20) \times (6+10)$.

In the second example above, if we replace the rows 18 and 120 by 138 and the rows 30 and 200 by 230, we get the standard algorithm! (This realization is one of the last steps in developing the algorithm using these models.)

A completely different algorithm?   The *lattice algorithm* is quite old. To use it, construct a "lattice" with one of the factors across the top and the other on the side. The calculation proceeds by multiplying each row number by each column number and placing the results (split along the 10's and 1's place value) in the corresponding row-column entry of the lattice. The results of the multiplication is obtained by adding the numbers along diagonals (and composing when necessary).

lattice multiplication

EXAMPLE 3.4. *Multiply* 162×64 *using the lattice algorithm.*

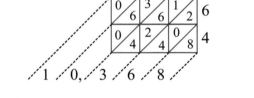

EXERCISE 3.5. *How does this algorithm keep track of place value? How is the distributive property used?*

After working out a few examples using the lattice algorithm you will find that the only differences between it and the standard multiplication algorithm are superficial; the steps that you follow are the same but in a slightly different order.

Homework Set 12

1. Compute using the lattice method: a) 21×14
   b) 57×39 c) 236×382.

2. (*Study the Textbook!*)   Read pages $39 - 47$ of Primary Math 3A. Give a Teacher's Solution to Problem 12 of Practice 3B and Problem 12 of Practice 3C. Model your solutions on those on pages 45 and 46.

   Why is there a multiplication word problem section just prior to the multiplication algorithm section which starts on page 49?

3. (*Study the Textbook!*)   Read pages $49 - 53$ of Primary Math 3A. What stage of the multiplication algorithm teaching sequence is being taught? Illustrate Problem 9g on page 53 using the chip model (as on the top of page 53). *Include the worked-out column multiplication.*

4. In Primary Math 3A, solve problems $8 - 12$ of Practice

3D and $10-11$ of Practice 3E doing the calculations mentally and simply writing down the numerical answer (with unit) on your homework.

5. (*Study the Textbook!*)   Read pages $36 - 39$ of Primary Math 4A. These pages develop the algorithm for multiplying by 2–digit numbers. The beginning of Stage 2 is multiplying by multiples of 10. Notice the method taught on page 36 for multiplying by a multiple of 10.

   a) Find 27×60 by each of the three methods of Problem 2 on page 37.

   b) Page 38 makes the transition to multiplying by general 2–digit numbers. What arithmetic property of multiplication is the little boy thinking about in the middle of page 38?

   c) Solve Problem 10e by column multiplication, modelling your solution on Problem 6a on page 38.

6. Give Teacher's Solutions to Problems 8 and 9 of Practice 2B of Primary Math 4A. (These are great problems!)

7. Illustrate and compute 37×3 and 84×13 as in Example 3.3 in this section.

8. Sam, Julie, and Frank each multiplied incorrectly. Explain each mistake.

Sam:	Julie:	Frank:
	2	2
32	27	37
$\times$ 7	$\times$ 4	$\times$ 4
2114	88	118

3.4 Long Division by 1–digit Numbers

Long division is the most important (and most complicated) algorithm taught in elementary school. Like the other algorithms, long division marks the end of learning about whole number division and helps to build students' confidence that they have mastered division. Long division also exposes students for the first time to ideas that will become important as they continue to learn mathematics, including the following.

1. It relates fractions and decimals (see Chapter 9). In particular, that helps students to understand irrational numbers.

2. It illustrates the ideas of a cyclic algorithm and of "successive approximation."

3. It is required for several topics in more advanced math, including factoring polynomials (in high school algebra) and 'Partial Fractions' (in calculus).

The items on this list are *concepts* in mathematics, computer programming, and science. Learning long division is an example of the 'upward spiral' of a balanced curriculum (see the Preface of this textbook): although it is a mechanical skill, learning it is essential for understanding concepts that come later.

A Curriculum Sequence

Long division is taught in two main stages: division by 1–digit whole numbers, and division by multi-digit whole numbers. Each stage consists of several short instructional periods requiring about a week of class time. These instructional periods are separated by a long period (at least six months) during which the algorithm is used in applications but not developed further. This gives time for both the calculational method and the associated place value concepts to "sink in."

All this takes time. In the Primary Mathematics curriculum long division is introduced early in grade 3, and is repeatedly returned to and developed in grades 4 and 5. It is completed in grade 6 with division of multi-digit decimals.

The first stage, division by 1–digit whole numbers, has two steps. The first step, done in Primary Math 3A pages 57–67 and Primary Math 4A pages 28–35, builds up to problems like $5\overline{)3685}$. The second step, done in Primary Math 4B pages 53–62 involves decimals and builds up to problems like $6\overline{)23.94}$. Primary Math 5A wraps up dividing by a 2–digit whole on pages 28–32. This section focuses on the first stage. Section 3.6 looks at the second stage on dividing by multi-digit whole numbers, and division with decimals is done in Section 9.1.

Prerequisites for long division by 1–digit whole numbers.

1. A good understanding of place value.

2. A solid knowledge of the meaning of multiplication and the basic multiplication facts up to 10×10.

3. A solid knowledge of the meaning of division (both partitive and measurement)

4. Multi-digit subtraction with regrouping.

5. Familiarity with the notation $3\overline{)15}$ to mean $15 \div 3$.

The most important of these is the first. Long division is essentially a tally system arranged in place value columns. Every step of the calculation respects this place value system. That puts a heavy burden on the students' understanding of place value. Consequently, in the Primary Mathematics curriculum *instruction on long division is punctuated by work on place value ideas*. For example, on pages 31-33 of Primary Math 4A long division practice problems are intermingled with a review of a place value concept — division by 10. Such place value knowledge helps students understand the algorithm and helps them calculate correctly.

The long division algorithm can be developed by either of two approaches:

• Partitive Division and

• Measurement Division.

Either way, one ends up writing down exactly the same numbers in the same positions. The difference lies in the *interpretation* of what one is doing. We will go through both approaches. In each case we will work through three examples which, together, show the development of the algorithm.

The Partitive Approach

Using the partitive approach, division is thought of as a problem of sharing or distributing equally. In such problems there are *three* numbers to keep track of, as in the following example.

EXAMPLE 4.1. *Jane put 14 dolls equally into 4 dollhouses. There were then _____ dolls in each dollhouse, a total of _____ dolls distributed into the dollhouses, and _____ left over.*

The first step toward the long division algorithm is learning to record those three numbers in the tabular format below (the arrows on the right provide the interpretations from Example 4.1).

```
          3                  < dolls in each dollhouse
    4 | 1  4
        1  2                 < dolls distributed
           2                 < left over
```

This tabular format has columns for tens and ones. The algorithm proceeds in steps, one for each place value column. Each step is the same: one distributes as above in one place value, then moves to the next and repeats. Here's how it works using a money model.

EXAMPLE 4.2. *Anna and Beth wish to split* 74 *cents (7 dimes and 4 pennies) equally.* They start by distributing the dimes, keeping a careful record in tabular form.

Tens Place. Distribute as many dimes as possible, recording the results in the tens column. Each girl gets 3 dimes; that distributes 6 dimes and leaves 1 dime (and 4 pennies).

```
          3              < dimes to each
    2 | 7  4
        6                < dimes distributed
        1                < remainder
```

The leftover 1 dime cannot be divided equally. Anna solves that problem by exchanging the dime for 10 pennies from her penny jar (she "unbundles a ten"); the girls then have 14 pennies. This unbundling is recorded by "bringing down the 4" and interpreting the digits 1 4 as 14 ones (rather than a ten and 4 ones).

Ones Place. Distribute 14 pennies. Each girl gets 7 pennies, so 14 pennies are distributed, and 0 are left.

```
          3  7           < pennies to each
    2 | 7  4
        6
        1  4
        1  4             < pennies distributed
           0             < remainder
```

Notice how place value is respected: numbers of tens (dimes) are consistently recorded in the tens column, and numbers of ones (pennies) are consistently recorded in the ones column. Students will need instruction calling their attention to that place value structure.

EXERCISE 4.3. *Example 4.2 involved a story and included 'teacher knowledge' details. Study pages 59 – 60 in Primary Math 3A to see how the same ideas can be introduced using other models and virtually no words.*

Larger dividends require more steps, but each step remains the same.

EXAMPLE 4.4. $627 \div 3$.

Here we have 6 hundreds, 2 tens, and 7 ones to distribute equally among three people.

Hundreds Place. Distribute 6 hundreds: each person gets 2 hundreds, so 6 hundreds are distributed, leaving 0 hundreds (plus 2 tens and 7 ones).

$$
\begin{array}{r}
2 \\
3\,\overline{)\,6\quad 2\quad 7} \\
6 \\
\hline
0
\end{array}
$$

< hundreds to each
< hundreds distributed
< remainder

Now switch attention to the tens place. Bring down the 2 to make clear that we have 2 tens.

Tens Place. Distribute the 2 tens. Since there are 3 people, we cannot even give 1 ten to each person! We distribute 0 tens, so we still have 2 tens (plus 7 ones) left.

We then "unbundle," interpreting the 2 tens and 7 ones as 27 ones, and continue.

Ones Place. Distribute the 27 ones: each person gets 9, so 27 are distributed and 0 are left.

$$
\begin{array}{r}
2\quad 0\quad 9 \\
3\,\overline{)\,6\quad 2\quad 7} \\
6 \\
\hline
0\quad 2 \\
0 \\
\hline
2\quad 7 \\
2\quad 7 \\
\hline
0
\end{array}
$$

Example 4.4 contains a subtlety that can give students difficulty. After realizing that no tens can be distributed, some students immediately proceed to the ones place; that produces the erroneous "answer" 29 (instead of 209). Thus it is important to realize that *each step produces a new digit of the quotient.* That digit is sometimes 0.

EXERCISE 4.5. *a) Study pages 62-64 in Primary Math 3A. In the illustration on page 62, how is the "sharing" depicted?*

b) Notice how quickly instruction passes from the model to the abstract calculation, and how the steps are neatly illustrated by the arrows within the pink rectangles. Is the subtlety which appears in the Example 4.4 above addressed? Where?

Examples 4.2 and 4.4 illustrate three features of the long division algorithm.

1. Long division is a repeating algorithm. Each step is the same: distribute, record, and shift to next place value ('bringing down' the next digit).

2. The algorithm is organized by place value — each step concerns a single place value.

3. The steps give better and better approximations to the answer, with each step generating one more correct digit of the quotient.

Once students understand the place value structure of long division there is no further need for interpretations — students proceed to doing the algorithm mechanically, calculating quickly without thinking of interpretations. Grid-lined paper ("graph paper") helps students recognize and maintain place-value columns in their computations.

The Measurement Approach

While the Primary Mathematics curriculum introduces long division using partitive interpretation, other curriculums use measurement division for that purpose. The next three examples illustrate the measurement division approach. As you will see, the two approaches are very similar.

EXAMPLE 4.6. *Find* $13 \div 4$ *using a measurement model.*

Lay out segments of length 4 along the number line, starting at 0 and stopping when there is no room for another segment. This process, which includes the multiplication $3 \times 4 = 12$, can be recorded in tabular form as before.

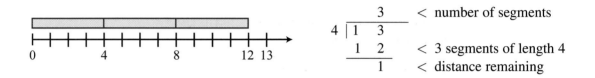

$$
\begin{array}{r}
3 \quad < \text{ number of segments} \\
4\,\overline{\vert\ 1\quad 3} \\
1\quad 2 \quad < \text{ 3 segments of length 4} \\
\overline{\quad 1} \quad < \text{ distance remaining}
\end{array}
$$

EXAMPLE 4.7. $945 \div 7$.

As before, we can visualize laying segments along the number line. However, it is difficult to count by sevens to 945. To save time and effort, we can think of laying out 10 or 100 such segments at a time. With that strategy, we can find $945 \div 7$ mentally in three easy steps.

1. 100 sevens gets us to 700, leaving 245 to go.

2. How many sevens in the remaining 245? 10 sevens get us to 70, 20 get us to 140, and 30 get us to 210. That leaves 35 to go.

3. How many sevens in the remaining 35? Exactly 5.

Thus $945 \div 7$ is $100 + 30 + 5 = 135$.

This Mental Math calculation has three iterations: count by 700s and subtract, count by 70s and subtract, and count by 7s and subtract. The iterations immediately translate into the long division shown below.

$$
\begin{array}{r}
1\quad 3\quad 5 \\
7\,\overline{\vert\ 9\quad 4\quad 5} \\
7\quad 0\quad 0 \quad < \text{ 1 segment of length 700} \\
\overline{2\quad 4\quad 5} \quad < \text{ 245 units left to go} \\
2\quad 1\quad 0 \quad < \text{ 3 segments of length 70} \\
\overline{3\quad 5} \quad < \text{ 35 units left to go} \\
3\quad 5 \quad < \text{ 5 segments of length 7} \\
\overline{0} \quad < \text{ remainder.}
\end{array}
$$

EXAMPLE 4.8. $6554 \div 8$.

With large dividends the cyclic nature of the algorithm and the role of the place value columns becomes clear. In this problem the divisor is 8, so we first count by 800s, then by 80's, then by 8s. The process gives the "intermediate algorithm" below on the left. After doing a dozen such problems students should see that there is no need to record all of these digits. Eliminating the unnecessary entries yields the efficient algorithm on the right — this is the standard form of long division.

```
              8  1  9   R2                                          8  1  9   R2
        8 | 6  5  5  4                                        8 | 6  5  5  4
          6  4  0  0    < 8 segments of length 800              6  4
          ─────────                           simplify         ─────────
             1  5  4    < 154 left               ⟹                1  5
                8  0    < 1 segment of length 80                     8
          ─────────                                             ─────────
                7  4    < 74 left                                      7  4
                7  2    < 9 segments of length 8                       7  2
          ─────────                                             ─────────
                   2    < 2 left                                          2
```

Homework Set 13

1. (*Study the Textbook!*)   After looking at page 57 of Primary Math 3A, make up a word problem (not the one illustrated!) that can be used to introduce the definitions of quotient and remainder.

2. (*Study the Textbook!*)   Draw your own version of Examples 1–4 on pages $58 - 59$ of Primary Math 3A using exactly the same numbers, but illustrating with dimes (white circles) and pennies (shaded circles) instead of stick bundles.

3. (*Study the Textbook!*)   Look at the pictures for Problems 4 and 5 on pages $59 - 60$ of Primary Math 3A. Why is it helpful to move to the chip model instead of staying with bundle sticks?

4. For the problem $243 \div 3$, draw the chip model and the 'box with arrows' as on page 62 of Primary Math 3A. Then do $521 \div 3$ as in Problem 4 on page 64.

5. Make up a measurement division word problem for $45 \div 8$ and solve it as in Example 4.6.

6. a) Using the same procedure as in Example 4.7, write down the reasoning involved in finding $17,456 \div 8$. Begin as follows: How many 8 are in 17,456? Well, 2000 eights gets us to 16,000. That leaves 1,456. Now begin again: . . . .

   b) Write down the long division for $17,456 \div 8$.

7. Give Teacher's Solutions for Problems 6–10 of Practice 3G of Primary Math 3A. At this point students have just learned to do long division; these word problems are intended to provide further practice. Thus the computational part of your Teacher's Solution should show a finished long division, without chip models and without breaking the computation into a sequence of steps. Your solutions should resemble the one given for Problem 11a, page 33 of Primary Math 4A.

3.5 Estimation

estimation

Estimation is the process of quickly finding an approximate answer to a given computation. Estimation is useful for solving problems where only an approximate answer is necessary. It can also be used to check answers to complex computations.

Teaching estimation is an excellent way of extending place value concepts to large numbers and decimals. It also helps to develop a sense of the relative sizes of numbers. For these reasons, estimation make it an especially useful topic in elementary school.

Incidentally, the word 'estimate' is commonly used for two distinct processes. The first is the one we are using: finding a rough answer to a *specific computation* such as 19.3×62. But one can also estimate a *measurement*, as when one says "it is about 5 miles to the mall." Both types of estimation are important, but because we are developing arithmetic this section focuses on estimating computations.

rounding off

Rounding. Estimation is done by judiciously choosing approximations and "rounding off." There is a standard, familiar method of "rounding off to the nearest ten" (or nearest hundred, etc.). This method is a straightforward algorithm which is easily taught, as the following exercise shows. It can be neatly illustrated using number lines. Only one subtlety is involved: the convention of "rounding fives up."

EXERCISE 5.1. *a) In Primary Math 4A, read pages 12–13 and do Problems 1, 4, and 6 on pages 14–16.*

b) In Primary Math 5A, read pages 11, 12, and the box at the top of page 13. Notice how the symbol $\approx$ is introduced. Do Problem 7 on page 13.

As one gains experience at estimation, one learns to spot other ways of rounding off and estimating. For example, one can estimate 26.4×6 by rounding it to the simple computation 25×6. There is no right or wrong way of estimating, but there is a guiding principle:

> Round off in a way that makes the resulting computation easy.

We next describe one method — which we call *simple estimation* — for doing this.

Simple Estimation

This method is beautifully developed in Primary Mathematics 4A and 5A. Rather than directly explain the method, these books present a set of carefully-chosen exercises that guide the student to discover it. We will explicitly describe the two steps involved. To fully understand the steps, and to appreciate how they can be taught, you should do Exercises 5.2 and 5.3 below as you read.

Step 1 — Rounding to 1–digit arithmetic facts. For addition and subtraction, we round off to reduce to addition or subtraction within 20. For example, rounding to the nearest hundred:

(a) $685 + 391 \approx 700 + 400 = 1100$.

(b) $1618 - 932 \approx 1600 - 900 = 700$.

For multiplication and division, we reduce to 1–digit facts such as 9×6 or $42 \div 7$ which are known from the multiplication table. Examples:

(c) $21.6 \times 7.7 \approx 20 \times 8 = 160$.

(d) $546 \div 7 \approx 560 \div 7 = 80$.

Notice that in (d) we rounded 546 not to the nearest ten, but instead to 560 because we know that 56 is a multiple of 7. Similarly, $645 \div 9$ rounds off to $630 \div 9 = 70$.

EXERCISE 5.2. (Study the textbook!) *(a) On page 17 of Primary Math 4A study the illustrations and do Problems 8 and 10. Notice how the wording of the questions evolves from "round off, then estimate" to just "estimate."*

(b) In Exercise 4 of Primary Math Workbook 5A , do Problems 1–4; these are examples of what we mean by "1-digit computations." Then do Problems 5abef, and 6abef; these ask the student to round the given problem to a 1-digit computation.

Step 2 — Keeping track of place value. For estimates involving large numbers we can still round to 1–digit facts, but the correct place value position may not be clear. For example, we can estimate 426×519 using the 1–digit fact $4 \times 5 = 20$, but how many zeros do we put after the 20? To settle that we note two facts familiar from Mental Math:

(i) In multiplication, "ending zeros" can be transferred from the factors to the product. Thus 400×500 is 4×5 with four appended zeros, or $200,000$ (it is $(4 \times 10 \times 10) \times (5 \times 10 \times 10) = (4 \times 5) \times 10000$).

(ii) In division, one can remove an equal number of zeros from the dividend and divisor without changing the answer (this is compensation for division).

Two examples:

(a) $805 \times 52.3 \approx \mathbf{800} \times \mathbf{50} = 40,\mathbf{000}$.

(b) $43,259 \div 580 \approx 42,\mathbf{000} \div \mathbf{600} = 420 \div 6 = 70$.

EXERCISE 5.3. (Study the textbook!) *(a) In Primary Math 5A, read page 15 and do Problems 6–8 on page 16. These show how to keep track of factors of 10 by counting ending zeros.*

(b) Continuing, read page 17 and do Problems 4–6 on page 18. These show how to keep track of factors of 10 in division problems by cancelling zeros.

Simple estimation is excellent for classroom use because it integrates 1–digit arithmetic with place value concepts. Teachers can also have students practice other ways of estimating in conjunction with Mental Math. For example, a student might estimate 27.8×8.9 by rounding to 28×9 and using the Mental Math method for multiplying by 9, obtaining $28 \times 9 = 280 - 28 \approx 250$. Such exercises provide opportunities for creative thinking. But they are difficult to teach and such sophisticated estimation techniques are not essential material for elementary school mathematics.

Remark. Compensation is also useful in making estimates. For example, we can estimate 35×75 by rounding 35 up to 40 and then, to compensate, rounding 75 *down* to 70, giving the approximate answer $40 \times 70 = 2800$. For division, we compensate by rounding dividend and divisor in the same direction (up or down). Thus to estimate $3845 \div 53$ we round 53 down to 50, and then, looking at the leading two digits of 3845, round down to a multiple of 5:

$$3845 \div 53 \approx 3500 \div 50 = 350 \div 5 = 70.$$

Teaching Considerations. Estimation problems are inherently ambiguous — there is always the issue of how accurate to be. The problem

"Estimate 18×35."

has many possible answers, including

$$
\begin{aligned}
20 \times 30 &= 600, \\
20 \times 40 &= 800, \\
20 \times 35 &= 700.
\end{aligned}
$$

It also has an exact answer by mental math, namely $(20 \times 35) - 70 = 700 - 70 = 630$. Which of these is an acceptable answer? Are some "more correct" than others? If 600 and 800 are good estimates, is 500 okay? How about 400? Is 650, obtained by "just guessing," acceptable?

Such a plethora of student answers creates a dilemma for the teacher. Accepting *all* answers makes the exercise rather meaningless. On the other hand, any choice which deems some of these answers unacceptable will seem arbitrary to the students, *as indeed it is.* Students face the same problem: should they just guess, or should they work hard to get a very good estimate? (When students first encounter estimation problems some are inclined to find the exact answer, round it off, and call that their estimate. This, of course, misses the point of estimation, which is to quickly find an approximate answer.)

Teachers can minimize these problems by carefully articulating (i) the purpose of the estimation, (ii) the accuracy of the level required, and (iii) a specific method for estimation. Ambiguities can also be reduced by selecting problems for which the exact calculation is difficult but there is an "obvious" way to estimate. Here are some examples.

(a) Estimate 97×204.

(b) Estimate 28×47 by rounding the factors to the nearest multiple of 10.

(c) Your shopping cart contains items which cost $4.95, $8.45, $1.95, $12.95, $28.95, and $14.32. What was the total cost to the nearest $10?

(d) Is $3464/54$ closest to 6.41, 64.1, or 641?

The numbers in (a) were chosen so there is an obvious estimate ($100 \times 200 = 20,000$) which is much easier to find than the exact answer. Questions (b) and (c) specify the accuracy required and also make the estimate particularly easy (after rounding, the numbers in (c) can be paired up to make multiples of 10). The multiple-choice question (d) asks us to estimate a fraction to within a factor of 10. Such "where does the decimal point go?" issues arise frequently when doing complicated calculations (even with a calculator) and when doing multi-digit long division as in the next section. Notice that each of these exercises simultaneously develops skill at place value and skill at estimation.

At first glance, it might seem that estimation is an easier skill than exact calculation and therefore should be taught first. Actually the opposite is true. To estimate, one must first mentally anticipate the steps in the exact calculation and judge which parts of the calculation are relatively unimportant. For example, to estimate

$$0.6 \times 213$$

a child must first realize that the exact answer is the sum of three products (0.6×200, 0.6×10, and 0.6×3) and then recognize that the one with the largest contribution is 0.6×200, so $0.6 \times 213 \approx 120$. Such thinking begins by envisioning some method for finding the exact answer. Thus from a teaching standpoint estimation is many separate skills, and each of those skills makes sense to children only *after* they are familiar with the corresponding exact calculation.

We conclude this section by describing a type of estimation problem which, because of its purpose, requires us to pay attention to whether we are underestimating or overestimating.

range
estimate

To produce a *range estimate* one does two rough calculations — one guaranteed to be less than the answer and one is guaranteed to be more than the answer. For example, 11.3234×18.8976 is more than $10 \times 18 = 180$ but less than $12 \times 20 = 240$. Such estimates have practical applications.

EXAMPLE 5.4. *Kristen has $10 and wants to buy a notebook costing $3.32, a pen costing $3.89 and an eraser costing $1.45. If the sales tax is 4%, does she have enough money?*

overestimate

Kristen should *overestimate* the cost. Rounding up, the cost of the three items is at most $3.50 + $4 + $1.50 = $9. Also rounding up, the sales tax is at most 9×5 cents $= 45$ cents. The total is at most $9.45, so she has enough money.

EXAMPLE 5.5. *If your car gets 31 miles a gallon, is a full 12.5 gallon gas tank enough to get to a city 319 miles away?*

underestimate

Clearly you want to know whether the car will go *at least* 319 miles. Rounding each factor down, the estimated driving range is $31 \times 12.5 > 30 \times 12 = 360$, so there is enough gas.

Homework Set 14

Write solutions to the estimation problems below by following the same guidelines as you did for writing Mental Math: write down the intermediate steps in a way that makes clear your thinking at each step.

1. *(Study the textbook!)* a) In Primary Math 4A, reread page 13 and problem 6 on page 16. Then draw similar pictures to illustrate Problems 7d and 7h on page 16.
   b) On page 18 of Primary Math 4A, what concept is being reinforced in Problems $1 - 5$?
   c) On page 12 of Primary Math 5A, read Problem 5 and do Problem 6.

2. *(Study the textbook!)* a) Reread page 17 of Primary Math 4A and do Problem 11 on that page.
   b) In Primary Math 5A, do Problems 8–12 on page 13. Notice the hints from the children in the margin!
   c) Do Problems 5cdgh and 6cdgh of Exercise 4 in Primary Math Workbook 5A.

3. *(Study the textbook!)* Do all problems in Exercise 5 and Exercise 6 in Primary Math Workbook 5A.

4. Estimate by giving a range: a) 57×23, b) 167×347 c) $54,827 \times 57$.

5. When one adds a list of numbers, roundoff errors can accumulate. For example, if we estimate $23 + 41 + 54$ by rounding to the nearest ten we get $20 + 40 + 50 = 110$, whereas the true sum 118 rounded to the nearest ten is 120. Write down two 3–digit numbers for which rounding to the nearest hundred and adding does not give the sum to the nearest hundred.

6. a) To give an overestimate, to the nearest hundred, for $1556 - 371$, would you round 1556 up or down? Would you round 371 up or down?

   b) To underestimate $3462 \div 28$, would you round 28 up or down? How about 3462?

   c) How many 800 pound gorillas can be lifted by an elevator with a capacity of 5750 pounds?

3.6 Completing the Long Division Algorithm

In Section 3.4 we saw how the algorithm for long division by a 1–digit number emerged from both the partitive and measurement interpretations of division. The algorithm involves just two ideas:

(a) We successively move through the place value positions from largest to smallest, generating one digit of the quotient at each step.

(b) Each step consists of writing a number as a multiple of the divisor plus a remainder (obtained by subtracting).

Idea (b) is exactly the Quotient–Remainder Theorem described in Section 1.6; it can be done for any whole number divisor. In fact, neither (a) nor (b) uses anything special about 1–digit divisors. Thus the long division algorithm of the previous section works *without change* for any whole number division problem. There is nothing new to learn!

You probably don't believe that statement. Here is an example to convince you.

EXAMPLE 6.1. *Find* $103,446 \div 21$.

First make a table of the multiples of 21 up to 9×21. The long division begins with the question, "How many 21's are in 103?" From the table the answer is 4, with $4 \times 21 = 84$. Of course, we really meant, "How many 21's are in 103 *thousand*?" so the answer is 4000 with $4000 \times 21 = 84,000$. Because there is no need to write the zeros, we simply record the numbers 4 and 84 in the appropriate columns. We can then subtract and repeat, using the table at each step. This is a fast, efficient, and totally mechanical process which always works — it is an algorithm.

$$1 \times 21 = 21$$
$$2 \times 21 = 42$$
$$3 \times 21 = 63$$
$$4 \times 21 = 84$$
$$5 \times 21 = 105$$
$$6 \times 21 = 126$$
$$7 \times 21 = 147$$
$$8 \times 21 = 168$$
$$9 \times 21 = 189$$

```
        4 9 2 6
21 ) 1 0 3 4 4 6
     - 8 4
       1 9 4
     - 1 8 9
         5 4
       - 4 2
         1 2 6
       - 1 2 6
             0
```

Now you try one.

EXERCISE 6.2. *Use the table below to complete the calculation of* $1,157,390 \div 145$.

$$1 \times 145 = 145$$
$$2 \times 145 = 290$$
$$3 \times 145 = 435$$
$$4 \times 145 = 580$$
$$5 \times 145 = 725$$
$$6 \times 145 = 870$$
$$7 \times 145 = 1015$$
$$8 \times 145 = 1160$$
$$9 \times 145 = 1305$$

```
             7
145 ) 1 1 5 7 3 9 0
      - 1 0 1 5
        1 4 2 3
```

This method has one drawback: we must first construct the multiplication table. That requires 9 multiplications, some of which might not even be used. For example, Example 6.1 above requires only four multiplications (one for each digit of the answer); the work done building the rest of the table was wasted effort. We can make the algorithm more efficient by using estimation to determine which multiplications are actually needed.

For that reason, long division by 2-digit numbers (in the form usually taught) requires the ability to estimate. Estimation is required because, as we work through the algorithm, we repeatedly encounter division problems with large numbers — beyond the range of the basic 1-digit multiplication table. In the first step of Exercise 6.2, for instance, we had to determine the largest multiple of 145 which is less than 1157. That is not easy to estimate. It is this need to estimate, not the procedure itself, which is the major conceptual problem students face in this last stage of learning the long division algorithm.

A Teaching sequence

In the Primary Mathematics books the long division algorithm is extended from 1-digit to 2-digit divisors in grade 5. This is fully two years after long division is first introduced. Thus the students are comfortably using long division with 1-digit divisors and understand at least one interpretation (partitive or measurement) of the algorithm. Classroom work on 2-digit divisors builds on that knowledge, and is done mostly at the abstract level where one is working with numbers and the algorithm itself. The transition is made remarkably quickly (Primary Math 5A pages 28-32).

The prerequisite skills needed for this transition should be clear.

1. Place value concepts for 4 and 5 digit numbers. (See pages 17–18 in Primary Math 5A.)

2. Facility at multiplication by 2–digit numbers.

3. Skill at estimating division by 2–digit numbers.

It is a good idea to verify that students have mastered these skills *before beginning 2–digit long division*. These skills are important because they reduce the short-term memory load as one works through the algorithm. Students who have difficulty with one or more of these component skills may become bogged down in one part of the procedure and fail to understand the algorithm as a whole. But when students are prepared, instruction time can be very short — this stage of long division is done in only *5 pages* in Primary Math 5A!

The following examples show a step-by-step development of the algorithm for 2-digit divisors.

2–digit division without estimation. The two interpretations (partitive and measurement) of long division continue to work with 2–digit divisors. Instruction begins with examples carefully chosen so as not to require estimation, as in the following example.

EXAMPLE 6.3. $422 \div 13$.

To check that the "sharing" interpretation applies, think of distributing $4.22 (4 dollars, 2 dimes, and 2 pennies) equally to 13 people. We first try to distribute the 4 dollar bills. That can't be done, so we convert the dollars into dimes; making a total of 42 dimes. We distribute 39 of these, 3 dimes to each person. That leaves 3 dimes and two pennies, which we can convert into 32 pennies and distribute.

$$
\begin{array}{r}
3\ \ 2 \quad \text{R}\,6 \\
13\,\overline{\big)\,4\ \ 2\ \ 2} \\
3\ \ 9 \\
\overline{3\ \ 2} \\
2\ \ 6 \\
\overline{6}
\end{array}
$$

Division with easy estimates. The "simple estimation" procedure described in the previous section usually yields the correct quotient for divisors whose last digit is 0,1,2 (where one rounds down) or 8 or 9 (where one rounds up).

EXAMPLE 6.4. $1230 \div 19$.

We first ask: how many times does 19 go into 123 tens? For that, we *estimate*: $19\overline{)123} \approx 20\overline{)120} = 6$. Distributing 6 tens into each of 19 bins uses 6 tens $\times$ 19 = 114 tens, and we are under way.

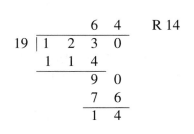

Note that the question $19\overline{)123}$ is a difficult problem for students not yet practiced in this kind of estimation. They will be unable to get past that step. Thus again, for emphasis:

> Skill at estimation is a prerequisite for 2–digit long division problems.

Errors in estimation. There is a second complication that arises for the first time in 2–digit division. *Estimates can be wrong!* Divisors that end in 4, 5, or 6 often create this difficulty.

EXAMPLE 6.5. $1138 \div 26$.

One might start like this.

Something is wrong here! Using the partitive interpretation, we are distributing 78 tens into 26 boxes. Since our remainder is larger than 26 tens we can distribute at least one more ten to each box; in fact *we should do that before moving to the next place value.* Thus our initial estimate was wrong. After correcting it to 4 tens per box we can finish.

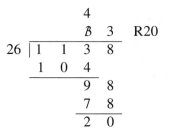

Thus each estimate must be checked and revised if necessary. The checking procedure, which is used at each step in each long division, is the following.

Check: is $0 \leq$ remainder $<$ divisor?

- If so, shift place value and bring down the next digit and shift attention to the next place value.

- If not, revise quotient by either (i) trying again, or
                      (ii) fixing by adding or subtracting 1 copy of the divisor.

EXAMPLE 6.6. $5387 \div 67$.

70 is larger than 5, and larger than 53, so we begin with the estimate $70\overline{)530} = 7\overline{)53} \approx 7$ and put the '7' at the top in the tens column. We then multiply 7 tens $\times$ 67 to get a total of 469 tens which we subtract.

$$\begin{array}{r} 7 \\ 67\,\overline{)\,5\quad 3\quad 8\quad 7} \\ 4\quad 6\quad 9 \\ \hline 6\quad 9 \end{array}$$

Oops! Doing the check, we see that this remainder is too large ($69 > 67$). Using the measurement interpretation, this means we can take one more step of size 67. The calculation can be fixed in two ways:

• Start over, estimating the quotient as 8 tens (instead of 7 tens), replacing the 469 tens by 8 tens $\times 67 = 536$ tens, and continuing.

• Better, simply replace the 7 tens by 8 tens and subtract 67 tens more (this avoids a new multiplication).

$$\begin{array}{r} 8 \\ \not 7 \\ 67\,\overline{)\,5\quad 3\quad 8\quad 7} \\ 4\quad 6\quad 9 \\ \hline 6\quad 9 \\ -\quad 6\quad 7 \\ \hline 2\quad 7 \end{array}$$

We are not yet done, and there is a pitfall lurking in the very last step! After checking that $27 < 67$ students may write the answer as $8\ R27$. Why is this wrong?

Asking "are you saying that 67×8 is roughly 5387?" will call attention to the error. Calling attention to the place value columns and asking "what if the last remainder had been 87 instead of 27?" should help lead the student to the correct answer — 8 tens with 27 remaining or 80 R27.

Homework Set 15

1. *(Study the textbook!)* Pages 17 – 18 of Primary Math 5A introduce the place value and approximation ideas needed for multi-digit long division. These ideas were briefly described in Section 3.5 as Step 2 of "simple estimation." To see how they are developed for students, carefully read Problem 7 on pages 31 – 32 in Primary Math 4A. Then do the following exercises related to pages 17, 18, and 21 of Primary Math 5A.

a) Study page 17. Then draw a similar picture for $3400 \div 100$, putting the student helper's thought bubble *first*. If you were explaining this to a class, would you explain the idea in the thought bubble before or after the chip picture?

b) On page 18, do Problem 1. Notice that (a) and (b)

can be solved by "removing all the zeros at the end," but that does not give the correct answer for (c). Make up a part (d) of the form ___ ÷ 100 which, like (c), cannot be solved by "removing all the zeros at the end."

c) Read Problem 2, paying attention to what the student helper is thinking. This introduces the idea of "cancelling zeros" for divisors which are multiples of 10, 100, and 1000, which effectively allows us to skip the first step of the solution written in color. Write down a similar solution, using two colors and a thought bubble, for $2400 \div 30$.

d) Do Problem 3.

e) On page 21 do Problems 4a, 5b, and 6adef. For 6d and 6f use (and show) the mental math method of repeatedly dividing by 2.

f) Returning to page 18, do Problem 4, read Problem 5, and do Problem 6. These are 'simple estimations" done by rounding to a problem like the ones just done.

2. *(Study the textbook!)*   Read pages $28 - 32$ of Primary Math 5A.

a) Do Problems 5adgj on page 29.

b) What component skill is being emphasized on pages $29 - 30$?

c) Still on pages $29 - 30$, why are there no chip model pictures?

d) Do Problems 16abd on page 31.

3. In Primary Math 5A, give Teacher's Solutions for Problems 9, 10, and 13 on page 32. Note that this is a teaching sequence that starts with a 1-step problem and builds up to a multi-step problem.

4. What do you tell Tracy when she writes the following?

$$
\begin{array}{r}
7\ \ 5\quad \text{R5} \\
6\,|\,\overline{4\ \ 2\ \ 3\ \ 5} \\
4\ \ 2 \\
\hline
0\ \ 3\ \ 5 \\
-\ \ 3\ \ 0 \\
\hline
5
\end{array}
$$

CHAPTER 4

Prealgebra

Prealgebra is simply arithmetic with one new feature: we use letters to represent numbers. Because the letters are simply stand-ins for numbers, *arithmetic is carried out exactly as it is with numbers*. In particular, the arithmetic properties (commutative, associative, distributive) hold because we are still doing arithmetic with numbers. Thus the identity

$$3(x + 1) = 3x + 3$$

holds because we know that it is true when $x = 2$, when $x = 5$, and in fact when x is any number at all.

That's it — that's all there is to prealgebra from a purely mathematical standpoint. Later, when students progress to algebra, this basic idea is used to define functions; as algebra continues it becomes increasingly focused on functions. The purpose of prealgebra is to prepare students for variables and functions without actually mentioning them. It is a crucial topic in the middle grades.

In the classroom the simplicity of prealgebra is crowded out by other considerations. Algebra is more abstract than arithmetic, although the abstraction is not nearly as great as is commonly perceived. In algebra, letters are used in several psychologically different ways, even though the calculations done with those letters are identical. And when applying algebra (as in word problems) students must often determine which quantities are usefully assigned letter names. This chapter focuses on the mathematical and pedagogical issues that students encounter in the transition from arithmetic to algebra.

4.1 Letters and Expressions

It is often useful to use letters to represent numbers. This is the case when

- the number is unknown,
- we want to state relationships which hold for all numbers,
- we want to work through a calculational procedure without specifying the numbers, or
- we want to show a relationship between quantities without specifying their values.

In the early grades, symbols such as ?, □, or __ are frequently used to represent unknown numbers. Using letters to represent unknown numbers is an abstraction only slightly beyond the level of arithmetic with those symbols. This step is easy for students who have mastered basic arithmetic. Thus the transition from arithmetic to beginning algebra is usually made in grades 5 through 7.

In some countries, the basic ideas of algebra are incorporated into the curricula from the beginning. In Russia, for instance, letters are introduced in the first grade! Students learn early to use letters for unknowns and see how this is useful in solving word problems.

EXERCISE 1.1. *(From a third grade Russian textbook)* *Find the unknown numbers.*

$$(x + 39) - 45 = 18 \qquad\qquad 92 - (43 - x) = 68$$
$$(24 + k) \cdot 2 = 72 \qquad\qquad 68 \div (a + 15) = 4$$

American curricula, old and new, tend to put off this transition until a "prealgebra" course in grade 7 or 8. That course often introduces algebra without emphasizing that algebra is firmly rooted in arithmetic. The transition is so brief that many students see algebra as an entirely new and useless subject, a game in which one manipulates letters according to arbitrary "rules" that must be memorized. They fail to recognize algebra as a powerful, practical extension of arithmetic.

The Primary Mathematics curriculum takes a third approach. Unknowns are, from the early grades, introduced through the bar diagrams as in the following example.

EXAMPLE 1.2. *There are 3 times as many boys as there are girls. If there are 96 children altogether, how many girls are there?*

A Teacher's Solution using bar diagrams incorporates unknowns in a natural way.

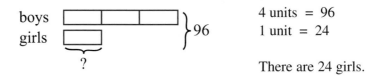

boys
girls
} 96
?

4 units = 96
1 unit = 24

There are 24 girls.

The question mark represents an unknown number (the answer to the problem). Replacing the question mark by a letter, one obtains a completely parallel "Teacher's Solution using algebra."

Number of girls: x
Number of boys: $3x$
Total: 96

$$x + 3x = 96$$
$$4x = 96$$
$$x = 24$$
There are 24 girls.

In this example the arithmetic is simple and there is no advantage to using letters instead of bar diagrams. But with larger numbers the advantage of using letters becomes obvious:

EXERCISE 1.3. *Give Teacher's Solutions for the following problem using (a) a bar diagram, and (b) algebra.*

A farmer has 33 times as many hens as roosters. If he has 442 chickens altogether, how many roosters does he have?

A Teacher's Solution using algebra has the following features.

Teacher's Solution using Algebra

Unknowns and quantities are clearly labelled.	Number of roosters: x Number of hens: $33x$ Total chickens: 442	$x + 33x = 442$ $34x = 442$ $x = 13$	$\begin{array}{r} 13 \\ 34\overline{)442} \\ -340 \\ \hline 102 \\ -102 \\ \hline 0 \end{array}$	*Computation explained with simple logic.*
Answer is clearly stated.	There are 13 roosters.		

Algebraic solutions to word problems are constructed by creating and solving algebraic equations. We next describe some ways of introducing those basic algebra ideas to students.

Expressions

The power of algebra lies in its ability to express not just numbers but calculational procedures such as "multiply a number by 3 and add the result to 2." The corresponding algebraic statement, $3m + 2$, is called an expression.

> **SCHOOL DEFINITION 1.4.** *A **numerical expression** is a combination of numbers, parentheses, and operation signs $(+, -, \times, \div, \sqrt{\ }, \dots)$ which represents a single number; examples include $3(4 + 17) - 12$, $(8 \div 5) \times 9$, and simply 15.*
>
> *More generally, an **algebraic expression** is a combination of numbers, parentheses, operation signs, and letters which represents a number for some choice of numerical values for the letters. Examples include $x + 8$, $3(2k + 5)$, and*
>
> $$\frac{3x + 7y^2}{15x^3y^2 + 2x}.$$

Statements like $57\div$, $\times 5$ or $+x$ are not expressions, nor is any statement that contains an equal sign. We have already seen that $5/0$ is not a numerical expression. On the other hand, $5/(x - 1)$ is an expression even though it does not specify a number when $x = 1$. By definition, any number or numerical expression is an algebraic expression.

Notice that the notation for multiplication is changed when one begins prealgebra. The notation 3×5, which is used through most of elementary school, is now replaced by a dot, as in $3 \cdot 5$ (the dot is needed for products of numbers to avoid confusing $3 \cdot 5$ with 35), or simply eliminated, as in $3x$ and cx. This new notation is shorter and clearer: writing $3xyz$ is certainly preferable to $3 \times x \times y \times z$.

Building and evaluating expressions. An expression can be *evaluated* by assigning specific values to the letters appearing in it. The expression then becomes a number (cases when this is not true, as in $1/x$ when $x = 0$, should be avoided in prealgebra). Returning to the expression

evaluating expressions

and assigning different values to the letters yields a different number. This notion of evaluation is the characteristic feature of expressions and the key to understanding their meaning and use.

The following examples give ways of building expressions and then evaluating them. In the first, the student builds an expression by generalizing special cases.

building expressions

EXERCISE 1.5. *Spiral notebooks cost $2 each.*

a) *The cost of 2 notebooks is $* _____

b) *The cost of 4 notebooks is $* _____

c) *The cost of 12 notebooks is $* _____

d) *The cost of x notebooks is $* _____

e) *The cost of z notebooks is $* _____

f) *The cost of $x + z$ notebooks is $* _____

These questions can be answered only because there is a simple expression that gives the cost of x notebooks. Bear that in mind as you read the next example, which uses a table to build an expression.

EXAMPLE 1.6. *Sam watched a copying machine make copies of a school newsletter. He recorded the number of copies in a table. How many copies can the machine make in m minutes?*

Minutes	Copies made
2	40
3	60
4	80
5	100

Solution. The machine makes copies at a constant rate which, the table shows, is 20 copies/minute. Knowing that, we can build the desired expression: in m minutes the machine makes $20m$ copies.

Notice how the table was used in this solution. We knew that the number of copies made was given by *some* expression because the machine made copies at a *constant* rate. The table allowed us to find that expression. However, there are many realistic situations in which a table does not lead to an expression.

EXAMPLE 1.7. *It started to rain.*
Every hour Sarah checked her rain gauge.
She recorded the total rainfall in a table.
How much rain will have fallen after h hours?

Hours	Rainfall
1	$\frac{1}{2}$ inch
2	1 inch
3	$1\frac{1}{2}$ inches

Solution. For the hours listed the amount of rainfall is given by the expression $\frac{1}{2}h$. But, of course, there is no reason why the rainfall will continue to be given by that expression, or *any* expression. The question cannot be answered!

In the Primary Mathematics texts, all examples that build expressions describe predictable situations governed by a specific expression. But watch out: most elementary textbooks are not so careful!

Asking a word problem first with numbers, then with letters, creates an exercise in building an expression.

EXERCISE 1.8. *Daniel has 3 times as much money as Juan.*

a) *If Juan has $8, how much money do they have altogether?*

b) *If Juan has $k, how much money do they have altogether?*

Alternatively, a word problem can specify an expression, which can then be evaluated.

EXERCISE 1.9. *Ms. Jackson bought T textbooks for $12 each and 2 teacher's guides for $8 each.*

　　a) Express the total cost in terms of T. _____

　　b) If Ms. Jackson bought 7 textbooks, what was the total cost? _____

Students first encounter letters in examples that are necessarily simple. But in simple examples the advantages of letters is not apparent. In all honesty, it is only after the curriculum has advanced further that students can fully appreciate the benefits of using letters and expressions.

A second use of letters is introduced in the middle grades: letters are used to described a calculational procedure as a formula.

EXAMPLE 1.10. *Express the area of a circle in terms of its radius r.*

EXAMPLE 1.11. *Megan deposited P dollars into a bank account that paid r% interest per year. Write an expression describing how many dollars she will have in the bank after t years.*

The answers, πr^2 and $P\left(1 + \frac{1}{100}r\right)^t$, are not easy to derive. But once found, they can be used over and over and never have to be derived again.

In word problems, letters always stand for numbers — they are not abbreviations. *The wording of every problem should make clear what number each letter stands for.* Poor wording can confuse students, as in the following problem.

> The Frog Mountain Spring Company examined their water business. They predicted that annual income from sales of their bottled water B would change according to the formula . . .

The problem continues, but the confusion is already planted. The wording suggests that B stands for "bottled water," leaving students wondering: how can bottled water be part of a formula? Of course, the authors meant for B to stand for the *annual income, in dollars, from sales of bottled water*, which is a number. That intention might be clear to experienced algebra students, but the wording in this problem is likely to baffle prealgebra students. As a teacher, you should be aware that textbooks do not always provide the clear, explicit wording needed by beginning algebra students. You should be prepared to proactively correct the text.

Arithmetic with expressions. Expressions can be added, subtracted, multiplied and divided. One can use models to provide examples motivating these operations. In fact, the models used for whole numbers are easily adapted to include unknowns.

　　• *Set model* — Containers holding a fixed number of objects work well.

Each box contain x crayons.

Total number of crayons = $3x + 5$.

- *Measurement model* — Bars b units long can be drawn with or without units.

- *Rectangular array or area model* — The number of rows and columns can be labeled by letters, say a and b. The number of squares in the rectangular array is then the product ab. Prealgebra students should already be familiar with area and the transition from rectangular arrays to the more abstract area model.

However, the caution mentioned in Section 1.5 still applies: whenever the area model (on the right above) appears, teachers should be sure all students understand that it is symbolic of the rectangular array on the left.

These models can be used to illustrate simple examples of adding and subtracting expressions. In the next two examples, the letter a stands for the number of crayons in each crayon box.

EXAMPLE 1.12. *Simplify $6a - 2a$.*

$$6a - 2a = \overbrace{a + a + a + a + \underbrace{a + a}_{2a}}^{6a}$$
$$= 4a.$$

This, of course, is just the distributive property: $6a - 2a = (6 - 2)a = 4a$.

EXAMPLE 1.13. *Simplify $3a + 5 + 2a - 2$.*

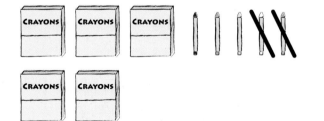

In boxes: $3a + 2a = (3 + 2)a = 5a$
Others: $5 - 2 = 3$
Total: $5a + 3$.

These two examples make clear how to sum expressions: add the terms involving a, and separately, the terms with no a. Guided by that observation, we can give a purely algebraic solution to the last problem:

$$
\begin{aligned}
3a + 5 + 2a - 2 &= (3a + 2a) + (5 - 2) \qquad &\text{Any-order property} \\
&= 5a + 3 &\text{Distributive property.}
\end{aligned}
$$

With that understood the model has served its purpose and need only be used occasionally as a reminder of the reasoning. Most problems can be solved using algebra alone.

EXAMPLE 1.14. *Simplify* $23x + 12 + 18x - 5 - 11x$.

For the solution we again apply the Any-order and distributive properties, this time without explicitly mentioning them:

$$
\begin{aligned}
23x + 12 + 18x - 5 - 11x &= (23 + 18 - 11)x + (12 - 5) \\
&= 30x + 7.
\end{aligned}
$$

Again, the principle at play is "separately add the terms involving x and those with no x." (This is reminiscent of the place value process used for adding two-digit numbers: "add the tens and the ones separately.") Simplifications of this sort are the beginnings of algebra.

The expressions in this section involve only *whole numbers*. In general, expressions can involve numbers of any type. As one moves beyond whole numbers to fractions, negative numbers, and real numbers, models become increasingly inadequate. It becomes essential to think in terms of the algebra alone.

Equations. Given two expressions, such as $x + 3x$ and 96, we can require that they be equal. The resulting statement, $x + 3x = 96$ in this case, is called an equation.

DEFINITION 1.15. *An **equation** is a statement that two expressions are equal.*

Some equations, such as $x + 3x = 96$, can be solved — they provide enough information to determine x. Others, such as $y = t + 3$, do not determine specific numerical values for y and t, but still provide information constraining which numbers those letters might represent. Still others, such as $6a - 2a = 4a$, are true no matter which number the letter represents; these are called *identities*. We will discuss identities in depth in the next section.

identities

Letters in Prealgebra

In mathematics, letters are sometimes used to name objects ("the intersection point P") or abbreviate words (12 g means 12 grams). Prealgebra begins when letters are used to represent numbers. Sometimes a letter simply represents a frequently used number, as when we write π for $3.14159 \cdots$. Beyond that, letters are used in two roles in prealgebra.

(i) Letters are used to represent specific but unknown numbers (which may in the end turn out not to exist, as is the case for the 'x' in the equation $x + 2 = x$).

(ii) Letters are also used to make statements — "identities" — that are true for all numbers (or a range of numbers, such as all $x > 0$ or all $x \neq 0$).

Many beginning algebra books refer to letters variously as "constants," "variables," and "parameters" and attempt definitions such as "a variable is a quantity that varies." Such definitions confuse both students and teachers. In fact, while these terms are used routinely in algebra, they cannot be precisely defined. The distinctions between constants and variables are subtle and depend on the context in which the letters appear. Those distinctions are important in advanced algebra, but they can only be appreciated by someone who has gone through several years of algebra, and hence are beyond the level of prealgebra.

A teacher's best course is to downplay definitions and simply make clear that, no matter what you call them, letters stand for numbers and are added, subtracted, multiplied, and divided as numbers are. Sometimes we have in mind a specific number, and sometimes we are making a statement that is true for all numbers.

We conclude by repeating and commenting on what is, for teachers, the most important point of this section:

- *In word problems, each letter should represent a number and its meaning should be clearly announced.*

Accordingly, letters can be introduced by a phrase such as *Let D be David's weight in pounds* or *David's weight: D pounds*. All solutions that use letters — by teachers and students alike — should begin with such a phrase. Notice that it is necessary to specify units. We can say *Let M be Maria's height in inches*, but we cannot say *M = Maria's height* because height is not a number until we specify whether we are using inches, feet, or meters. And we certainly cannot say *M=Maria* — Maria herself is not a number!

Defining letters carefully does not come naturally. Beginning algebra students will indeed write *M=Maria*, or will simply start using the letter M, thinking of it vaguely as something associated with Maria. Then, plunging ahead with the algebra, they become confused and frustrated. Teachers must guide students by emphasizing the importance taking the time to write careful definitions as the first step toward solving a word problem. When the teacher succeeds, the students come away with a valuable lesson about reasoning: a clear beginning promotes clear thinking.

Homework Set 16

1. *(Mental Math)* Make a list of the squares from $11^2 = 121$ through $20^2 = 400$. *Memorize these.* We will use these facts later for Mental Math exercises.

2. *(Mental Math)* Recall that $2^3 = 2 \times 2 \times 2 = 8$. Memorize the "Mental Math tags" $2^5 = 32$, $2^8 = 256$, and $2^{10} = 1024$ and the list of the first 12 powers of 2 (2, 4, 8, 16, 32, 64, 128, 256, 512, 1024, 2048, 4096). Using the three tags, you can mentally reconstruct the other powers of 2. For example, 2^7 is $2^5 \times 2 \times 2 = 128$ (two numbers after 32 on the list) and is also $2^8 \div 2 = 128$ (one before 256 on the list). Use the Mental Math tags to find:

    a) 2^4 b) 2^9 c) 2^6 d) 2^{11}

3. Which of the following are algebraic expressions?

    a) $32(52 + 7) - 38 \times \dfrac{1}{4}$ b) $3 + \div 7$
    c) $a + 3$ d) $5\pi + 4$
    e) $3x + 2 = 7$ f) $(a + b)(a - b)$
    g) x h) $12,304$
    i) $y \div 0$

4. a) Illustrate the expression $a + 7$ using a measurement model.
    b) Illustrate the expression $6x + 2$ using a rectangular array model.

5. Fred is confused about the meaning of the equal sign. His answer to the problem "Simplify $3(x+2) - x + 8$" is written below. Which of his equal signs are incorrect? What should he have written?

$$3(x + 2) = 3x + 6 - x = 2x + 6 + 8 = 2x + 14.$$

6. Write the indicated expressions.

    a) The number of inches in m feet.
    b) The perimeter of a square of side s cm.
    c) The value in cents of x nickels and y dimes.
    d) The number of pounds in $6z$ ounces.
    e) Three consecutive whole numbers the smallest of which is n.
    f) The average speed of a train that travels w miles in 5 hours.
    g) Ann is 18 years younger than Bill. Carmen is one-fifth as old as Ann. Dana is 4 years older than Carmen. If Bill is B years old, what is Dana's age in terms of B?

7. Give a Teacher's Solution using algebra (see the template given in this section) for the following problem:

    The lengths of the sides of a triangle, measured in inches, are consecutive whole numbers, and the perimeter is 27 inches. What is the length of the shortest side?

8. You have previously solved the problems on page 25 of Primary Math 5A using bar diagrams. Now do some of those problems again, making the transition to algebra as follows.

    a) For Problem 6, give a Teacher's Solution using a bar diagram.
    b) For Problems 6, 8, and 10 give a Teacher's Solution using algebra only.

9. *(Study the textbook!)* Pages $6 - 14$ of Primary Math 6A introduce students to algebraic expressions.

    a) Do Problems $1 - 14$ (beginning on page 7). For each problem write the answer and then write B or E to indicate whether the problem is building an expression or is evaluating one. Your answer for Problem 1 should read $13, x + 8$; B.
    b) How many different letters are used in the expressions that appear in Problems $1 - 14$? Why?
    c) The boy at the bottom of page 8 is calling attention to which arithmetic property?

10. *(Study the textbook!)* In Primary Math 6A:

    a) Illustrate Problems 21ac on page 13 with equations similar to those in the pink boxes on page 12 and Problem 21g with a picture similar to those in Problem 19.
    b) Do Problem 5ab on page 14 by *explicitly* showing the use of the distributive property (see Example 1.14 in this section).
    c) Answer Problems $6 - 9$ on page 14.

11. Make up a short word problem which builds the given expression in the given context. Be sure to make clear what each letter represents.

    a) The expression $12c$ in the context of baking cookies.
    b) The expression $13r + 3s$ in the context of shopping (cf. Exercise 1.9).
    c) The expression $2w + 13$ in the context of money saved from an allowance.
    d) The expression $(240 - x)/50$ as the time needed to complete a trip to another city.

4.2 Identities, Properties, Rules

algebraic identity

Algebraic identities are equations that are true no matter which numbers their letters represent. A simple example is the equation

$$5x + 3x + 7 = 8x + 7,$$

which is true for every choice of x. A much more important example is the commutative property for addition, which can be stated as

$$a + b = b + a \qquad \text{for all numbers } a \text{ and } b.$$

This is a precise statement of the first grade phrase "we can add two numbers in either order." In spirit, it is the same as saying that "$3 + 5 = 5 + 3$ no matter what the numbers 3 and 5 are." That awkward wording is rendered clear and precise by using letters. The ability to make precise statements that hold for all numbers is one of the motivations for algebra, and one of its great achievements.

The discussion in this section will distinguish three types of identities. The most basic identities are called *properties*. Identities which are so simple and useful that they are worth memorizing are called *rules*, and ones which occur less often are simply called identities.

arithmetic properties and rules

The commutative property is one of the four fundamental properties of arithmetic stated in Sections 1.3 and 1.5. The complete list is as follows.

Arithmetic Properties

The following identities hold for all whole numbers a, b, and c:

- commutative: $a + b = b + a$ and $ab = ba$,

- associative: $a + (b + c) = (a + b) + c$ and $a(bc) = (ab)c$,

- distributive: $a(b + c) = ab + ac$,

- additive identity and multiplicative identity: $a + 0 = a$ and $a \cdot 1 = a$.

We have been using these properties since addition and multiplication were first introduced. Previously they were described through examples; now we have used letters to write them down succinctly and precisely. Nothing else has changed. In particular, these properties remain statements about *numbers*. They are not properties of letters, nor are they new rules introduced for the first time when one starts algebra. They are simply statements about the familiar ways numbers behave when added and multiplied, now phrased in a more precise and powerful language.

The arithmetic properties are used whenever we manipulate numbers or expressions. In arithmetic they are usually used without being explicitly named. In prealgebra, however, the arithmetic properties are named and brought to the forefront. They serve as foundational identities and are repeatedly used in simplifications and in deriving other identities.

EXAMPLE 2.1. *Simplify* $6(3 + a) + 7$.

$$
\begin{aligned}
6(3 + a) + 7 &= (6 \cdot 3 + 6a) + 7 && \text{distributive property} \\
&= (6a + 18) + 7 && \text{commutative property} \\
&= 6a + (18 + 7) && \text{associative property} \\
&= 6a + 25 && \text{addition.}
\end{aligned}
$$

All expressions above are equal to one another for every value of a. For example, if $a = 2$ then every line above is equal to 37.

Arithmetic Rules

Proficiency at arithmetic obviously increases as one learns more arithmetic facts. Someone who knows that $12 \times 12 = 144$ can more easily find 12×13. In the same way, learning algebra identities increases one's proficiency at algebra. You are no doubt familiar with how the "invert and multiply" identity

$$
\frac{a}{b} \div \frac{c}{d} = \frac{ad}{bc}
$$

greatly speeds up some algebra calculations. Algebra identities of this type — simple identities which can be recalled and applied when needed — are commonly called *arithmetic rules*.

arithmetic rules

The word "rule" is unfortunate. In English it almost always means "a prescribed law," but in mathematics it is used with a different meaning: "something that is true without exception." Students must be warned about this shift in meaning, otherwise they may come to think of arithmetic rules as laws invented and prescribed by teachers or textbook authors, like the rules of chess or basketball. That creates a deep mistaken impression about what algebra is. In fact, 'arithmetic rules' are identities — statements that are true for all numbers, without exception. They are nobody's invention and there is nothing arbitrary about them.

Rules are especially simple and useful identities. Being simple, they can be explained, using examples and models, in ways that make sense (recall the teaching principle that "everything in mathematics makes sense"). An identity becomes a rule after it is understood, practiced, memorized, and applied often. Last year's identity becomes this year's rule. Each rule is acquired with effort, but once mastered it becomes part of the student's developing toolbox of algebra skills.

Identities can be introduced using models or derived algebraically from already-known facts such as the distributive property. But they are learned and understood by repeatedly building and evaluating the algebraic identity, as we did with expressions in the previous section . That can be done in word problems and in Mental Math exercises. Such exercises are essential in prealgebra because an algebraic identity makes sense only when students realize that it is a general expression of many (infinitely many!) arithmetic facts.

Examples of Identities.   Here are two identities that should be familiar from your algebra courses:

- $(a + b)(a + b) = a^2 + 2ab + b^2$, and

- $(a + b)(a - b) = a^2 - b^2$.

Such identities can be developed using models and specific numbers and reinforcing through Mental Math. The following three steps give one approach to developing the first identity above.

• **Step 1.** One begins by using rectangular arrays to illustrate special cases, such as $(10 + 3)(10 + 3)$.

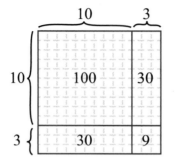

Total number of squares:
$100 + 30 + 30 + 9$
$100 + 2(30) + 9$.

This same model was used in Section 3.3 in one approach to explaining the multiplication algorithm.

• **Step 2.** The above picture is easily modified to show more general cases like $(a + 1)^2 = a^2 + 2a + 1$. These can be used in Mental Math exercises, which provide an entertaining way of understanding the identity by repeatedly evaluating it.

EXERCISE 2.2. *Use the identity* $(a + 1)^2 = a^2 + 2a + 1$ *to mentally calculate* $21^2, 31^2, 41^2$.

For example,
$$21^2 = (20 + 1)^2 = 400 + 2 \cdot 20 + 1 = 441.$$

• **Step 3.** In a middle school course, the same identity can be motivated with a rectangular array model using letters. This time it is important to show that it follows directly from the distributive property using algebra.

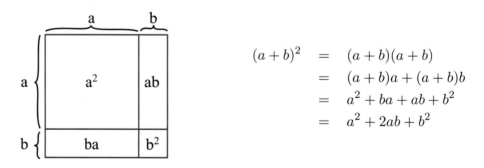

$$
\begin{aligned}
(a + b)^2 &= (a + b)(a + b) \\
&= (a + b)a + (a + b)b \\
&= a^2 + ba + ab + b^2 \\
&= a^2 + 2ab + b^2
\end{aligned}
$$

Even in this final step the focus should be on connecting algebra to students' knowledge of arithmetic, so many special cases should be calculated. The goal is the same as earlier: to be sure that students realize that identities are simply new ways of expressing their knowledge of numbers, rather than strange sequences of letters to be memorized.

The identity $(a + b)(a - b) = a^2 - b^2$ can also be modelled with rectangular arrays (try it as a challenge!). But it has a different geometric interpretation, which leads to some wonderful

Mental Math exercises. On the number line, $a + b$ and $a - b$ are a pair of numbers equally spaced about their average. Thus if we are told the numbers $a + b$ and $a - b$, we can easily find a (their average) and b (the difference from the average), and therefore find $a^2 - b^2$.

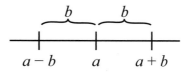

For example, we can use the identity to find 19×21 by taking $a = 20$ (the average) and $b = 1$ (the difference from the average) to get $19 \times 21 = 20^2 - 1^2 = 399$. Another example: $28 \times 32 = 30^2 - 4 = 896$.

EXERCISE 2.3. *Use this method to find* $8 \times 12,\quad 11 \times 13,\quad 17 \times 23,\quad and\quad 7 \times 9.$

You can use this method to quickly find almost all products of numbers less than 20 provided you know the squares of the numbers 11 through 20 (Problem 6 below). For example, $13 \times 17 = 15^2 - 4 = 221$.

binomials

The two identities we have just discussed involve the binomials expressions $a + b$ and $a - b$ (the word "binomial" literally means "two numbers"). Both are special cases of the identity for the product of two binomials, namely

$$(a + b)(c + d) \;=\; ac + ad + bc + bd.$$

This is easily derived by applying the distributive property in two stages:

$$(a + b)(c + d) \;=\; (a + b)\,c + (a + b)\,d \;=\; ac + bc + ad + bd.$$

double distributive rule

In fact, this identity can be thought of as the "double distributive rule."   That explanation conveys the essential mathematics of the formula and suggests why it is a particularly useful identity.

EXERCISE 2.4. *Draw a rectangular array like the one on the previous page to illustrate and complete the identity*

$$(a + b)(c + d) \;=\; \underline{\hspace{2cm}}.$$

Caution on FOIL mnemonic

The identity in Exercise 2.4 is often "explained" using the mnemonic "FOIL — first, outer, inner, last." FOIL may be an effective way to get students to mechanically do some algebra calculations, but it is a teaching device that has the potential to do more harm than good.

What's wrong with just having students memorize FOIL? First, teaching the mnemonic completely bypasses the key point — the distributive property. Algebra is easier to learn when students see how identities follow from facts and principles they already know. Second, many students regard FOIL as a rote procedure special to algebra; they fail to realize that the letters they are rearranging are actually numbers and they are using manipulations which are clear for numbers. Finally, the FOIL mnemonic does not generalize — see Homework Problem 7.

Homework Set 17

1. (Mental Math) Use the Mental Math tags $2^5 = 32$, $2^8 = 256$, and $2^{10} = 1024$ to find the following mentally.

a) 2^9 b) 2^4 c) 2^6 d) 2^7

e) 2^{11} f) 2^{12} g) 2^{13} h) 2^{14}.

2. (Mental Math) Calculate the following mentally (and show how you did it!).

a) 13×15 b) $(15 + 1)(15 - 1)$
c) $2^8 \cdot 2^3$ d) $2^{13} \div 8$
e) 48×25 f) $354 - 139 + 46$
g) $34\,200 \div 50$ h) $142^2 - 140^2$.

3. How might you teach your class to simplify $(x^2 + 3x + 4) + (2x^2 + x + 7)$? Here is one approach.

a) Draw a picture involving rectangular arrays of areas x^2, x, and 1 which makes clear the principle "total the x^2 terms, the x terms, and the constant terms separately."

b) Simplify the expression algebraically in several steps using the Any-order and distributive properties. Label each step as in Example 2.1.

4. (Mental Math) Use the identity $(a+b)^2 = a^2 + 2ab + b^2$ to calculate 21^2, 31^2, 41^2, 51^2 (show your method). Do the same for 19^2, 29^2, 39^2, 49^2 using the identity $(a-b)^2 = a^2 - 2ab + b^2$.

5. (Mental Math) What is 15^2? 150^2? Show how to calculate 151^2 mentally.

6. (Mental Math) The following Mental Math problems are applications of the identity $(a+b)(a-b) = a^2 - b^2$. You will need to know your squares up to 20.

a) Numbers which differ by 2: Calculate mentally using the identity $(a+1)(a-1) = a^2 - 1$.

14×16, 18×20, 13×15, 17×19, 16×18, 19×21, 139×141, 6×8.

b) Numbers which differ by 4: Calculate mentally using the identity $(a+2)(a-2) = a^2 - 4$.

14×18	12×16	13×17
17×21	9×13	58×62
188×192	4×8	

7. Consider the identity

$$(x + y)(a + b + c) = xa + xb + xc + ya + yb + yc.$$

a) Illustrate this identity by a rectangular array.

b) Derive the identity using the distributive property.

c) Does the FOIL mnemonic work for this identity?

8. By repeatedly using the distributive property, derive an identity for $(a + b)^3$.

9. Write an identity of the form

$$(a + b)^2 - (a - b)^2 = \underline{\hspace{2cm}}$$

by considering the figure below.

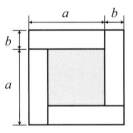

10. (A Teaching Sequence) For this problem, let a and b be two whole numbers. Show how each of the following identities follow from the distributive property.

a) $(20 + 4)^2 = 20^2 + 2 \cdot 20 \cdot 4 + 4^2$.

b) $(a + 4)^2 = a^2 + 2 \cdot a \cdot 4 + 4^2$.

c) $(a + b)^2 = a^2 + 2ab + b^2$.

Identity c) implies infinitely many equalities like a) and b), and you have just verified them all at once. This is one example of the power of algebra.

11. (A Teaching Sequence) Following the directions of the previous problem, build up to an identity for $(a+b)(a-b)$.

a) $(7 + 3)(7 - 3) = 7^2 - 3^2$.

b) $(a + 3)(a - 3) = a^2 - 3^2$.

c) $(a + b)(a - b) = a^2 - b^2$.

4.3 Exponents

exponential
notation

The number 1024 is the product of ten 2's: $1024 = 2 \cdot 2 \cdot 2 \cdot 2 \cdot 2 \cdot 2 \cdot 2 \cdot 2 \cdot 2 \cdot 2$. Such products occur often in mathematics, and writing them can be quite tedious. *Exponential notation* is a common way of abbreviating repeated products. We have already used exponential notation for the powers of 2, and the notation is similiar for any positive number a:

$$
\begin{aligned}
2 &= 2^1 & a &= a^1 \\
2 \cdot 2 &= 2^2 & a \cdot a &= a^2 \\
2 \cdot 2 \cdot 2 &= 2^3 & a \cdot a \cdot a &= a^3 \\
2 \cdot 2 \cdot 2 \cdot 2 &= 2^4 & a \cdot a \cdot a \cdot a &= a^4 \\
&\vdots & &\vdots \\
\underbrace{2 \cdot 2 \cdots 2}_{n \text{ times}} &= 2^n & \underbrace{a \cdot a \cdots a}_{n \text{ times}} &= a^n
\end{aligned}
$$

DEFINITION 3.1. *Let m be a nonzero whole number. For any number a, we write*

$$a^m = \underbrace{a \cdot a \cdot a \cdots a}_{m \text{ times}}.$$

*The number a is called the **base** and m is called the **exponent** or the **power**.*

This definition generalizes to fractional exponents and leads ultimately to exponential and logarithmic functions. But at the prealgebra stage the definition simply says that a^m is an abbreviation for the product of m factors of a. According to this definition, a^1 is a, while a^0 is not yet defined.

For powers of 10, exponential notation is intimately related to place value. Thus

$$
\begin{aligned}
10^1 &= 10 \\
10^2 &= 10 \times 10 = 100 \\
10^3 &= 10 \times 10 \times 10 = 1000,
\end{aligned}
$$

and 10^5 is 1 followed by 5 zeros. The expanded form can then be written using powers of 10 as in

$$3629 = \left(3 \times 10^3\right) + \left(6 \times 10^2\right) + \left(2 \times 10^1\right) + (9 \times 1).$$

Mental Math with powers of 10 can also be expressed using exponential notation. For example, compare the calculations

$$\underbrace{100 \times 100 = 10,000}_{\text{Mental Math}} \quad \text{and} \quad \underbrace{10^2 \times 10^2 = 10^4}_{\text{exponential notation}}.$$

Such comparisons help students understand both place value and exponential notation.

Because exponents record the number of factors, when we multiply powers of a fixed number, the total number of factors adds. That principle can be introduced using Mental Math or by a sequence of examples.

EXAMPLE 3.2. *In Homework Set 17 you learned the "memory tags"* $2^5 = 32$, $2^8 = 256$ *and* $2^{10} = 1024$. *You can use those to multiply powers of 2 mentally, for example,*

$$32 \cdot 8 = 2^5 \cdot (2 \cdot 2 \cdot 2) = 2^{5+3} = 2^8 = 256.$$

Use that method to mentally find $32 \cdot 32$ *and* $64 \cdot 64$.

EXAMPLE 3.3. *Below is a teaching sequence for multiplying powers.*

(i) $10^4 \cdot 10^5 = \underbrace{(10 \cdot 10 \cdot 10 \cdot 10)}_{4\ factors} \cdot \underbrace{(10 \cdot 10 \cdot 10 \cdot 10 \cdot 10)}_{5\ factors} = 10^9.$

(ii) $10^4 \cdot 10^m = (10 \cdot 10 \cdot 10 \cdot 10) \cdot \underbrace{(10 \cdot 10 \cdot 10 \cdots 10)}_{m\ factors} = 10^{4+m}.$

(iii) $x^4 \cdot x^5 = (x \cdot x \cdot x \cdot x) \cdot (x \cdot x \cdot x \cdot x \cdot x) = x^9.$

(iv) $a^3 \cdot a^m = (a \cdot a \cdot a) \cdot \underbrace{(a \cdot a \cdots a \cdot a)}_{m\ factors} = a^{3+m}.$

The general rule is then clear.

Rule 1: $a^m \cdot a^n = a^{m+n}$ for whole numbers m and n.

As was emphasized in the previous section, such arithmetic rules are not just made up — they follow logically from definitions and the arithmetic properties. In fact, Rule 1 is a simple consequence of the definition of exponents and the Any-order property:

$$a^m \cdot a^n = \underbrace{(a \cdot a \cdots a)}_{m\ \text{factors}} \cdot \underbrace{(a \cdot a \cdot a \cdots a \cdot a)}_{n\ \text{factors}} \qquad \text{Definition of exponents (Def. 3.1)}$$

$$= \underbrace{(a \cdot a \cdot a \cdots \cdot a)}_{m+n\ \text{factors}} \qquad \text{Any-order property}$$

$$= a^{m+n} \qquad \text{Definition of exponents.}$$

To see how to divide numbers that have exponents, use fraction notation. For example, to divide 2^{10} by 2^4, we simply write these out as products, cancel, and tally up the remaining factors.

$$\frac{2^{10}}{2^4} = \frac{\cancel{2} \cdot \cancel{2} \cdot \cancel{2} \cdot \cancel{2} \cdot 2 \cdot 2 \cdot 2 \cdot 2 \cdot 2 \cdot 2}{\cancel{2} \cdot \cancel{2} \cdot \cancel{2} \cdot \cancel{2}} = 2 \cdot 2 \cdot 2 \cdot 2 \cdot 2 \cdot 2 = 2^6.$$

In this calculation, the numerator originally has 10 factors of two, but 4 of those cancel with factors in the denominator, leaving 6 factors of two. In the general case, we separate the factors in the numerator into two groups, with the first group having the same number of factors as the denominator.

$$\frac{a^m}{a^n} = \frac{\overbrace{(a \cdot a \cdots \cdot a \cdot a \cdot a \cdots \cdot a)}^{m}}{\underbrace{(a \cdot a \cdots \cdot a)}_{n}} \qquad \text{Definition of exponents}$$

$$= \frac{\overbrace{(a \cdot a \cdots \cdot a)}^{n} \overbrace{(a \cdot a \cdots \cdot a)}^{m-n}}{\underbrace{(a \cdot a \cdots \cdot a)}_{n}} \qquad \text{Any-order property}$$

$$= \underbrace{(a \cdot a \cdots \cdot a)}_{m-n} \qquad \text{Below}$$

$$= a^{m-n} \qquad \text{Definition of exponent}$$

In the middle step, we used the fact that $a^n/a^n = 1$. That follows because $a^n \div a^n$ is 1 by the missing factor definition of division (since $a^n \times \underline{1} = a^n$). In algebra, one must frequently divide numbers with exponents (e.g. $\frac{x^6}{x^3}$). One can avoid going though the above steps every time by remembering the result as a second rule of exponents.

Rule 2: $\dfrac{a^m}{a^n} = a^{m-n}$ for whole numbers m and n with $m \geq n$, provided that $a \neq 0$.

Next consider expressions like $(2^4)^3$. By definition this is the product $2^4 \cdot 2^4 \cdot 2^4$. Writing each factor of 2^4 as $2 \cdot 2 \cdot 2 \cdot 2$ makes this a product of 12 twos. Thus $(2^4)^3 = 2^4 \cdot 2^4 \cdot 2^4 = 2^{12}$.

EXERCISE 3.4. *Complete the table.*

$(x^3)^2$	$x^3 \cdot x^3$	x^{3+3}	$x^{3\cdot 2}$
$(x^3)^4$		$x^{3+3+3+3}$	$x^{3\cdot \square}$
$(x^3)^n$	$\underbrace{x^3 \cdot x^3 \cdot x^3 \cdots x^3}_{n \text{ times}}$	$x^{\overbrace{3+3+3+\cdots+3}^{n \text{ times}}}$	$x^{\square \cdot \square}$
$(x^m)^n$	$\underbrace{x^m \cdot x^m \cdot x^m \cdots x^m}_{n \text{ times}}$	$x^{\overbrace{m+m+m+\cdots+m}^{n \text{ times}}}$	$x^{\square \cdot \square}$

The observation $x^3 \cdot x^3 \cdot x^3 \cdot x^3 = x^{3+3+3+3}$ in the second row is essentially Rule 1. Changing letters, the last line of the table gives our third power rule, which you will verify in Homework Problem 4d.

Rule 3: $(a^m)^n = a^{mn}$ for whole numbers m and n.

Finally, products of numbers raised to *equal powers* can be simplified by pairing up factors.

EXERCISE 3.5. *Complete the table.*

$5^3 \cdot y^3$	$(5 \cdot 5 \cdot 5)(y \cdot y \cdot y)$	$(5y)(5y)(5y)$	$(5y)^{\square}$
$x^4 \cdot y^4$			$(\quad)^4$
$x^n \cdot y^n$	$\underbrace{(x \cdot x \cdots x)}_{n \text{ times}}\underbrace{(y \cdot y \cdots y)}_{n \text{ times}}$	$\underbrace{}_{n \text{ times}}$	

In each line of this table, we rearrange the factors to form pairs (the rearrangement, of course, does not change the product — that is the Any-order property). There are no leftover factors because the exponents of the two factors are equal. After changing letters, the last line of the table can be stated and justified as follows.

Rule 4: $a^m \cdot b^m = (ab)^m$ for any whole number m.

$$a^m \cdot b^m \quad = \quad \underbrace{(a \cdot a \cdot a \cdots a)}_{m \text{ times}} \cdot \underbrace{(b \cdot b \cdot b \cdots b)}_{m \text{ times}} \qquad \text{Def. of exponents}$$

$$= \quad \underbrace{(ab)(ab) \cdots (ab)}_{m \text{ times}} \qquad\qquad \text{Any-order property}$$

$$= \quad (ab)^m \qquad\qquad\qquad\qquad \text{Def. of exponents.}$$

The four power rules are summarized in the box below. Once students understand why these rules are true, they should do problems using them, first with numbers and then with letters. At first students may have to write out the definition of exponents and "discover" the rules while doing each problem. With practice they will learn the rules and use them as natural facts about "the way exponents work" in the same way that they think of the Any-order property is simply "the way addition works." This is important — the fluent use of exponents is essential for high school mathematics.

> ### Power Rules
>
> For any whole numbers m and n, we have
>
> **(1)** $a^m \cdot a^n = a^{m+n}$ **(3)** $(a^m)^n = a^{mn}$
>
> **(2)** $\dfrac{a^m}{a^n} = a^{m-n}$ for $m \geq n$ and $a \neq 0$ **(4)** $a^m \cdot b^m = (ab)^m.$

Here are some examples illustrating the use of the power rules for numbers.

a) $1000 \cdot 1000 = 10^3 \cdot 10^3 = 10^{3+3} = 10^6 = 1,000,000.$

b) $8^4 = (2^3)^4 = 2^{12} = 2^{10+2} = 2^{10} \cdot \cdot 4 = 1024 \cdot 4 = 4096.$

c) $2^4 \cdot 3^4 = (2 \cdot 3)^4 = 6^4.$

d) $\dfrac{6^5}{3^4} = \dfrac{(2 \cdot 3)^5}{3^4} = \dfrac{2^5 \cdot 3^5}{3^4} = 2^5 \cdot \dfrac{3^5}{3^4} = 2^5 \cdot 3^{5-4} = 32 \cdot 3 = 96.$

We can also use the power rules repeatedly to simplify more complicated expressions. When those expressions involve whole numbers, it is helpful to replace each whole number by its prime factorization.

EXERCISE 3.6. *Fill in the boxes to simplify.*

$$\frac{6^4 \cdot 12^3 \cdot 15^2}{9^2 \cdot 8^2 \cdot 5} = \frac{(2 \cdot \Box)^4 (2 \cdot 2 \cdot 3)^3 (3 \cdot \Box)^2}{(3 \cdot 3)^2 (2^3)^2 \cdot 5} = \frac{2^4 \cdot 3^4 \cdot 2^3 \cdot 2^3 \cdot \Box \cdot 3^2 \cdot 5^2}{3^4 \cdot 2^6 \cdot 5}$$

$$= \frac{2^{4+3+3}}{2^6} \cdot \frac{3^{4+3+2}}{3^4} \cdot \frac{5^2}{5}$$

$$= 2^4 \cdot 3^5 \cdot 5.$$

Such expressions can always be reduced until they become a product of different primes, each raised to a power. In your homework you will be asked to simplify until your answer has that form.

EXERCISE 3.7. *Simplify* $\dfrac{x^4 \cdot (xy)^3}{x^3 y^2}$.

Zero as an exponent

Definition 3.1 stipulates that the exponent m is strictly positive, so does not cover the case when the exponent is zero. Is it possible to make sense of a^0? The pattern

$$
\begin{aligned}
10^4 \div 10 &= 10^3 \\
10^3 \div 10 &= 10^2 \\
10^2 \div 10 &= 10^1 \\
10^1 \div 10 &= \underline{}
\end{aligned}
$$

suggests that 10^0 should be defined as $10 \div 10 = 1$. Similarly a^0 should be 1 for any non-zero number a. In fact, if we want Rule 2 to hold that choice is forced on us:

$$
a^0 = a^{1-1} = \frac{a^1}{a^1} = \frac{a}{a} = 1.
$$

We can also check that setting $a^0 = 1$ is consistent with each of the other power rules.

(1) $a^0 \cdot a^m = a^{0+m} = a^m \Longleftrightarrow a^0 = 1.$

(2) $a^0 = a^{m-m} = \frac{a^m}{a^m} = 1.$

(3) $(a^0)^m = a^{0 \cdot m} = a^0 \Longleftrightarrow a^0 = 1.$

(4) $1 = (a \cdot b)^0 = a^0 \cdot b^0 = 1 \cdot 1 = 1.$

Since everything is consistent, we can extend the definition of exponents to include exponent zero by setting $a^0 = 1$ for every non-zero number a.

That still leaves 0^0 with no assigned meaning. This time there is *no* choice that is consistent with the rules of exponents. Patterns suggest (but do not prove!) that there is a problem.

$$
\begin{array}{ll}
0^3 = 0 & \qquad 3^0 = 1 \\
0^2 = 0 & \qquad 2^0 = 1 \\
0^1 = 0 & \qquad 1^0 = 1 \\
0^0 = ? & \qquad 0^0 = ?
\end{array}
$$

(One pattern suggests defining 0^0 to be 0, the other suggests $0^0 = 1$.) But there is a simple and definitive mathematical argument: if our choice is to be consistent with Rule 2 we must define

$$
0^0 = 0^{1-1} = 0 \div 0.
$$

Thus 0^0 is undefined in precisely the same way that $0 \div 0$ is undefined (see Section 1.6).

Homework Set 18

1. *(Mental Math)* Calculate the following mentally, using the Mental Math tags 2^5, 2^8, and 2^{10}.

   a) $32 \cdot 32$

   b) $1024 \div 256$

   c) $4096 \div 32$

   d) 64×128

   e) $1024 \times 64 \div 512$

   f) $2048 \div 256 \times 16$

2. *(Mental Math)* Calculate the following mentally and show how you did it.

   a) $2^8 \cdot 2^7 \div 2^{11}$

   b) $(2^3)^5 \div 2^9$

   c) $256 \cdot 128 \div 2048$

   d) $8^5 \div 512$

   e) 48×15

   f) 256×99

   g) $512\,000 \div 320$

   h) 80^3

3. Read page 11 of Primary Math 6A and do Problems 15, 16, and 17ghi (just list the answers separated by commas).

4. *(A Teaching Sequence)* Let m, n and $a \neq 0$ be whole numbers. Simplify the following using the definition of exponents as done in Example 3.3 and Exercise 3.4.

   a) $(5^2)^3$

   b) $(5^2)^m$

   c) $(a^2)^3$

   d) Now simplify $(a^n)^m$, including labels justifying each step, as done in this section for Rules 1, 2, and 4. You may use Rule 1 and "Definition of multiplication" as justifications.

5. *(A Teaching Sequence)* Follow the instructions of Problem 4. Remember to justify Part d)!

   a) $3^4 \cdot 5^4$

   b) $3^4 \cdot b^4$

   c) $3^n \cdot 5^n$

   d) $a^n \cdot b^n$

6. Let a and b be non-zero whole numbers. Simplify as much as possible, factoring the numbers and leaving the answer in exponential form.

   a) $\dfrac{2^5 \cdot 6^2 \cdot 18^2}{3^4 \cdot 4^2}$

   b) $\dfrac{2^5 \cdot (2b)^2 \cdot (2b^2)^2}{b^4 \cdot 4^2}$

   c) $\dfrac{a^5 \cdot (ab)^2 \cdot (ab^2)^2}{b^4 \cdot (a^2)^2}$

   d) For what values of a and b do your three simplifications become identical?

7. Simplify as in Problem 6 (a, b and c are non-zero).

   a) $\dfrac{5^3 \cdot 24^2 \cdot 10^0}{8 \cdot 15^2 \cdot 3}$

   b) $\dfrac{a^3 \cdot (bc^3)^2 \cdot (ac)^0}{c^3 \cdot (ab)^2 \cdot b}$

   c) How can you obtain simplification a) from b)?

8. Let m and n be two whole numbers. Simplify as in the previous two problems.

   a) $\dfrac{6^{21} \cdot 10^{18} \cdot 15^{22}}{30^{11} \cdot 16^7}$

   b) $\dfrac{6^{3n} \cdot 10^{n+11} \cdot 15^{22}}{30^{11} \cdot 16^n}$

   c) Use the power rules to show that:

   $$\frac{6^{3n} \cdot 10^{n+m} \cdot 15^{2m}}{30^m \cdot 16^n} = 3^{3n+m} \cdot 5^{n+2m}.$$

   d) Plug $n = 7$ and $m = 11$ into $3^{3n+m} \cdot 5^{n+2m}$. Is the result the same as your answer to a)?

9. *(Calculator)* Describe how to calculate the square of the number $N = 23805723$ using a calculator that displays only 8 digits, plus one pencil-and-paper addition (with possibly more than two summands). *Hint*: Write $N = 2380 \times 10^4 + 5723$ and use the identity for $(a+b)^2$.

10. *(Scientific Notation)* Very large numbers can be conveniently written in the form $c \times 10^N$ where c is a number between 1 and 10 ($1 \leq c < 10$) written as a decimal, and N is a whole number. For example, $1,200,000$ is 1.2×10^6. Scientific notation is covered in most middle school curricula.

   Write each of the following in scientific notation.

   a) The numbers 1030, 15600 and $345,000,000$.

   b) The sums $(3.4 \times 10^7) + (5.2 \times 10^7)$ and $(6 \times 10^8) + (9.3 \times 10^8)$.

   c) The products $(2 \times 10^4) \times (3.2 \times 10^5)$ and $(8 \times 10^4) \times (96 \times 10^{23})$.

   d) The quotients (written in fraction form) $\dfrac{6 \times 10^9}{3 \times 10^4}$ and $\dfrac{5.4 \times 10^8}{9 \times 10^5}$.

   e) The powers $(2 \times 10^7)^3$ and $(5 \times 10^4)^3$.

CHAPTER 5

Factors, Primes, and Proofs

In Chapters 1–4 we introduced, developed, and completed the basic operations on whole numbers — addition, subtraction, multiplication, division, and powers. We also made the very first steps toward algebra by beginning to use letters to represent unspecified numbers. The use of letters enables us to explore properties of whole numbers in a new way: instead of making statements about specific numbers, such as $17 \cdot 3 = 51$, we can make statements which are true for *all* whole numbers. The topic of factors, multiples, and prime numbers includes many such statements.

Of course, when a statement is claimed to be true for all whole numbers we cannot verify it by checking every case — that would require checking infinitely many cases. Over the centuries, mathematicians have devised various clever ways of proving the truth of such statements using reasoning. Thus this chapter is about both the topic of factors, multiples, and prime numbers, and the idea of a mathematical proof.

5.1 Definitions, Explanations and Proofs

Mathematics is built on precise definitions and proceeds using clear reasoning. In the classroom the reasoning occurs in explanations and guided investigations, while in mathematics textbooks the reasoning often occurs in formal and informal "proofs." This section is an introduction to the roles of definitions and reasoning both in mathematics and in the classroom. These notions will be crucial for our discussion of factors and primes later in this chapter.

To understand the importance of clear definitions, let us consider the definition of *even number*. When asked, a class of third grade students may offer *four* different definitions of even number:

a) a number which occurs as we skip count by twos ("$0, 2, 4, 6, 8, 10, 12, 14, \ldots$"),

b) an even number of objects can be paired up (with none left unpaired),

c) a number which is twice a whole number,

d) a number whose last digit is $0, 2, 4, 6,$ or 8.

These definitions are not obviously the same. For example, the question "Is 3738 even?" can be answered instantly by a child who knows Definition d), while the child using Definition c) cannot answer it until she has calculated $3738 \div 2$. With one definition the problem is trivial, with another it is frustratingly difficult!

The classroom repercussions are obvious. Suppose that a third grade teacher begins a discussion of even numbers without mentioning any definition. As she talks, the students will each be trying to relate her words to the definition they have chosen. Different students will understand the discussion differently, and many will be confused.

A better teaching strategy examines the definitions sequentially. The teacher might choose and clearly state one of the above definitions and then link it to the others. Alternatively, the teacher could solicit definitions from children, write them succinctly on the board, and then relate them with help from the class. The goal, of course, is for everyone to be aware that any of the definitions can be used to specify even numbers, and that each has its advantages.

In this section we will discuss even numbers taking Definition c) as the starting point.

> **DEFINITION 1.1.** *An **even number** is a number which is twice a whole number. An **odd number** is a number which is 1 more than twice a whole number.*

EXERCISE 1.2. *a) Read Problem 7 on page 25 of Primary Math 4A. It is a simple classroom exercise which relates Definitions a) and c) to Definition _____.*
   b) According to the Definition 1.1, is 0 an even number?

The phrase "which is twice a whole number" in Definition 1.1 can be also expressed using a letter name, say k. That gives the form of Definition 1.1 that we will use later in this section:

odd and even numbers using letters

- An *even number* is a number that can be written as $2k$ for some whole number k. An *odd number* is one of the form $2k + 1$ for some whole number k.

Proofs as explanations

Once students understand a definition they are in a position to derive and explain facts based on that definition. In mathematics, new facts are not established by experiment. Instead, they are built from assumptions and previously known facts by a form of reasoning called a proof.

proof theorem

> A **proof** of a mathematical statement is a detailed explanation of how that statement follows logically from statements already accepted as true.
>
> A **theorem** is a mathematical statement with a proof.

Read the above words carefully: a proof is not an explanation of what the fact is, it is a chain of reasoning that explains *why the fact is a consequence* of assumptions and previously known facts. In this sense proofs are detailed versions of classroom explanations.

In teaching (and in this book) the allowed "assumptions" are the familiar ones of arithmetic, such as the Any-order property or the fact that adding equals to both sides of an equation maintains equality. The list of "previously known facts" depends on the grade level and grows as students become increasingly familiar with arithmetic and algebra.

lemma

Mathematics books are often formatted with theorems typeset in clearly delineated blocks of text starting with the word "theorem" followed by the statement to be proved, and demarcating where the proof begins by the word "proof" and where it ends with the symbol □. When a theorem is used in the course of establishing a more important fact it is called a *lemma*.

You may recall proofs from your high school classes with some anxiety. This is most likely the unfortunate byproduct of encountering proofs without the necessary prerequisite skills. To prepare students for the rigorous proofs of high school mathematics, students need exposure to proof-like thinking much earlier; they must develop what are often called "critical thinking skills." Proofs in elementary school serve that purpose; they are informal and the focus is on getting students to reason out why an idea is true and to explain it using models, pictures, or arithmetic (and later with letters and algebra).

We will use even and odd numbers as an example. We can model even and odd numbers by rectangular arrays, using dots to indicate that we are not specifying the number of squares.

An even number   An odd number

EXERCISE 1.3. *a) Why does Definition 1.1 imply that an even number of squares can be arranged as in the first diagram?*

b) Do you see how these diagrams show that the definitions b) and c) at the beginning of this section are the same?

Students can readily guess the following fact from numerical examples. It can then be proved using diagrams.

THEOREM 1.4. *The sum of two even numbers is even.*

Picture Proof.

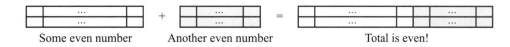

Some even number   Another even number   Total is even!

□

This is a complete proof! Notice the role of the dots in these diagrams. One cannot prove a fact about *all* even numbers by drawing diagrams for a few examples, such as $4 + 6 = 10$ or $6 + 8 = 14$ — even a million examples is not enough. But the dots leave the number of squares ambiguous; they show a collection of squares arranged in two equal rows, but never specify how many squares are in the row. This makes the picture slightly more abstract and allows us to depict all cases at once.

To obtain an algebraic proof of Theorem 1.4, we draw the same picture, replacing the first label by "$2k$" (2 rows of k squares), the second label by "$2m$," and the third label by "$2(k+m)$" (2 rows of $k + m$ squares). Having done that, we can omit the picture — the letters provide a language for giving the picture proof without the pictures!

Algebraic proof. Represent two even numbers by $2k$ and $2m$ where k and m are whole numbers. Then $2k + 2m = 2(k + m)$ by the distributive property. Thus the sum is twice the whole number $k + m$, so is even. □

The main idea in *both* of these proofs is the Distributive property. Can you recognize the above picture proof in the rectangular array illustration of the Distributive property given in Section 1.3?

To finish this section, here is a similar theorem with the picture proof and algebraic proof.

THEOREM 1.5. *The sum of an even number and an odd number is an odd number.*

Picture proof.

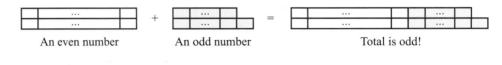

An even number   An odd number   Total is odd!

□

Algebraic proof. Represent an even number by $2k$ and an odd number by $2\ell + 1$ where k and ℓ are whole numbers. Then $2k + (2\ell + 1) = (2k + 2\ell) + 1 = 2(k + \ell) + 1$ using the associative property and then the distributive property. This sum $(2k + 2\ell) + 1$ is 1 more than an even number, so is odd.   □

Homework Set 19

1. Illustrate $16 + 18 = 34$ with diagrams as in Theorem 1.4 but draw every square. Do the same for $112 + 326 = 438$ using the "$\cdots$" notation and labels.

2. Illustrate $332 + 449 = 781$ with diagrams similar to Theorem 1.5 using the "$\cdots$" notation.

3. Illustrate $323 + 615 = 938$ using the "$\cdots$" notation.

4. a) Give a picture proof of the fact "The sum of two odd numbers is an even number."

   b) Give an algebraic proof of the same fact.

5. Use the Quotient-Remainder Theorem (page 35) to explain why every whole number A can be modelled by one of the two diagrams shown above Exercise 1.3. (*Hint*: when we write $A = 2q + r$, what are the possibilities for r?)

6. Even and odd numbers can also be illustrated by single-row diagrams:

The first diagram depicts two groups of k boxes; the second depicts two groups of k boxes plus one more box.

Multiplication by even or by odd numbers can be illustrated by stacking copies of these diagrams on top of one another to form rectangular arrays.

   a) Give a picture proof that an even number $2k$ times any whole number ℓ is an even number (suggestion: use colors to show that your picture has two equal parts).

   b) Given an algebraic proof of the same fact.

   c) Give *both* a picture proof and an algebraic proof that the product of two odd numbers is always odd (the picture proof is more complicated!).

7. Give algebraic proofs of the following two statements about whole numbers.

   a) Suppose A is even. If B is even, then $A + B$ is even.

   b) Suppose A is even. If $A + B$ is even, then B is even.

5.2 Divisibility Tests

divisibility test

If someone tells you that "the students in the class are wearing a total of 47 shoes" you immediately know that something is peculiar. You are alerted because this statement contrasts with the fact that all even numbers end with the digits 0, 2, 4, 6 or 8. This familiar fact is one example of a "divisibility test." It allows us to quickly spot which numbers — even very large numbers — are divisible by 2. In this section we will develop tests for divisibility by 2, 3, 4, 5, 8, 9, 10, and 11.

In the remainder of this chapter, we will often use letters $A, B, \ldots, k, l, \ldots$ and $a, b, \ldots$ to represent whole numbers. At any time you may assign them specific values (like $A = 30, k = 5$) to aid your understanding. For clarity, multiplication will be denoted by either a dot (as in $3 \cdot 5$) or no symbol (as in $3A$), rather than by the symbol $\times$ used in early elementary school.

We launch the topic with a clear definition. In this case it is especially important to be clear because there are at least *four* phrases commonly used for this one concept.

DEFINITION 2.1. *We say "A is divisible by k" whenever A is a multiple of k, that is, if $A = k \cdot a$ for some whole number a. The following phrases all have the same meaning:*

- *A is divisible by k*
- *k divides A*
- *A is a multiple of k*
- *k is a factor of A*

Divisibility can be illustrated by rectangular arrays. A number A is divisible by 4 if A squares can be arranged in a rectangular array with 4 rows of the same length.

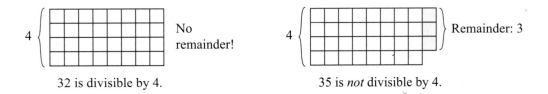

32 is divisible by 4.   35 is *not* divisible by 4.

One also sometimes hears the phrase "k goes into A evenly" used as an informal expression meaning "if we divide A by k we get a whole number, with no remainder." In fact, that procedure — divide and see whether the remainder is zero — is the most direct way of checking divisibility, and the one students begin with.

EXAMPLE 2.2. *Is 537 divisible by 7?*

The long division at right has a remainder of 5, so 537 is not divisible by 7.

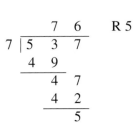

One can also use Mental Math methods.

EXAMPLE 2.3. *Is 618 divisible by 3?*

600 *is a multiple of 3.*
18 *is a multiple of 3.*
Therefore 618 is also.

EXAMPLE 2.4. *Is 1626 divisible by 8?*

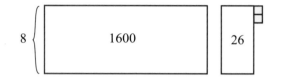

1600 *is a multiple of 8.*
26 *is not a multiple of 8.*
Therefore 1626 isn't either.

Examples 2.3 and 2.4 use the same strategy: separate the given number into a large part which is clearly divisible by the given number, and a "leftover" part. Then check whether the leftover part is also divisible. We will repeatedly use that strategy to answer questions about divisibility. For that purpose we state the strategy as a lemma.

LEMMA 2.5 (Divisibility Lemma). *Suppose A is a number divisible by k. Then B is divisible by $k \iff A + B$ is divisible by k.*

EXAMPLE 2.6. *Taking $A = 1600$, the Divisibility Lemma says that*

$$1626 \text{ is divisible by } 8 \iff 26 \text{ is divisible by } 8.$$

That is exactly the reasoning we used in Example 2.4. It reduces a hard problem to an easy one.

The double arrow $\iff$ is read "if and only if." It means the statements to its left and right are equivalent, that is, if one is true, both are true. Thus the lemma is making two statements. The first is "if two numbers are divisible by k, then so is their sum." The second is the other way around: "if the sum of two whole numbers is divisible by k and one of the addends is also, then the other addend is also divisible by k." To prove Lemma 2.5 we must prove both statements.

Picture proof. Since A is divisible by k we can assemble A squares in a rectangular array with k squares in each column.

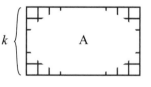

If B is also divisible by k we can draw a similar rectangular picture for B and add pictorially.

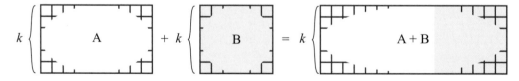

Thus whenever B is divisible by k then $A + B$ is also divisible by k.

Now for the other way around ("the converse"). If A and $A + B$ are divisible by k, we can arrange our rectangular arrays in a comparison model picture.

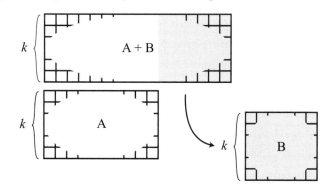

This shows that B is also a multiple of k. □

The above pictures should seem familiar: they are rectangular arrays illustrating two versions of the Distributive Property (cf. Section 1.5). Apparently the Distributive Property is the key idea in both parts of the proof! With that in mind, we can convert the picture proof into an algebraic proof by (i) introducing additional letters to label the (horizontal) lengths of the rectangles and (ii) using the Distributive Property.

Algebraic Proof. Because A is divisible by k we can write $A = ka$ for some whole number a (cf. the first picture above). If B is also divisible by k, then $B = kb$ for some whole number b. By the Distributive Property, $A + B = ka + kb = k(a + b)$, so $A + B$ is divisible by k.

To go the other way, suppose that $A + B$ is divisible by k. Then $A + B = kc$ for some whole number c. Again using the Distributive Property, we have $B = (A + B) - A = kc - ka = k(c - a)$, which shows that B is divisible by k. □

We are now ready to state and prove some specific divisibility tests. These are all derived and proved in essentially the same way, using the method of Examples 2.3 and 2.4. Given a number n and a test number t, we use expanded form to write n as a sum of a large number which is a multiple of t and a remainder. The Divisibility Lemma then tells us that n is divisible by t if and only if the remainder is divisible by t. Checking the divisibility of the remainder is relatively easy, and that becomes the test.

THEOREM 2.7 (Divisibility Tests for $2, 4, 5, 8, 10$). *A number is divisible*
- *by 10 if and only if its last digit is 0,*
- *by 5 if and only if its last digit is 0 or 5,*
- *by 2 if and only if its last digit is $0, 2, 4, 6,$ or 8,*
- *by 4 if and only if its last two digits are a number divisible by 4,*
- *by 8 if and only if its last three digits are a number divisible by 8.*

EXAMPLE 2.8.

a) $32,424$ *is even and is divisible by 4 because 24 (the last two digits) is divisible by 4.*

b) $98,234,484$ *is divisible by 4 because 84 is a multiple of 4 (since 80 is a multiple of 4). However, this number is not divisible by 8 since $484 = 480 + 4$ is not a multiple of 8.*

c) $1,943,537,208$ *is divisible by 8 because $208 = 200 + 8$ is a multiple of 8.*

The following two paragraphs show how divisibility tests are proved. Read these very carefully; they can be used as models for the proofs of other divisibility tests that you will do for homework. The idea of the first proof is to write the given number as a multiple of 10 plus its last digit. This is always possible by expanded form. For example, $4837 = 4000 + 800 + 30 + 7 = 4830 + 7 = 10 \cdot 483 + 7$. The second proof similarly uses expanded form to write the given number as a multiple of 100 plus its last two digits, as in $3762 = 3700 + 62 = 100 \cdot 37 + 62$.

Proof of the Divisibility Test for 2. Using expanded form, any whole number N can be written

$$N = 10a + b$$

where b is the last digit. But $10a = 2(5a)$ is divisible by 2, so the Divisibility Lemma (using $10a$ for A) says that N is divisible by 2 if and only if b is divisible by 2, i.e., $b = 0, 2, 4, 6, 8$. □

Proof of the Divisibility Test for 4. Using expanded form we can write any whole number N as

$$N = 100a + b$$

where b is the last two digits. But $100a = 4(25a)$ is divisible by 4 so, by the Divisibility Lemma, N is divisible by 4 if and only if b is. □

EXERCISE 2.9. *Write down a proof for the Divisibility Test for 5 by duplicating the above proof of the Divisibility Test for 2 and modifying the last sentence appropriately.*

THEOREM 2.10 (Divisibility Tests for 3 and 9). *A number is divisible*
- *by 3 if and only if the sum of the digits is divisible by 3,*
- *by 9 if and only if the sum of the digits is divisible by 9.*

EXAMPLE 2.11. *a) The number 378 is divisible by both 3 and 9 because the sum of the digits $3 + 7 + 8 = 18$ is divisible by 3 and 9.*
b) The number 3822 is divisible by 3 but not by 9. Why?

Proof of the Divisibility Test for 3 and 9. Consider a three digit number N with digits abc (the proof with more digits is similar). In expanded form

$$N = 100a + 10b + c.$$

Note that $100a = 99a + a$ and $10b = 9b + b$, we can rewrite this as

$$N = (99a + 9b) + (a + b + c).$$

Now $(99a + 9b) = 9(11a + b)$ is divisible by both 3 and 9. By the Divisibility Lemma, N is divisible by 3 (or 9) if and only if $a + b + c$ is divisible by 3 (or 9). But $a + b + c$ is the sum of the digits! □

"Casting out nines." Here is a simple trick that makes checking divisibility by 3 and 9 very fast and easy: When checking divisibility by 9, it is not actually necessary to find sum of the digits; we need only determine whether the sum is a multiple of 9. Thus we can ignore any digits that are 9, and pairs of digits that sum to 9. For example, to check 429761, we can "cast out" the 9 and the $2 + 7$; that leaves $4 + 6 + 1 = 11$ so this number is not divisible by 9. Similarly, when checking divisibility by 3 one can "cast out threes."

THEOREM 2.12 (Divisibility Test for 11). *A number is divisible by* 11 *if and only if the number formed by*

$$(sum\ of\ odd\text{-}position\ digits) - (sum\ of\ even\text{-}position\ digits)$$

is a multiple (positive, negative, or zero) of 11.

For example, the number $82,819$ is divisible by 11 since $(8 + 8 + 9) - (2 + 1) = 22$ is a multiple of 11. Similarly, the number 123 is not divisible by 11 since $(1 + 3) - (2) = 2$ is not a multiple of 11. Other examples:

$$3894 \quad \longrightarrow \quad (8 + 4) - (3 + 9) = 0 \quad \text{therefore 3894 is divisible by 11,}$$
$$7491 \quad \longrightarrow \quad 5 - 16 = -11 \quad \text{therefore 7491 is divisible by 11,}$$
$$618,392 \quad \longrightarrow \quad 6 - 23 = -17 \quad \text{therefore 618,392 is not divisible by 11.}$$

Proof of the Divisibility Test for 11. We only give the proof for a four digit number N. Writing N in expanded form and rearranging,

$$\begin{aligned} N &= 1000a + 100b + 10c + d \\ &= (1001a + 99b + 11c) + (-a + b - c + d). \end{aligned}$$

But $1001a + 99b + 11c = 11(91a + 9b + c)$ is divisible by 11. By the Divisibility Lemma, 11 divides N if and only if 11 divides $-a + b - c + d$. But that is exactly the difference $(b + d) - (a + c)$ between the odd-position and the even-position digits of N. □

Homework Set 20

1. Which of the following numbers is divisible by 3? by 9? by 11?

   a) $2,838$ b) $34,521$
   c) $10,234,341$ d) 792
   e) $8,394$ f) $26,341$
   g) $333,333$ h) 179

2. Which of the numbers below divide the number $5,192,132$?

   $$3 \quad 4 \quad 5 \quad 8 \quad 9 \quad 11$$

3. Which of the numbers below divide the number $186,426$?

   $$2 \quad 3 \quad 4 \quad 5 \quad 8 \quad 9 \quad 10 \quad 11$$

4. *(Study the textbook!)* Read all of page 25 of Primary Math 4A. Which Divisibility Tests are described on that page?

5. Let m be a whole number. If 18 divides m, then 3 and 6 divide m as well. Show that the converse is not necessar-ily true by writing down a number which is divisible by 3 and 6 but not 18.

6. To apply the Divisibility Test for 9 to the 4-digit number 2435, we can write

   $$\begin{aligned} 2435 &= 2(1000) + 4(100) + 3(10) + 5 \\ &= 2(999 + 1) + 4(99 + 1) + 3(9 + 1) + 5 \\ &= [2(999) + 4(99) + 3(9)] + [2 + 4 + 3 + 5] \end{aligned}$$

   and note that $[2(999) + 4(99) + 3(9)]$ is a multiple of 9. By the Divisibility Lemma, 2435 is a multiple of 9 if and only if the leftover part $2 + 4 + 3 + 5$ is a multiple of 9, which it is not. Thus 2435 is not a multiple of 9.

   a) Similarly show how the Divisibility Test for 3 applies to the number 1134 and the number $53,648$.

   b) Similarly show how the Divisibility Test for 11 applies to the number 1358.

7. Prove the Divisibility Test for 9 for 4–digit numbers.

8. Prove the Divisibility Test for 8 (adapt the proof of the Divisibility Test for 4 given in this section).

5.3 Primes and the Fundamental Theorem of Arithmetic

Most whole numbers can be expressed as products of smaller whole numbers. For example,

$$42 = 6 \cdot 7.$$

factors
factorization

The whole numbers 6 and 7 are called *factors* of 42, and $6 \cdot 7$ is a *factorization* of 42. (When discussing factorizations, order does not matter, so $6 \cdot 7$ and $7 \cdot 6$ are considered the same factorization). The number 6 can be factored further, giving the factorization

$$42 = 2 \cdot 3 \cdot 7.$$

The process stops there: none of the numbers $2, 3, 7$ are products of smaller whole numbers. In general, a number that cannot be written as a product of smaller whole numbers is called prime. More formally,

DEFINITION 3.1. *A **prime number** is a whole number $p > 1$ whose only factors are 1 and p. A whole number $N \geq 2$ that is not prime is called* composite.

The prime numbers less than 20 are $2, 3, 5, 7, 11, 13, 17$ and 19. The numbers $4, 6, 8, 9$, etc., are composite because they can be written as products of smaller numbers. Note that, by definition, the numbers 0 and 1 are neither prime nor composite.

Listing Primes. One can create a list of the prime numbers by writing down the whole numbers $2, 3, 4, 5, \ldots$ and successively checking each one. Of course, the even numbers larger than 2 are not prime, so there is no need to check them. Likewise the multiples of 3 after 3 needn't be checked. Thus we can proceed as follows. First, circle 2 and cross out every multiple of 2 in the list.

$$\boxed{2} \quad 3 \quad \cancel{4} \quad 5 \quad \cancel{6} \quad 7 \quad \cancel{8} \quad 9 \quad \cancel{10} \quad 11 \quad \cancel{12}$$
$$13 \quad \cancel{14} \quad 15 \quad \cancel{16} \quad 17 \quad \cancel{18} \quad 19 \quad \cancel{20} \quad 21 \quad \cancel{22} \quad 23 \quad \cancel{24}$$
$$\vdots$$

Next, circle 3 and cross out every third number (even if it has been crossed out).

$$\boxed{2} \quad \boxed{3} \quad \cancel{4} \quad 5 \quad \cancel{6} \quad 7 \quad \cancel{8} \quad \cancel{9} \quad \cancel{10} \quad 11 \quad \cancel{12}$$
$$13 \quad \cancel{14} \quad \cancel{15} \quad \cancel{16} \quad 17 \quad \cancel{18} \quad 19 \quad \cancel{20} \quad \cancel{21} \quad \cancel{22} \quad 23 \quad \cancel{24}$$

Continue this procedure, at each step circling the first number that is not circled or crossed out, and then crossing out all its multiples.

$$\boxed{2} \quad \boxed{3} \quad \cancel{4} \quad \boxed{5} \quad \cancel{6} \quad \boxed{7} \quad \cancel{8} \quad \cancel{9} \quad \cancel{10} \quad \boxed{11} \quad \cancel{12}$$
$$\boxed{13} \quad \cancel{14} \quad \cancel{15} \quad \cancel{16} \quad \boxed{17} \quad \cancel{18} \quad \boxed{19} \quad \cancel{20} \quad \cancel{21} \quad \cancel{22} \quad \boxed{23} \quad \cancel{24}$$

Sieve of
Eratosthenes

In the end, the circled numbers are the list of primes. This method is called the *Sieve of Eratosthenes* (Eratosthenes, c. 275 – 195 B.C., was a Greek scholar who made a map of the world, devised a system of chronology, and accurately estimated the circumference of the Earth and the distance to the moon). Notice that listing the numbers in rows of 12 makes it especially easy to cross out the multiples of 2 and 3.

Primes are important because they are "building blocks" from which all whole numbers are made. This "building" is done by multiplication. Thus discussions of primes involve factors, multiples, products, and powers (all related to multiplication and division), but *do not involve addition or subtraction.* Here is one such simple fact about primes.

LEMMA 3.2. *Every whole number $N > 1$ is a multiple of a prime.*

Proof. Given N, list all of its factors and let p be the smallest factor greater than 1. Then N is a multiple of p, say $N = pq$. Suppose that p factors as rs. Then r is a factor of N (since $N = pq = rsq$) and also $r \leq p$. But no factor of N is smaller than p except 1. Thus r is either 1 or p. We conclude that p is prime and N is a multiple of p.   □

EXAMPLE 3.3. *The complete list of factors of 45 is $\{1, 3, 5, 9, 15, 45\}$. The smallest factor larger than 1 (namely 3) is prime and 45 is a multiple of that prime.*

Lemma 3.2 is an exemplary "lemma" — it is a simple fact that is repeatedly useful. This case is particularly striking because, by simply applying Lemma 3.2 over and over, we arrive at an extraordinarily important fact about whole numbers.

THEOREM 3.4 (Fundamental Theorem of Arithmetic). *Every whole number $N > 1$ can be written as a product of primes, and this can be done in only one way (except for reordering).*

Proof. By Lemma 3.2 we can write

$$N = p_1 n_1$$

for some prime p_1. If $n_1 = 1$ then $N = p_1$ is prime and we are done. Otherwise n_1 can be factored as $n_1 = p_2 n_2$ for a prime p_2, so

$$N = p_1 p_2 n_2.$$

Again, if $n_2 = 1$ we are done; otherwise we can repeat and write

$$N = p_1 p_2 p_3 n_3,$$

etc. The numbers $n_1, n_2, n_3 \ldots$ form a list of decreasing whole numbers, so must end. But the list ends only when we encounter a factor n_k which is 1, and at that point we have written N as a product of primes.

The proof that N is a product of primes *in only one way* is surprisingly hard; it is done at the end of Section 5.5.   □

EXAMPLE 3.5. *For the number $N = 1430$, the procedure used to prove Theorem 3.4 gives* $1430 = 2 \cdot 715 = 2 \cdot 5 \cdot 143 = 2 \cdot 5 \cdot 11 \cdot 13.$

prime
factorization

Of course, 1430 has other factorizations, such as $10 \cdot 143$ and $55 \cdot 26$, but $2 \cdot 5 \cdot 11 \cdot 13$ is the only factorization that involves only primes — it is the only *prime factorization*. In that language, the Fundamental Theorem of Arithmetic says *every whole number bigger than 1 has a unique prime factorization.*

Finding prime factorizations is even easier than the above proof suggests. There is no need to factor out primes first, or to go in any systematic order (but see Homework Problem 1). Just keep factoring until you can factor no further.

EXAMPLE 3.6. *We can factor 80 by building the* factor tree *on the left. The same procedure is written more compactly on the right.*

$$\begin{aligned} 80 &= 8 \cdot 10 \\ &= 2 \cdot 2 \cdot 2 \cdot 2 \cdot 5 \end{aligned}$$

It is shorter to write the prime factorization of 80 as $2^4 \cdot 5$. We can similarly express any number as a product of powers of distinct primes, listed in ascending order. For example,

exponential form
of prime factorization

$$591,600 = 2^4 \cdot 3 \cdot 5^2 \cdot 17 \cdot 29.$$

When prime factorizations are written in this *exponential form* no reordering is possible — the exact way of writing the prime factorization is determined.

Most curricula include work on factorizations and primes sometime in grades 4–6: the Common Core Mathematics Standards places this topic in grade 4 and grade 6. This work solidifies understanding of multiplication, division, and divisibility tests, and many students find the topic interesting. Usually, the Fundamental Theorem of Arithmetic is not proved — it is assumed to be obvious to students who have learned to construct factor trees. But the Fundamental Theorem of Arithmetic is the central concept, and a clear statement of Theorem 3.4 should be part of any classroom treatment of this topic.

The Fundamental Theorem of Arithmetic shows that each whole number is built out of primes, much as molecules are built out of atoms (in both cases everything is assembled from a collection of indivisible 'particles'). This same idea shows up again before the end of high school mathematics in the context of factoring polynomials such as

$$x^2 - 5x + 6 \qquad \text{and} \qquad 9x^5 + 3x^4 - 12x^3 + 45x^2 - 18x + 348.$$

Fundamental Theorem
of Algebra

Monomials such as $x + 3$ and $x - 12$ are especially simple polynomials. The *Fundamental Theorem of Algebra* states that, if we consistently use complex numbers, every polynomial $p(x)$ can be written as a constant times a product of monomials:

$$p(x) = k(x - r_1)(x - r_2) \cdots (x - r_n)$$

for some number k and some monomials $(x - r_i)$. These monomials can be considered as "prime factors" of $p(x)$.

Homework Set 21

1. Find the prime factorizations of

   a) 700   b) 1560

   c) 3465   d) 70840.

TIP: Build factor trees by spotting large factors and dividing by them. Thus to factor 280, begin with $280 = 10 \cdot 28$ rather than $280 = 2 \cdot 140$.

2. Use the divisibility tests to determine whether the following numbers are prime (P), composite (C), or neither. Give one factor for each composite number.

   a) 12   b) 123

   c) 1234   d) 12345

   e) 154   f) 102302320

   g) 1   h) 97

3. Write the prime factorizations of the following numbers in exponential form.

   a) 63   b) 768

   c) 324   d) 361

   e) 196   f) 1024

   g) 480   h) 10,000

4. The complete list of factors of 30 can be arranged in pairs so that the product of each pair is 30:

$$\begin{array}{cccc} 1 & 2 & 3 & 5 \\ 30 & 15 & 10 & 6 \end{array}$$

   a) Make similar lists of all the factors of 56, of 84, and of 144.

   b) Prove that a number N has an even number of factors unless it is the square of a whole number. (*Hint:* Each factor a has a "partner" $b = N/a$ and a and b are different unless... unless what?)

5. The number $1 \cdot 2 \cdot 3 \cdot 4 \cdot 5$ is commonly written as 5! and pronounced "5 factorial." Similarly, 7! is shorthand for the number $1 \cdot 2 \cdot 3 \cdot 4 \cdot 5 \cdot 6 \cdot 7$. The prime factorization of such numbers can be found by writing down the definition and factoring further. For example, $7! = 1 \cdot 2 \cdot 3 \cdot (2 \cdot 2) \cdot 5 \cdot (2 \cdot 3) \cdot 7 = 2^4 \cdot 3^2 \cdot 5 \cdot 7$.

   a) Write the prime factorization of 10! in exponential form.

   b) Is 10! divisible by 10? by 30? by 120? by 1000? *Hint:* For divisibility by 30, pull out factors of 3 and 10 to write $10! = (3 \cdot 10) \cdot (\text{remaining factors})$.

   c) Is 30! divisible by 2,400,000?

   d) Find the largest N such that 18! is divisible by 12^N.

6. How many zeros are at the end of the decimal form of the numbers?

   a) 10! *Hint:* Count factors of 10 in the factorization.

   b) 40!

   c) 1000!

7. The description of the Sieve of Eratosthenes in this section states that, at each step, the first number which is not circled or crossed out is prime. Use Lemma 3.2 to explain why that is always true. For example, if you circle 2 and cross out its multiples, then do the same for 3, 5, and 7, the first number not circled or crossed out is 11. Why is that automatically prime?

5.4 More on Primes

This section gives two applications of the Fundamental Theorem of Arithmetic. The first is a way to determine if a number is prime. To check whether a number N is prime, we must look for factors other than 1 and N; if there are no such factors then N is prime. That testing process can be simplified by looking for the *smallest factor* larger than 1 and making two observations:

- The smallest factor — call it p — is *prime*, as we saw in the proof of Lemma 3.2.

- That factor p is *no greater than* $\sqrt{N}$: If $N = pn$ with $n > 1$, then $p \leq n$ (since p is the smallest factor). Multiplying both sides by p shows that $p^2 \leq pn = N$, so $p \leq \sqrt{N}$.

These observations give a useful test for primes.

FACT 4.1 (Primality Test). *A whole number $N > 1$ is prime unless it has a prime factor $p \leq \sqrt{N}$. Thus to test whether N is prime one need only check divisibility by the primes $p = 2, 3, 5, \ldots$ satisfying $p^2 \leq N$.*

EXAMPLE 4.2. *Is 179 prime?*

The square root of 179 is less than 14 (since $14^2 = 196$). With the help of the divisibility tests, one can check that 179 is not divisible by $2, 3, 5, 7, 11, 13$. Hence 179 is prime.

Notice that divisibility by $2, 3, 5, 11$ can be quickly checked by divisibility tests, while divisibility by 7 and 13 must be checked "by hand." This can be done mentally by subtracting off multiples and using the Divisibility Lemma. For example, is 179 divisible by 13? Well, 130 is, leaving $179 - 130 = 49$. But 49 is not divisible by 13, so 179 isn't divisible either.

EXAMPLE 4.3. *Is 221 prime?*

We need to check for divisibility by primes up to $\sqrt{221} \approx 15$. Checking $2, 3, 5, 7, 11, 13$ one finds that 221 is divisible by 13, in fact $221 = 13 \cdot 17$.

To determine which primes satisfy $p^2 \leq N$, it is helpful to familiarize yourself with the table below.

$$
\begin{array}{rclrclrcl}
10^2 &=& 100 & 25^2 &=& 625 & 40^2 &=& 1600 \\
15^2 &=& 225 & 30^2 &=& 900 & 45^2 &\approx& 2000 \\
20^2 &=& 400 & 35^2 &\approx& 1200 & 50^2 &=& 2500
\end{array}
$$

TIP: It is not necessary to find the square root. If you are unsure whether it is necessary to check divisibility by a certain prime p, just check the condition $p^2 \leq N$ by squaring. For example, to determine whether 827 is prime, must we check divisibility by 29? Well no, since the square $29^2 = 841$ is more than 827.

EXAMPLE 4.4. *Is 1067 prime?*

Since 1067 is less than $35^2 \approx 1200$ there is no need to check primes beyond 35, and that means the last prime we need check is 31. Divisibility tests immediately show that 1067 is not a multiple of 2, 3, or 5, but *is* a multiple of 11. Hence 1067 is not prime.

Our second application is to answer an obvious question about primes: does the list of primes

$$2,\ 3,\ 5,\ 7,\ 11,\ 13,\ 17,\ 19,\ 23,\ \ldots$$

end? Well, either

- this list ends, or

- it never ends.

In other words, the set of all primes is either *finite* (the first case) or *infinite* (the second case). Infinite simply means "not finite." Of course, finite sets are easier to work with because their elements can be listed — they can be lined up to form a list, however long, with a first element and a last element.

finite
infinite

Only one of these possibilities can be true, but which one? Is there a largest prime?

One possible hint comes from the fact that primes become increasingly scarce as one moves along the number line. In one of your homework problems you will find 1000 consecutive numbers which are composite. By the same reasoning, one can find strings of 100,000, or a million consecutive composite numbers. Of course prime numbers might continue to appear, tucked between long strings of composite numbers. So which is it: is the set of all primes finite or infinite?

This question was answered by the ancient Greeks. Remarkably, the answer does not involve calculating primes. The problem is solved by pure logic. Here is the clever solution.

THEOREM 4.5. *There are infinitely many prime numbers.*

Proof. The list of all prime numbers is either finite or infinite. We will show that it is logically impossible for it to be finite.

If there were finitely many primes, we could write them in order: $2, 3, 5, 7, 11, \ldots, P$ where P is the largest prime number.

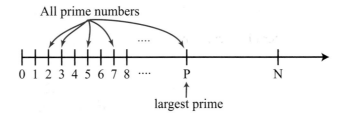

We could then multiply all the primes together, add 1, and call the resulting number N:

$$N = (2 \cdot 3 \cdot \cdots \cdot P) + 1.$$

If we divide N by any prime on the list, the remainder is 1. Thus N is not a multiple of any prime. But that contradicts the fact (Lemma 3.2) that every whole number *is* a multiple of a prime! That contradiction means that our assumption that there is a largest prime P is not true. The list of primes never ends. $\square$

This method of proof is called *proof by contradiction*. Proofs using this technique boil down to the following logic.

(i) Either a statement or its negation must be true — but not both. For instance, the negation of "There is an infinite number of primes" is "There is a finite number of primes"; one and only one of these statements is true.

(ii) We assume that the negation is true and show how that assumption leads to a logical contradiction. In the above proof, the assumption that the number of primes is finite was shown to be incompatible with a known fact (Lemma 3.2).

(iii) We conclude that our assumption is wrong, so the original statement is true.

Proof by contradiction is a powerful logical technique. Very similar reasoning can be used in the classroom—see Exercise 3 below.

Homework Set 22

1. Which of the following numbers are prime? Provide a factorization for those which are not prime.

   a) 127   b) 129

   c) 327   d) 221

   e) 337   f) 389

   g) 223   h) 859

2. What is the largest prime less than 1000? *Hint*: Try 999, 998, etc.

3. A *counterexample* to a mathematical statement is an example where the statement is false. To prove that a statement is true, one must prove it true for *all numbers*, but to show that it is false requires *only one* counterexample. Counterexamples are useful for teaching. Use the idea of *instructional counterexamples* to answer the questions below.

   a) A student claims that all odd numbers are prime. How do you convince her that it is not true?

   b) An algebra student claims that $(a + b)^2 = a^2 + b^2$ is true for all numbers a and b. Show his claim is false by counterexample.

   c) Tiana conjectures that for each whole number n, the expression $n^2 + n + 11$ always produces a prime. She presents the table below as evidence. Is she right?

n	$n^2 + n + 11$
1	13
2	17
3	23
4	31
5	41

4. Prove that the sum of any three consecutive numbers is divisible by 3. *Hint*: Call the first number x.

5. Notice that the number $6! = 1 \cdot 2 \cdot 3 \cdot 4 \cdot 5 \cdot 6$ is divisible by 2, 3, 4, 5, and 6.

   a) Prove that the numbers $6! + 2$, $6! + 3$, $6! + 4$, $6! + 5$, $6! + 6$ are all composite by giving a factor of each.

   b) Name a factor of $31! + 29$ — the number 29 more than $31!$.

   c) Find 1000 consecutive numbers that are composite. *Hint:* A good first try is to consider the numbers starting with $1000! + 2$.

6. Prove that every prime $p > 3$ is either one more or one less than a number divisible by 6.

   Hint: Start with the sentence "By the Quotient-Remainder Theorem of Section 1.6, we can write $p = 6q + r$ for some whole numbers q and r with $0 \le r < 6$." Knowing that p is prime, which remainders can you eliminate?

7. Michelle claims that the proof of Theorem 4.5 gives a way of making an infinite list of primes. She demonstrates

with this list:

$$q_1 = 2,$$
$$q_2 = 2 + 1 = 3,$$
$$q_3 = 2 \cdot 3 + 1 = 7,$$
$$q_4 = 2 \cdot 3 \cdot 7 + 1 = 43.$$

At each step, she multiplies all the previous numbers in her list and then adds 1. Use a calculator to find q_5 and q_6 and to determine if q_5 is prime. Is Michelle's method correct?

8. Kyle has a different method for extending a list of primes.

He takes the ones he already has, multiplies them together and adds one to get a number N; he then finds *the smallest prime factor* of N and includes it in his list. Then he repeats this procedure with the new list.

a) *(Calculator)* Use a calculator to carry out Kyle's procedure, starting with $p_1 = 2$, $p_2 = 3$, and finding 4 more primes.

b) Make Kyle's argument into a proof that there are infinitely many primes. *Hint*: Suppose, at some stage, Kyle's list is $\{p_1, p_2, \ldots, p_k\}$. Form N as Kyle does (but using the letters p_k) and show that the smallest prime factor of N is a prime not already on the list.

5.5 Greatest Common Factors and Least Common Multiples

Factors and multiples have been a reoccurring theme in this chapter. We have seen how studying factors and multiples leads, rather quickly, to prime numbers and the Fundamental Theorem of Arithmetic. This section pursues that same theme, now looking at more than one whole number at a time. Given two (or more) whole numbers, we can consider their *common* factors and multiples and, among those, the greatest common factor and least common multiple. These important mathematical concepts lead to many wonderful problems and investigations suitable for students at all levels, beginning at the end of elementary school. Consequently, this topic is included in most middle school curricula.

The ideas discussed in this section cannot be learned by simply reading — to understand you must do examples of the calculations described. Thus it is especially beneficial in this section to do the exercises in the text (Exercises 5.3, 5.5, 5.11) as you read.

Our starting point is the following important definition.

DEFINITION 5.1. *The **Greatest Common Factor** of two nonzero whole numbers a and b, written $GCF(a, b)$, is the greatest whole number which is a factor of both a and b.*

We also set $GCF(a, 0) = a$ for all nonzero whole numbers a.

To remember the meaning of "GCF," it is helpful to read the letters "GCF" backwards: to find the GCF one thinks of the factors, then the common factors, and then the greatest of the common factors. (In many textbooks the GCF is called the "Greatest Common Divisor" and written GCD.)

EXAMPLE 5.2. *To find $GCF(18, 30)$, we list all the factors of 18 and 30*

Factors of 18:   1, 2, 3, 6, 9, 18
Factors of 30:   1, 2, 3, 5, 6, 10, 15, 30,

find the numbers that appear on both lists (1, 2, 3 and 6), and take the largest of those. Thus $GCF(18, 30) = 6$.

EXERCISE 5.3. *Find GCF*$(42, 70)$.

With large numbers, it is not practical to list all the factors. Fortunately, there are two easier ways to find greatest common factors. The first uses prime factorizations, which you can find using factor trees.

EXAMPLE 5.4. *Calculate GCF*$(96, 144)$.

Solution: Find the prime factorizations and match the primes which appear in both factorizations:

$$
\begin{array}{ccccccccccc}
96 & = & 2 & \cdot & 2 & \cdot & 2 & \cdot & 2 & \cdot & 3 & \cdot & 2 \\
 & & \updownarrow & & \updownarrow & & \updownarrow & & \updownarrow & & \updownarrow & & \\
144 & = & 2 & \cdot & 2 & \cdot & 2 & \cdot & 2 & \cdot & 3 & \cdot & 3.
\end{array}
$$

Clearly 2 is a common factor of 96 and 144, as is $2 \cdot 2$. In fact, the greatest common factor is *the product of the primes which appear in both factorizations*, namely $2 \cdot 2 \cdot 2 \cdot 2 \cdot 3 = 48$. This calculation can be streamlined by writing the prime factorizations in exponential form; the GCF is then found by looking at the primes one at a time (first 2, then 3, etc.) and taking the smaller of the exponents that appear in the prime factorizations. For example,

$$96 = 2^5 \cdot 3, \qquad 144 = 2^4 \cdot 3^2 \qquad \Rightarrow \qquad \text{GCF}(96, 144) = 2^4 \cdot 3 = 48.$$

In doing this, consider only those primes which appear in both factorizations, and remember that $3 = 3^1$.

EXERCISE 5.5. *a) Find GCF*$(1000, 1440)$.

b) Find GCF$(2^4 \cdot 3^4 \cdot 5^2 \cdot 13, \ \ 2^6 \cdot 3^2 \cdot 7^3 \cdot 11 \cdot 29)$.

The second computational method for finding greatest common factors is even more efficient because it eliminates the need to find prime factorizations. It is called *Euclid's Algorithm*.

Euclid's
Algorithm

Euclid's Algorithm is based on long division. Given whole numbers a and b with $a > b$, it is a simple matter to use long division to find the quotient q and remainder r and write $a = b \cdot q + r$. The following observation is the key point.

LEMMA 5.6. *If* $a = bq + r$ *then* $GCF(a, b) = GCF(b, r)$.

Proof. If n is a factor of both b and r then it is also a factor of $a = bq + r$ (because $bq + r$ is a multiple of n). Similarly, if n is a factor of both a and b then it is also a factor of $r = a - bq$. Thus the lists

$$\{\text{common factors of } a \text{ and } b\} \qquad \text{and} \qquad \{\text{common factors of } b \text{ and } r\}$$

are identical. Consequently, the largest number in the first list, which we named $\text{GCF}(a, b)$, is the same as the largest number in the second list, which we named $\text{GCF}(b, r)$. □

Lemma 5.6 replaces the problem of finding $\text{GCF}(a, b)$ by an easier "find the GCF" problem — easier because the remainder r is smaller than both a and b. Euclid's idea was to apply Lemma 5.6 repeatedly.

EXAMPLE 5.7. *To find GCF(348, 72), Shana used long division to find* $348 = 4 \cdot 72 + 60$, *then applied Lemma 5.6 to conclude that*

$$\text{GCF}(348, 72) \quad = \quad \text{GCF}(72, 60).$$

Starting again, she noted that $72 = 1 \cdot 60 + 12$, so

$$\text{GCF}(72, 60) \quad = \quad \text{GCF}(60, 12).$$

Since 60 is a multiple of 12, Shana concluded

$$\text{GCF}(348, 72) = 12.$$

Here is an example with large numbers. The accompanying divisions (which we omit) can be done by long division or with a calculator.

$$
\begin{aligned}
\text{GCF}(2139858, 692344) \quad &= \quad \text{GCF}(692344, 62826) \\
&= \quad \text{GCF}(62826, 1258) \\
&= \quad \text{GCF}(1258, 1184) \\
&= \quad \text{GCF}(1184, 74) \\
&= \quad \text{GCF}(74, 0) \\
&= \quad 74.
\end{aligned}
$$

A zero appeared in the next-to-last line because the corresponding division has no remainder (1184 is a multiple of 74). We then used the fact that $\text{GCF}(a, 0) = a$ for any whole number a, which is true by Definition 5.1. With that observation, Euclid's algorithm is simply described: *Repeatedly apply Lemma 5.6 until a 0 appears, then use GCF(a, 0) = a.*

In addition to looking at the common factors, we can look for common multiples. We do just that when we add fractions by finding a "common denominator," as in the example

$$\frac{1}{6} + \frac{1}{15} = \frac{5}{30} + \frac{2}{30} = \frac{7}{30}$$

(we will discuss such calculations in the next chapter). The following idea is useful in that context.

DEFINITION 5.8. *The **Least Common Multiple** of two nonzero whole numbers a and b, written LCM(a, b), is the least whole number (larger than 0) which is a multiple of both a and b.*

Again, it is helpful to read the letters backwards: to find the LCM think about the multiples, then the common multiples, then the smallest of the common multiples.

EXAMPLE 5.9. *To find LCM(9, 12), we list the multiples of 9 and the multiples of 12 (both lists are infinite) and find the smallest number which appears on both lists. Thus LCM(9, 12) = 36.*

Multiples of 9:   *9, 18, 27, $\boxed{36}$, 45, 54, 63, 72, 81, 90, . . .*
Multiples of 12:   *12, 24, $\boxed{36}$, 48, 60, 72, 84, 96, . . .*

There are also two more efficient ways of calculating least common multiples: using prime factorizations and using Euclid's Algorithm.

EXAMPLE 5.10. *Find LCM(180, 1848).*

Solution: We again begin by finding the prime factorizations and matching the primes which appear in both factorizations.

$$
\begin{array}{ccccccccccc}
180 & = & 2 & \cdot & 2 & \cdot & 3 & \cdot & 3 & \cdot & 5 \\
 & & \updownarrow & & \updownarrow & & & & \updownarrow & & \\
1848 & = & 2 & \cdot & 2 & \cdot & 2 & \cdot & 3 & \cdot & 7 & \cdot & 11
\end{array}
$$

The prime factorization of the least common multiple includes only one prime factor from each pair, together with all the unpaired factors. Thus

$$
\mathrm{LCM}(180, 1848) \;=\; \underbrace{2 \cdot 2 \cdot 3}_{\substack{\text{one factor} \\ \text{from each pair}}} \cdot \underbrace{2 \cdot 3 \cdot 5 \cdot 7 \cdot 11}_{\substack{\text{unpaired} \\ \text{factors}}} \;=\; 27,720.
$$

Alternatively, using prime factorizations in exponential form, $\mathrm{LCM}(a, b)$ is found by looking at the primes one at a time and taking the larger of the exponents.

The other way to compute $\mathrm{LCM}(a, b)$ is to first use Euclid's Algorithm to find $\mathrm{GCF}(a, b)$ and then use the formula

$$
\mathrm{LCM}(a, b) \;=\; \frac{ab}{\mathrm{GCF}(a, b)}
$$

(cf. Homework Problem 11).

EXERCISE 5.11. *Use Euclid's Algorithm to find GCF(8361, 75), then use the above formula to find LCM(8361, 75).*

To finish this section, we return to greatest common factors. The following question provides a geometric interpretation of the GCF.

EXAMPLE 5.12. *Which whole numbers can be obtained by adding and subtracting multiples of 6 and multiples of 15?*

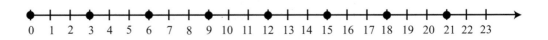

Solution: On the number line, mark the whole numbers obtained by adding and subtracting multiples of 6 and 15. All must be multiples of 3 (since 6 and 15 are multiples of 3). The marked numbers include 3 (which is $15 - 2 \cdot 6$), and therefore include every multiple of 3. Thus the marked numbers are exactly the multiples of 3. Notice that 3 is GCF(15, 6).

The same picture is true in general: for any whole numbers a and b, the numbers obtained by adding and subtracting multiples a and b are exactly the multiples of GCF(a, b). The key point is the following.

LEMMA 5.13. *For any whole numbers a and b, there is a multiple of a and a multiple of b which differ by GCF(a, b).*

This follows from Euclid's Algorithm. To see how, we can look back at Example 5.7, where Shana found that GCF(348, 72) = 12. The two division facts that Shana used can be written as

$$
\begin{aligned}
60 &= 348 - 4 \cdot 72 \\
12 &= 72 - 60.
\end{aligned}
$$

Substituting the first equation into the second gives $12 = 72 - (348 - 4 \cdot 72) = 5 \cdot 72 - 348$. Thus GCF(348, 72) = 12 is the difference of a multiple of 348 and a multiple of 72. The same method — writing down the division facts used in Euclid's Algorithm and substituting one into the next — works in general and proves Lemma 5.13.

LEMMA 5.14. *If p is a prime factor of ab, then p is a factor of either a or b.*

Proof. Since p is prime, its only factors are 1 and p. If p is also a factor of a, we are done. Otherwise, GCF(p, a) = 1, so by Lemma 5.13 we can write 1 as the difference of a multiple mp of p and a multiple na of a: $1 = mp - na$ (or $1 = na - mp$). Multiplying by b then gives

$$
b = \pm(mpb - nab).
$$

Since p is a factor of ab, the righthand side of this equation is a multiple of p, and therefore p is a factor of b. □

proof of uniqueness of prime factorizations

Lemma 5.14 enables us to finish the proof of the Fundamental Theorem of Arithmetic. Recall that in Section 5.1 we showed that each whole number has a prime factorization, but did not show that it has only one prime factorization (except for reordering the factors).

To show the reasoning, we will work with a particular number. Here is the proof that the number 34485 has only one prime factorization. The same reasoning applies to any whole number $N > 1$.

One prime factorization is $34485 = 3 \cdot 5 \cdot 11 \cdot 11 \cdot 19$. Suppose that there is another, written as $34485 = p_1 p_2 \cdots p_n$. Since 3 is a factor of 34485, Lemma 5.14 (and a little thinking) implies that one of the primes $p_1, p_2, \cdots, p_n$ is 3; in fact, we can choose the order so that $p_1 = 3$. Dividing both factorizations by 3 gives $11495 = 5 \cdot 11 \cdot 11 \cdot 19$ and $11495 = p_2 \cdots p_n$. We can then repeat the reasoning for the prime 5 to conclude that $p_2 = 5$ (after reordering). Continuing, we conclude that $p_3 = 11$, $p_4 = 11$, $p_5 = 19$, and, if n is 6 or more, $1 = p_6 \cdots p_n$. This last equation is impossible since every prime is at least 2. Thus $n = 5$ and the two prime factorizations are identical.

Homework Set 23

1. *(Study the textbook!)* Read pages $19 - 26$ of Primary Math 4A. Notice how the ideas of factors and multiples are introduced, and how common multiples are defined on page 26.

   a) Use the method shown by the little girl in Problem 11 of page 26 to find a common multiple of 15 and 12.

   b) In Practice 1B of Primary Math 4A, do Problems 1 and 4–7.

2. Using only Definition 5.1, prove that $\text{GCF}(a, b) = a$ whenever b is a multiple of a. *Hint:* Why is $\text{GCF}(a, b) \le a$? Why is $\text{GCF}(a, b) \ge a$?

3. Using only Definition 5.1, prove that if p is prime then $\text{GCF}(p, a) = 1$ unless a is a multiple of p.

4. Use the method of Example 5.4 to find

   a) $\text{GCF}(28, 63)$

   b) $\text{GCF}(104, 132)$

   c) $\text{GCF}(24, 56, 180)$.

5. Use Euclid's Algorithm to find

   a) $\text{GCF}(91, 52)$

   b) $\text{GCF}(812, 336)$, and

   c) $\text{GCF}(2389485, 59675)$.

   Use long division for b) and a calculator for c).

6. Use the method of Example 5.10 to find
   a) $\text{LCM}(32, 1024)$ and b) $\text{LCM}(24, 120, 1056)$.

7. a) On pages 38 and 39 of Primary Math 5A, common multiples are used for what purpose?

   b) Find

   $$\frac{2}{84} + \frac{5}{147} = \underline{\quad}$$

   by converting to fractions whose denominator is $\text{LCM}(84, 147)$.

8. a) Use Euclid's Algorithm to find the GCF of the numbers $2n + 3$ and $n + 1$. *Hint:* Start by writing $2n + 3 = 2(n + 1) + 1$.

   b) Show that the fraction $\dfrac{8n + 1}{20n + 2}$ cannot be reduced for any whole number n.

9. Two gears in a machine are aligned by a mark that is drawn from the center of the first gear to the center of the second gear. If there are 192 teeth on the first gear and 320 teeth on the second gear, how many revolutions of the first gear are needed to realign the mark?

10. The following problem was taken from a fifth grade German textbook. It is for the better students.

    The gymnastics club is having an event, and they want to group all the participants neatly in rows. However, whether they try to use rows of 2, 3, 4, 5, 6, 7 or 8, there is always one gymnast leftover. There are fewer than 1000 gymnasts in all. How many are there?

    Hint: Suppose that one gymnast left the room.

11. a) Write down the prime factorizations of 72 and 112. Then find $\text{GCF}(112, 72)$ and $\text{LCM}(112, 72)$, and verify that $\text{GCF}(112, 72) \cdot \text{LCM}(112, 72) = 112 \cdot 72$.

    b) By referring to the 'prime factorization' methods of finding the GCF and LCM , prove that for any numbers a and b one has

    $$\text{GCF}(a, b) \cdot \text{LCM}(a, b) = a \cdot b.$$

    If we know $\text{GCF}(a, b)$, this formula can be used to find $\text{LCM}(a, b)$

    c) *(Mental Math)* Find $\text{GCF}(16, 102)$ and use the above formula to find $\text{LCM}(16, 102)$.

12. Use Euclid's Algorithm to find $\text{GCF}(57, 23)$, recording the division facts you use. Then use those division facts to write the GCF as the difference between a multiple of 57 and a multiple of 23 (as explained after Lemma 5.13).

CHAPTER **6**

Fractions

A fraction is a point on the number line. For example, to locate 7/5 we start at 0, find the step size so that 5 equal steps gets us to 1, and then take 7 such steps, landing at the points called $\frac{1}{5}, \frac{2}{5}, \frac{3}{5}, \ldots$ until we get to $\frac{7}{5}$. By this definition the fraction 3/1 is the same point on the number line as the whole number 3. Thus each whole number is a fraction.

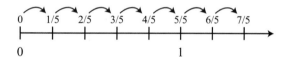

Like whole numbers, fractions can be added, subtracted, multiplied, and divided — we can do arithmetic with fractions. In fact, extending arithmetic from whole numbers to fractions fixes a deficiency of whole number arithmetic: division problems like $13 \div 4$ cannot be solved unless we use fractions. Furthermore, once developed, fractions allow one to *eliminate* division in favor of multiplication ($x \div 6$ is the same as $x \times \frac{1}{6}$). In this sense arithmetic becomes *easier* when we enlarge our notion of 'number' to include fractions.

Learning fractions is a fundamental part of elementary school mathematics. Coherent curricula introduce fractions in grades 1 or 2 and repeatedly return to the subject, exploring the interpretations and uses of all four arithmetic operations and developing computational skills until fractions are mastered at the end of grade 6. In this chapter we will examine how fractions are developed in the Primary Mathematics curriculum.

6.1 Fraction Basics

When counting or measuring we always have some unit in mind. When measuring distances we may use inches, feet, or miles; when counting students we may count individuals, classes, or schools. The unit is sometimes made very explicit for clarity (as in "3 cups of flour"), while at other times one has to think for a moment to recognize the presence of a unit (as in "the table seats six"). But the count makes no sense without a unit ("I have 3 water").

whole unit
fractional unit

We use fractions when there is a given unit, called the *whole unit*, but we want to measure using a smaller unit, called the *fractional* unit. For example, if 4 laps around a track is 1 mile,

131

then *mile* is the whole unit and *lap* is the fractional unit. We write

$$1 \text{ lap} = \tfrac{1}{4} \text{ mile} \qquad 3 \text{ laps} = \tfrac{3}{4} \text{ mile} \qquad 5 \text{ laps} = \tfrac{5}{4} \text{ mile}$$

with the numerator counting the number of fractional units and the denominator specifying the fractional units.

numerator

denominator

$$\frac{3}{4} \text{ mile}$$

Numerator is the number of fractional units.

Denominator names a fractional unit by specifying how many fractional units make one whole unit.

This standard notation for fractions is confusing when first encountered. Teachers should be on the lookout for two common student misconceptions:

(i) thinking of $\tfrac{3}{4}$ as a pair of numbers (rather than a single number), and

(ii) thinking that larger fractions have larger denominators (thereby concluding, for instance, that $\tfrac{1}{5} > \tfrac{1}{3}$).

Language is also important. For many students, the imposing terms "numerator" and "denominator" hinder understanding. These terms have to be learned, but some students are better able to focus on the mathematics when the informal terms "top" and "bottom" are used instead in classroom conversations. ("Numerator" and "denominator" can be re-introduced later, once fractions are safely mastered.) The use of "top" and "bottom" is especially successful when teaching remedial arithmetic or remedial algebra.

Curriculum Sequence

In the next several sections we will work through the Primary Mathematics curriculum, tracing the development of fractions. Along the way we will point out some common student errors and call attention to some student exercises which help eliminate misconceptions (including (i) and (ii) above) before they take root.

Stage 1 — Introducing Fractions. Most children start school already informally knowing the simplest fractions: halves and quarters. They understand and use these as adjectives, always speaking of fractions *of something*, as in "my glass is half full." Grades K–2 mathematics builds on that understanding by developing fractions using words ("three quarters") and the following models. In all cases, *one starts by drawing or identifying the whole unit,* making it clear to the students.

always identify
the whole unit

Area or Regional Model — Useful pictures include: pie diagrams, squares (or rectangles), and volumes of liquids. All are important.

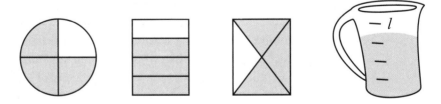

Linear Measurement Model — Here one thinks of fractions as points on the number line. Useful examples include the fractional markings on rulers, clocks, and scales. Bar diagrams are thickened number lines.

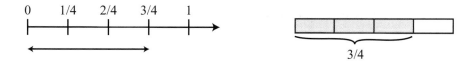

Students benefit from hands-on practice reading measurements on rulers, clocks, balance scales, etc. that contain fractional rulings *that are not explicitly labeled.*

Set Model — Here one thinks of fractions as a count of a subset. For instance, if a class of 20 contains 15 girls and 5 boys, then $\frac{3}{4}$ of the students are girls.

This model requires care — one can get into trouble because sets cannot be arbitrarily subdivided. (What is $\frac{1}{3}$ of 20 students?)

draw whole unit first

TIP: Whenever you illustrate such partitions, start by drawing the whole unit (the part of your picture that corresponds to the number 1). To interpret an illustration, students must know what you are taking fractions of!

These are the same three models previously used for whole number operations (with the area model replacing the rectangular array pictures). All of these models occur in real-world applications of fractions, so it is important for students to become comfortable with each of them.

Stage 2 — Counting and Ordering. As mentioned above, the notation of fractions is confusing for children. Obviously, teachers should attend to this issue first. The Primary Math texts introduce fractions at the end of grade 2, but do not proceed to the next step (addition of fractions) until grade 4. Students have plenty of time to internalize the notation.

The key points are that a fraction is a single number (not two!), and that a fraction is specified by two whole numbers which play different roles: the denominator specifies a fractional unit and the numerator specifies the number of those units. Here are two types of exercises which help children assimilate the notation.

First, counting by fractional units ("1 fourth, 2 fourths, 3 fourths, 4 fourths, 5 fourths, . . . "), both verbally and in writing, shows how the numerator counts fractional units.

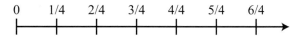

Second, exercises asking children to *compare fractions* point out the different roles of numerator and denominator. Those roles are evident when comparing fractions with either

- the same denominator. $\frac{3}{8} < \frac{5}{8}$

• the same numerator. $\frac{3}{4} > \frac{3}{7}$

In the first case we are comparing the number of fractional units. In the second we are comparing the size of the fractional units. The second type of comparison is often overlooked in elementary school curricula. Such comparison exercises help students understand the role of the denominator, and the ideas learned carry over to other situations, including algebra inequalities (encountered in later grades) such as

$$\frac{3}{x^2 + 4} \; < \; \frac{3}{x^2}.$$

Another way to quickly compare two fractions is to compare both to an intermediate fraction. For example, to compare $\frac{2}{5}$ and $\frac{4}{7}$ one needs only observe that $\frac{2}{5}$ is less than $\frac{1}{2}$, while $\frac{4}{7}$ is more than $\frac{1}{2}$.

Of course, when comparing fractional amounts it is important to use the same whole unit: $\frac{1}{2}$ of a yard is not greater than $\frac{1}{10}$ of a mile. The whole unit is often obvious or implicit. It is helpful to call attention to its presence. For example, when a student announces that the answer is $\frac{3}{4}$, the teacher can respond by asking "$\frac{3}{4}$ *of what?*"

Already at this level there are many marvelous "early fractions exercises." Two are shown below (for more, see Primary Math 2B and Workbook 2B).

(a) What fraction of each shape is shaded?   (b) Circle the smallest fraction.

$$\frac{1}{4} \qquad \frac{1}{7} \qquad \frac{1}{5}$$

Stage 3 — Renaming Fractions.   Each fraction can be represented in many ways: $\frac{2}{3}$, $\frac{4}{6}$, and $\frac{8}{12}$ all represent the same fraction. Students who miss this fundamental fact will be mystified by the arithmetic of fractions. Fortunately, the idea can be easily illustrated and understood at the beginning of students' exposure to fractions.

• Fraction Strips (a concrete approach).

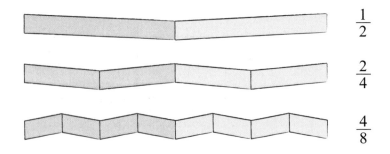

$$\frac{1}{2}$$

$$\frac{2}{4}$$

$$\frac{4}{8}$$

- Subdivided Areas (a pictorial approach). Rectangles are particularly useful because they can be partitioned in both directions.

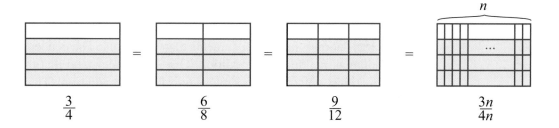

$$\frac{3}{4} \qquad \frac{6}{8} \qquad \frac{9}{12} \qquad \frac{3n}{4n}$$

- Numbers. Students who understand the above pictures are ready to rename fractions using standard notation:

$$\frac{3}{5} = \frac{\square}{10} \qquad\qquad \frac{8}{\square} = \frac{2}{3}.$$

renaming fractions
equivalent fractions

This process is called *renaming the fraction* — we are changing the notation without changing the fraction. Different notations for the same fraction, such as $\frac{3}{5}$ and $\frac{6}{10}$, are called *equivalent fractions*. In this context, the word "equivalent" means "equal" — equivalent fractions are equal.

The goal of this stage of teaching fractions is for students to become comfortable and proficient at renaming fractions (eventually without needing to refer to pictures). Speaking at the "teacher's level," the concept to be learned is expressed in algebraic form as

Rule 1 (Equivalent Fractions). $\dfrac{a}{b} = \dfrac{an}{bn}$ for any nonzero whole number n.

Rule 1 is most useful when used in the other direction, to make both numerator and denominator smaller:

$$\frac{18}{42} = \frac{9}{21} = \frac{3}{7}.$$

irreducible
simplest form

When this 'reducing' or 'simplifying' process can no longer be done we say the fraction is *irreducible* or in *simplest form*.

Stage 4 — Addition and subtraction with same denominators. Spoken statements such as

"2 fifths $+$ 2 fifths $=$ 4 fifths"   and   "2 sevenths $+$ 3 sevenths $=$ ____ sevenths"

are immediately clear to children. In these, one is simply adding fractional units in the obvious way. Such verbal exercises convey the key principle used to introduce fraction addition:

Key Principle of Fraction Addition

Once we agree on the fractional unit, we count, add, and subtract just like whole numbers.

Once this principle is understood, it would seem to be straightforward to translate into fraction notation (with the denominators recording the fractional unit), as in the additions

$$\frac{2}{5}+\frac{2}{5}=\frac{4}{5} \quad \text{and} \quad \frac{2}{7}+\frac{3}{7}=\frac{5}{7}.$$

This translation is harder for students than it appears. The conceptual difficulty is understanding the notation, not doing the addition. One must understand that the denominator simply records the fractional unit, and hence plays no role in the addition. That aspect of fraction notation is not intuitive and requires practice.

Thus instruction in fraction addition (and subtraction) initially focuses on fractions with the same denominator, and allows time for students to internalize the meaning and the notation. Again speaking at the "teacher's level," the goal is to develop the facts expressed in algebraic form as

Rule 2 (Fraction Addition). $\dfrac{a}{b}+\dfrac{c}{b}=\dfrac{a+c}{b} \quad \text{and} \quad \dfrac{a}{b}-\dfrac{c}{b}=\dfrac{a-c}{b}.$

It is clear from this formula (or from pictures such as those below) that *addition of fractions satisfies the Any-order and the additive identity properties.* Also notice that in the special case when the denominators are 1, Rule 2 gives "numerator only" additions such as

$$\frac{3}{1}+\frac{5}{1}=\frac{3+5}{1}=\frac{8}{1}.$$

Of course, $\frac{3}{1}$ is an awkward way of writing the whole number 3, and the above equation is the whole number fact $3+5=8$. In that sense *fraction addition includes and extends whole number addition.* It expands on what students already know; it is not a brand new way of adding.

To add fractions with unlike denominators we need to rename them so they have the same fractional unit. Then we add as before. That process is easiest when the denominators are small and one is a multiple of the other. In those cases addition and subtraction is done by "counting in terms of the smallest fractional unit" (in teacher's language, these are problems where one of the denominators is the common denominator). Problems of this type can readily be done by students at this stage, as the following problems illustrate.

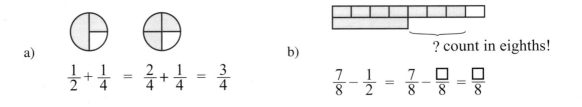

a) $\frac{1}{2}+\frac{1}{4}=\frac{2}{4}+\frac{1}{4}=\frac{3}{4}$

b) ? count in eighths! $\frac{7}{8}-\frac{1}{2}=\frac{7}{8}-\frac{\square}{8}=\frac{\square}{8}$

The general case of adding fractions with different denominators is conceptually harder. We will discuss it in the next section.

Stage 5 — Word Problems. Fractions are amazingly useful in many real-world situations! Students understand and appreciate fractions better when they learn from word problems that display the uses of fraction. Here is such a problem.

EXAMPLE 1.1. *Mother opened a quart of milk and poured $\frac{1}{5}$ of the quart for Kate, and $\frac{2}{5}$ for Ryan. How much was left?*

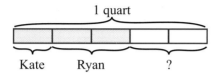

Together, Kate and Ryan received $\frac{3}{5}$ quart, so

$\frac{2}{5}$ of the quart was left.

Homework Set 24

1. *(Study the textbook!)* [Do this problem only if you have access to Primary Math 3B] Read and work through pages 64 − 77 of Primary Math 3B. Answer the following problems as you go.

   a) On page 69, draw pictures illustrating Problems 4abc, 5c, 6b, 7b.

   b) On page 73, draw pictures (like those on the same page) for 5e and 5f.

2. *(Study the textbook!)* Read pages 42 − 49 of Primary Math 4A and answer the following problems.

   a) Parts a, b, c, f, i, and j of Problem 9 on page 45.

   b) Parts a, b, c, f, i, and j of Problem 10 on page 49.

   c) Create bar diagrams, similar to those on pages 42 − 49, for Problems 4ab and 5ab on page 50.

3. *(Study the textbook!)* Pages 50 − 51 of Primary Math 4A give some simple fraction word problems.
   Give Teacher's Solutions for Problems 6 − 9 on page 50 and 6 − 8 on page 51. For each subtraction problem, specify whether it is using the part-whole, take-away, or comparison interpretation of subtraction.

4. *(Study the textbook!)* Read Review B (pages 66 − 69) in Primary Math 4A. Review sets like this are designed to evaluate and consolidate student learning.

   a) Answer Problems 12 − 16 of Review B (pages 66 − 69). For each problem, write the answers as a list of the form 12: $\frac{5}{8}, \frac{1}{3}, \ldots$.

   b) Problems 12, 13, 15, and 16 evaluate and consolidate knowledge of what?

5. Using the definition of fractions described in the first few sentences of this chapter, give a "teacher's explanation" (consisting of a number line and one or two sentences) for the equality $\frac{4}{5} = \frac{8}{10}$.

6. Give Teacher's Solutions to the following problems using a picture or diagram based on the indicated model.

   a) Mrs. Smith used $\frac{3}{10}$ of a bottle of cooking oil, which measured 150 $m\ell$. How much oil did the bottle hold? (use an area model).

   b) $\frac{4}{5}$ of the children in a choir are girls. If there are 8 boys, how many children are there altogether? (measurement model).

   c) Jim had 15 stamps. He gave $\frac{2}{5}$ of them to Jill. How many stamps did he give to Jill? (set model).

   d) Beth made 12 bows. She used $\frac{1}{5}$ meter of ribbon for each bow. How much ribbon did she use altogether? (measurement model).

   e) A shopkeeper had 150 kg of rice. He sold $\frac{2}{5}$ of it and packed the remainder equally into 5 bags. Find the weight of rice in each bag. (measurement model).

   f) Peter had 400 stamps. $\frac{5}{8}$ of them were Singapore stamps and the rest were U.S. stamps. He gave $\frac{1}{5}$ of the Singapore stamps to his friend. How many stamps did he have left? (bar diagram).

7. Find a fraction smaller than $1/5$. Find another fraction smaller than the one you found. Can you continue this process? Is there a smallest fraction greater than zero? Explain (give an algorithm!).

6.2 More Fraction Basics

This section continues our survey of the development of fractions in the Primary Mathematics curriculum. In that curriculum, the material of the previous section (Stages $1 - 5$) is covered in grades 2, 3 and 4, and the material in this section (Stages $6 - 8$ below) is covered in the grades 4 and 5.

Stage 6 — Mixed numbers and Improper fractions. Fractions greater than one can be written either as mixed numbers or improper fractions.

mixed number

improper fraction

- A *mixed number* is a fraction expressed as the sum of a whole number and a fraction less than one. The mixed number $2\frac{1}{8}$ is an abbreviation for $2 + \frac{1}{8}$.

- An *improper fraction* is a fraction $\frac{a}{b}$ with $a \geq b$ such as $\frac{8}{5}$ or $\frac{7}{7}$.

Notice that whole numbers can be written as improper fractions; for example, 2 is $\frac{2}{1}$ or $\frac{4}{2}$ or $\frac{6}{3}$.

Conversions between mixed numbers and improper fractions can be illustrated with area and measurement models, as in the following example and exercise.

EXAMPLE 2.1. $3\frac{1}{2}$ *is how many halves?*

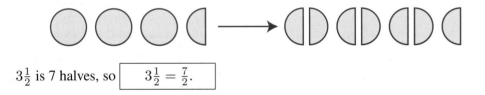

$3\frac{1}{2}$ is 7 halves, so $\boxed{3\frac{1}{2} = \frac{7}{2}.}$

EXERCISE 2.2. *Convert $\frac{14}{5}$ to a mixed number (fill in the two boxes).*

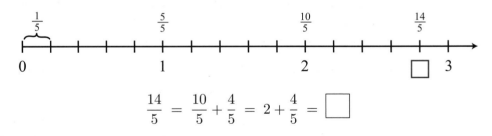

$$\frac{14}{5} = \frac{10}{5} + \frac{4}{5} = 2 + \frac{4}{5} = \boxed{}$$

converting to mixed numbers

Exercise 2.2 points to the general computational method for converting fractions to mixed numbers: use division to write the numerator as a multiple of the denominator plus a remainder, then simplify. For example, noting that $14 = (2 \times 5) + 4$, we have

$$\frac{14}{5} = \frac{(2 \times 5) + 4}{5} = \frac{2 \times 5}{5} + \frac{4}{5} = 2\frac{4}{5}.$$

For larger numbers one can use long division. For example, to rewrite $\frac{391}{12}$, we can use long division to see that $391 \div 12$ has quotient 32 with remainder 7, and consequently

$$\frac{391}{12} = \frac{(12 \times 32) + 7}{12} = 32\frac{7}{12}.$$

Stage 7 — Fractions as an expression of division. Fractions provide an answer (a quotient) to division problems like $5 \div 3$ or $17 \div 11$ which do not have whole number solutions. This can be illustrated for children using partitive ("sharing") division, as in the following example.

EXAMPLE 2.3. *5 children want to share 3 giant cookies equally. How much should each get?*

One approach is to split each cookie into five equal parts.

We then have 15 fifths, which can be divided equally among the 5 children. Each child gets 3 fifths $= \frac{3}{5}$ of a cookie, showing that

$$3 \div 5 = \frac{3}{5}.$$

The same reasoning applies with different numbers of cookies and children showing, for example, that $3 \div 10 = \frac{3}{10}$. Such exercises lead to another basic fraction fact, stated in "teacher's language" as follows.

Rule 3 (Fraction-division Equivalence). $a \div b = \dfrac{a}{b}$.

This rule can be read in two ways. It shows that whole number division problems can always be answered using fractions. For example, $240 \div 38$ is $\frac{240}{38}$; the fraction can then be simplified if desired. The rule also reveals a new way of thinking about fraction notation: the horizontal bar separating numerator from denominator can be interpreted as a division sign: $\frac{3}{5}$ *means* $3 \div 5$. That interpretation becomes increasingly important as students progress to algebra.

In fact, understanding Rule 3 changes the way students think about whole number division. Division is originally learned at a time when only whole numbers are available as "answers," so the result of a division must be expressed as a quotient plus a remainder. That "whole number" viewpoint of division is, for most purposes, replaced by Rule 3 when fractions are learned. However, confusion can arise if instruction is not designed to help students make this transition.

rethinking division

Classroom Example. *When asked how 4 people should equally split a 17-ounce fudge bar, Colleen declares that they should get "4 R1" ounces each.*

Colleen has recognized that this is the division problem $17 \div 4$, and has given the formal answer she learned for that problem. But what does it mean to give each person "4 R1 ounces?" She undoubtedly means "4 ounces each, with 1 ounce left over," but that still overlooks the fact that fudge bars can be subdivided. If the fudge were cut with a knife, the answer would involve fractions: each should get $\frac{17}{4} = 4\frac{1}{4}$ ounces. That reasoning is different from Colleen's "whole number division" thinking.

Fractions give students a new and more flexible perspective on division. Students should emerge from elementary school knowing that the question "what is 17 divided by 4?" has four answers ($4R1, \frac{17}{4}, 4\frac{1}{4}, 4.25$) and that it is up to them to choose the one that best fits the context.

Stage 8 — Adding fractions with unlike denominators. In the Primary Mathematics curriculum, fourth grade students learn to add and subtract fractions first when the denominators are the same, and then when one denominator is a multiple of the other. Addition of fractions with general denominators is developed in grade 5.

Remember, we cannot add two fractions until we have the same fractional unit. When one denominator is a multiple of the other we need only rename one fraction. But in general we need to rename both fractions.

Pictorial Approach — Fraction addition can be illustrated by rectangular area models, chopping vertically to show the first summand and horizontally to show the second. (The two rectangles represent the same whole unit, so must be identical).

EXAMPLE 2.4. *Find* $\frac{1}{2} + \frac{2}{5}$.

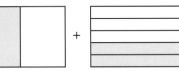

The fractional
unit is 1/2.

The fractional
unit is 1/5.

I need the same
unit to add.

Chopping both rectangles in both directions creates a common fractional unit $\frac{1}{10}$ and neatly illustrates the equivalent fractions with that denominator.

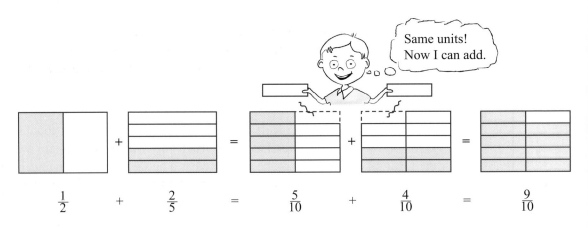

$$\frac{1}{2} \quad + \quad \frac{2}{5} \quad = \quad \frac{5}{10} \quad + \quad \frac{4}{10} \quad = \quad \frac{9}{10}$$

EXERCISE 2.5. *Find* $\frac{2}{3} - \frac{2}{7}$ *by appropriately shading the rectangles and completing the arithmetic.*

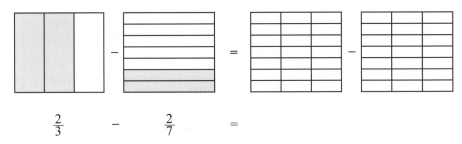

$$\frac{2}{3} \quad - \quad \frac{2}{7} \quad =$$

We are using Rule 1 (equivalent fractions) to get the same denominator, then using Rule 2 (addition with like denominators) to add. Algebraically, we write this as

$$\frac{a}{b} + \frac{c}{d} = \frac{ad}{bd} + \frac{bc}{bd} = \frac{ad+bc}{bd}.$$

In some curriculums this formula is given as the definition of fraction addition with little or no explanation of what it means. That, of course is backwards — this formula is the *last* step in teaching fraction addition, not the first. Be careful not to make this mistake as a teacher!

Abstract Approach — Finding common fractional units ("common denominators") is the same as finding common multiples of the denominators. The Least Common Multiple, if easily found, is an especially efficient common denominator (although no teacher should require its use).

LCM as a common denominator

EXERCISE 2.6. *Add $\frac{3}{8}$ and $\frac{1}{6}$.*

Mixed numbers are usually added by separately adding their whole number and fractional parts, then combining and "regrouping" if necessary. For example, $2\frac{1}{2} + 3\frac{2}{3} = (2+3) + (\frac{1}{2} + \frac{2}{3}) = 5\frac{7}{6} = 6\frac{1}{6}$. But other methods can be used, such as the "counting-up" technique in the following example.

EXAMPLE 2.7. *Find $7\frac{1}{4} - 3\frac{3}{4}$.*

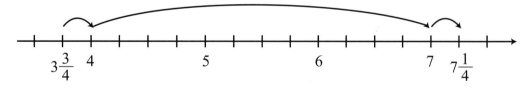

Starting at $3\frac{3}{4}$ and "counting on" as shown, we find that $7\frac{1}{4} - 3\frac{3}{4}$ is $\frac{1}{4} + 3 + \frac{1}{4} = \boxed{3\frac{1}{2}}$.

We conclude this section by discussing another common student error — one mentioned at the beginning of this section.

Common Student Error: *When asked to find $\frac{1}{3} + \frac{2}{5}$, Mark writes $\frac{3}{8}$. How can you help Mark?*

Apparently, Mark is thinking of each fraction as a *pair* of numbers (numerator and denominator) and guessing that the way to add fractions is to separately add numerator and denominator. If he is shown another way of adding his reaction is likely to be "yes, but my way is easier!" But if Mark is first shown that his method is wrong, he will temporarily have no way to add fractions, and will be open to suggestions. With that in mind, here is one way for a teacher to proceed.

instructional
counterexample

i) Begin by using an *instructional counterexample* (cf. HW Set 22), saying "Mark, if your method was the correct way to add fractions, then by the same logic,

$$\frac{1}{2} + \frac{1}{2} = \frac{2}{4} = \frac{1}{2}.$$

How can that be?!"

ii) Next, use pictures to expose the key issue — that we cannot add until we convert to fractional units of the same size. That can be done as in Example 2.4, or as follows.

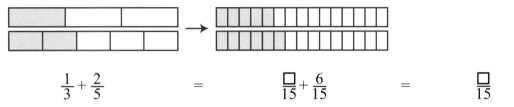

$$\frac{1}{3} + \frac{2}{5} \qquad = \qquad \frac{\square}{15} + \frac{6}{15} \qquad = \qquad \frac{\square}{15}$$

iii) Once Mark has understood the need for common denominators, one can return to the original problem and ask Mark to solve it without pictures:

$$\frac{1}{3} + \frac{2}{5} = \frac{\square}{15} + \frac{\square}{15} = \frac{\square}{15}.$$

This example serves as a warning not to take the step Pictorial ⇒ Abstract too quickly! Pictures and word problems have an important role in helping students gain a clear understanding of the meaning of fraction notation and the ideas of equivalent fractions and common denominators. Mark and his classmates should have a firm grasp of these notions before they begin adding fractions.

Homework Set 25

1. (*Study the textbook!*)   Read pages 52 − 57 of Primary Math 4A, computing mentally as you read. Mixed numbers and improper fractions help students to see that fractions can be bigger than 1.

   a) Illustrate Problems 8a and 8b on page 57 using a number line.

   b) Illustrate Problems 10a and 10b on page 57 using an area model. Start by drawing the whole unit.

2. (*Study the textbook!*)   Read pages 33 − 36 of Primary Math 5A. Do the following problems as you read.

   a) On page 33, Rule 3 is illustrated using which interpretation (partitive or measurement)?

   b) Give Teachers' Solutions to Problems 6 − 8 of Practice 3A.

3. (*Study the textbook!*)   Read pages 37 − 43 of Primary Math 5A. Notice how the problems on pages 38 and 39 teach addition of fractions as a 2-step process (find a common denominator, then add) with the student helpers in the margin finding the least common multiple.

   a) Illustrate Problems 1c, 2c, and 3c of Practice 3B using pictures similar to Examples 2.4 and 2.5 of this section.

   b) Give a Teacher's Solution to Problems 7 and 8 of Practice 3B.

   c) Illustrate Problems 1c, 2c, and 4c of Practice 3C using a measurement model similar to Example 2.7 of this section.

4. (*Mental Math*) Do the following Mental Math problems, using compensation for a) and b). Show your intermedi-

ate steps.

a) $28\frac{2}{7} - 3\frac{6}{7}$

b) $9\frac{1}{6} - 5\frac{5}{6}$

c) $\left(1\frac{3}{4} + 4\frac{5}{11}\right) + \left(2\frac{8}{11} + 5\frac{1}{4}\right)$

d) $12\frac{1}{8} - 4\frac{5}{8}$

e) $\frac{4}{9} + \left(\frac{3}{5} + 3\frac{5}{9}\right)$

5. Give range estimates for
   a) $3\frac{8}{9} + 7\frac{3}{13}$,   b) $2\frac{2}{11} + 4\frac{8}{9} + 12\frac{1}{12}$.

6. Estimate by rounding to the nearest $\frac{1}{2}$ unit:

   a) $2\frac{4}{9} + 7\frac{5}{12}$ b) $22\frac{4}{11} + 19\frac{8}{9} + 13\frac{7}{12}$.

7. Use long division to convert a) $\frac{735}{37}$ and b) $\frac{4271}{9}$ to mixed numbers.

8. A student claims that $\frac{46}{6}$ cannot be equal to $\frac{23}{3}$ because $46 \div 6$ is $7\mathbf{R}4$, while $23 \div 3$ is $7\mathbf{R}2$. How would you respond?

9. a) Use Euclid's Algorithm (cf. Section 5.5) to reduce the fraction $\dfrac{5829}{18879}$. *Hint*: find GCF(18879, 5829).

   b) Use Euclid's Algorithm to show that the fraction $\dfrac{13837}{24827}$ cannot be simplified.

6.3 Multiplication of Fractions and a Review of Division

By grade 5 in the Primary Mathematics curriculum students have begun thinking of fractions, more and more, as numbers — quantities which can be added, subtracted, multiplied, and divided, and which obey the arithmetic properties:

- commutative,
- associative,
- distributive, and
- additive and multiplicative identities.

These arithmetic properties guide the development of fractions. In this section we will use models and interpretations to guide us to the correct definition of fraction multiplication.

Thought Experiment.   One might try to define fraction multiplication by the procedure used to add fractions: find a common denominator and then multiply the numerators as in whole number multiplication:

$$\frac{2}{5} \star \frac{3}{5} = \frac{2 \times 3}{5} = \frac{6}{5}.$$

While this proposed "multiplication" is commutative (why?), it is inconsistent with the associative, distributive, and multiplicative identity properties. For instance, it implies that

$$\frac{1}{3} \star 1 = \frac{1}{3} \star \frac{3}{3} = \frac{1 \times 3}{3} = \frac{3}{3} = 1,$$

contradicting the multiplicative identity property (multiplying by 1 should not change the number!). Thus we must reject this interpretation of fraction multiplication *because it violates the arithmetic properties*.

A Teaching Sequence

Students' understanding of multiplication for whole numbers is based on the three models pictured in Section 1.5 on page 25. Fraction multiplication can be taught by adapting those models to fractions. The first step involves fractions, but no new ideas about multiplication. The second step requires a new interpretation of multiplication.

Step 1 — Whole number times a fraction. This case is natural and intuitive because all of the familiar interpretations of multiplication apply: number of units, groups of, repeated addition, and rectangular arrays.

$$3 \times \frac{1}{4} \;=\; 3 \text{ quarters} \;=\; \frac{3}{4}.$$

$$3 \times \frac{1}{4} \;=\; 3 \text{ groups of } \frac{1}{4} \;=\; \frac{3}{4}.$$

$$3 \times \frac{1}{4} \;=\; \frac{1}{4} + \frac{1}{4} + \frac{1}{4} \;=\; \frac{3}{4}.$$

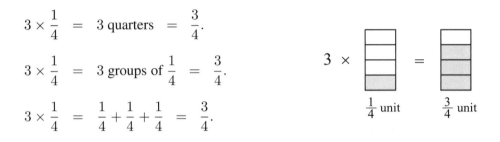

Step 2 — Fraction times a whole number. This step requires a conceptual shift in the way students understand multiplication. Most of the familiar interpretations of multiplication, including repeated addition and "groups of" in the set model, do not give sensible interpretations for $\frac{1}{4} \times 3$. What does it mean to "add 3 to itself $\frac{1}{4}$ times?" What does "$\frac{1}{4}$ groups" mean? These interpretations must be replaced.

The new interpretation is simple: we interpret $\frac{1}{4} \times 3$ as "$\frac{1}{4}$ *of* 3." That can be illustrated by drawing 3 units and taking $\frac{1}{4}$ *of* that region. (Here again rectangular arrays models are especially clear because we can chop both horizontally and vertically.)

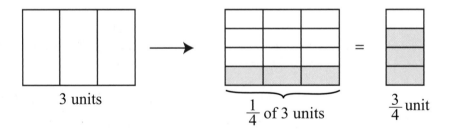

Since this is the same picture as in Step 1, we see that

$$\frac{1}{4} \times 3 \;=\; 3 \times \frac{1}{4}.$$

Thus this interpretation makes fraction multiplication commutative. The other arithmetic properties (Any-order, distributive, etc.) hold as well, as you will show in HW Set 29.

Step 3 — Fraction times a fraction. We continue to interpret "$\frac{1}{4} \times$" to mean "$\frac{1}{4}$ of" and illustrate it using a rectangle chopped in both directions.

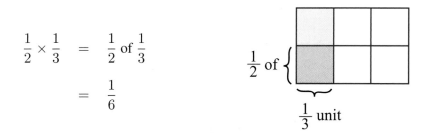

$$\frac{1}{2} \times \frac{1}{3} \;=\; \frac{1}{2} \text{ of } \frac{1}{3}$$

$$=\; \frac{1}{6}$$

The chopping creates the fractional unit corresponding to the product of the denominators.

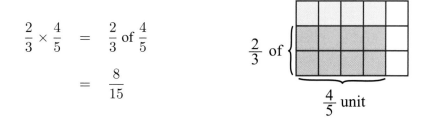

$$\frac{2}{3} \times \frac{4}{5} \;=\; \frac{2}{3} \text{ of } \frac{4}{5}$$

$$=\; \frac{8}{15}$$

The doubly-shaded region is a rectangular array which shows that the numerator of the product is the product of the numerators.

After practicing many such problems students will discover — and understand — the short-cut

$$\frac{2}{3} \times \frac{4}{5} \;=\; \frac{2 \times 4}{3 \times 5}$$

(multiplying both numerators and denominators). For later use we record this shortcut in algebraic form.

Rule 4 (Fraction Multiplication). $\dfrac{a}{b} \cdot \dfrac{c}{d} = \dfrac{a \cdot c}{b \cdot d}.$

Clearly, it is much easier to multiply fractions than to add them. Tell that to your students! Also point out to your students that the Any-order, distributive, and multiplicative identity properties continue to hold for fractions. For example,

$$\frac{4}{5} \times 1 = \frac{4}{5} \times \frac{1}{1} = \frac{4}{5} \qquad \text{and} \qquad \frac{2}{3} \times \frac{5}{8} = \frac{2 \times 5}{3 \times 8} = \frac{5}{8} \times \frac{2}{3}.$$

Thus fraction multiplication, given by Rule 4, retains the arithmetic properties that students have been routinely using since first grade.

After multiplying numerator and denominator, it is often convenient to rewrite the resulting fraction in simplest form. One approach is to multiply, then simplify. Do that for the following example:

$$\frac{9}{10} \times \frac{5}{12} \;=\; \frac{45}{120} \;=\; \boxed{}.$$

But that is not the easiest way! It is clearer and simpler to *factor and cancel before multiplying*:

factor and cancel before multiplying

$$\frac{9}{10} \times \frac{5}{12} \;=\; \frac{9 \times 5}{10 \times 12} \;=\; \frac{3 \times \cancel{3} \times \cancel{5}}{2 \times \cancel{5} \times \cancel{3} \times 4} \;=\; \boxed{}.$$

Finally, word problems help students to understand why the interpretation of fraction multiplication is a useful one.

EXAMPLE 3.1. *Mrs. Smith had $\frac{13}{20}$ liters of cooking oil. She used $\frac{5}{7}$ of it to fry shrimp crackers. How much oil did she use?*

The large rectangle below represents 1 liter.

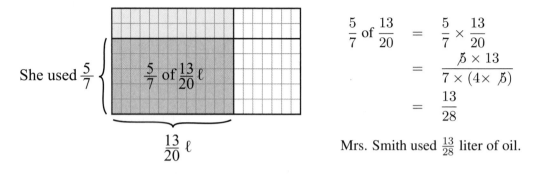

$$\frac{5}{7} \text{ of } \frac{13}{20} = \frac{5}{7} \times \frac{13}{20}$$

$$= \frac{\cancel{5} \times 13}{7 \times (4 \times \cancel{5})}$$

$$= \frac{13}{28}$$

Mrs. Smith used $\frac{13}{28}$ liter of oil.

Notice that the dark inner rectangle is exactly the amount that she used, so the word problem, model, and arithmetic are all consistent.

Review of partitive and measurement division

Recall that there are two ways to view the division problem $12 \div 3$ (See Section 1.6). In measurement division, one uses the divisor as a yardstick and asks "12 is how many 3's?" In partitive division, one partitions 12 into 3 equal parts and asks "How big is each part?"

Interpretation	Interpretive question	Diagram
Measurement division:	12 is how many 3's?	
Partitive division:	12 is 3 groups of what size?	

Word problems implicitly specify one of the meanings of division. For division problems involving whole numbers one can distinguish the two interpretations using either the interpretative question or the bar diagram.

EXAMPLE 3.2. *a) Kim bought 12 oranges and put them in bags of 3. How many bags did she have?*

b) A 12 foot rope is cut into 3 equal pieces. What is the length of one piece?

Problem a) corresponds to the first diagram above, so is a measurement division question. Problem b) corresponds to the second picture above, so is partitive division.

With fractions, measurement and partitive division can still be distinguished by the interpretative questions. Measurement division asks "A is how many Bs?" Partitive division asks "A is B of what size?"

One can also use diagrams to distinguish measurement and partitive division. However, the diagrams for fraction division problems do not always look like those in the chart above. As you do problems, you will discover that the diagrams corresponding to the two interpretative questions have a different form when the divisor is smaller than the dividend.

EXAMPLE 3.3. *If a road is created at $\frac{1}{2}$ miles per week, how many weeks will it take to build $1\frac{3}{4}$ miles?*

Initially it is not even clear that this is a division problem! But the diagram

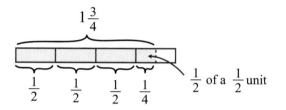

shows that the question is, "$1\frac{3}{4}$ miles is how many $\frac{1}{2}$ miles?" and this is measurement division. In this case the diagram also gives the answer: it will take $3\frac{1}{2}$ weeks constructing $\frac{1}{2}$ miles a week to complete $1\frac{3}{4}$ miles. The underlying arithmetic is the division

$$1\frac{3}{4} \div \frac{1}{2} = 3\frac{1}{2}.$$

Notice that, in the question of Example 3.3, the dividend and the divisor have the same units—both are expressed in miles. *In measurement division, dividend and divisor are multiples of the same whole unit.* Attention to units gives another way of distinguishing between partitive and measurement division.

units in division problems

Diagrams for partitive division do not always look like the one on the previous page. But we can still recognize partitive division by the interpretive question, and by observing units.

EXAMPLE 3.4. *If $\frac{1}{2}$ of a jug is $1\frac{3}{4}$ gallons, how many gallons does the jug hold?*

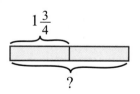

This asks, "$1\frac{3}{4}$ gallons are $\frac{1}{2}$ of what size?" so we are using partitive division. (Notice that dividend and divisor use different units, 'gallon' and 'jug.') The diagram makes clear that the jug holds $3\frac{1}{2}$ gallons. Again the underlying division problem is

$$1\frac{3}{4} \div \frac{1}{2} = 3\frac{1}{2}.$$

How to draw a bar diagram for partitive division. Given a problem like $4 \div \frac{5}{6}$, follow these steps.

1. Write out the interpretive question, "4 is $\frac{5}{6}$ of what size?" It is your guide. Construct the diagram by reading it *backwards*.

2. Draw "what size?" as a bar labeled with a question mark.

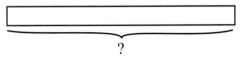

3. Identify "$\frac{5}{6}$ of what size?" by chopping the bar and shading:

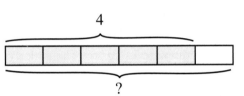

4. We're told that "$\frac{5}{6}$ of what size" is equal to 4. Label the shaded region to show this.

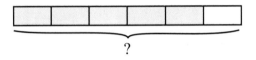

This is your bar diagram!

EXERCISE 3.5. *Use the above procedure for the whole number problem $20 \div 5$ ("20 is 5 groups of what size?").*

Exercise 3.5 shows that the same procedure for drawing a partitive division diagram works for whole number divisors and fraction divisors alike. Hence the partitive models for whole numbers and fractions are fundamentally the same.

Caution. When dividing by a fraction larger than 1, as in $4 \div \frac{5}{3}$, the steps are the same as above but the resulting picture looks different. To answer the question "4 is $\frac{5}{3}$'s of what size?" one must *extend* the original bar (the unit) to a longer bar:

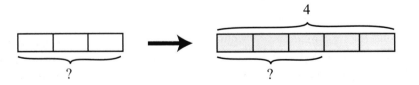

Because of this extra difficulty, it is probably wise for teachers to initially avoid the partitive diagrams where the divisor is larger than 1 (unless it is a whole number). It is also wise to avoid drawing bar diagrams for measurement division if the divisor is larger than the dividend.

EXERCISE 3.6. *Try to draw a bar diagram for $\frac{1}{3} \div \frac{1}{2}$ using the measurement division interpretation. Do you see why the partitive interpretation is easier to understand in this case?*

The implication is clear: wait until students are comfortable with drawing the simpler diagrams before moving on to more complicated diagrams.

Homework Set 26

1. *(Mental Math)* Another way to write the shortcut for multiplying by 25 is to use fractions:

$$25 \times 48 = \frac{100}{4} \times 48 = 100 \times \frac{48}{4} = 100 \times 12.$$

Use this way to find the following products mentally.

   a) 25×64 b) 25×320

   c) 884×25 d) 3212×25.

2. *(Mental Math)* Calculate mentally using the arithmetic properties (remember to show your thinking).

   a) $44 \cdot \frac{3}{8} + 44 \cdot \frac{7}{8}$ b) $(\frac{4}{7} + \frac{7}{9}) - \frac{3}{7}$

   c) $48 \times 99\frac{5}{12}$ d) $1234 \cdot \frac{331}{783} + 1234 \cdot \frac{452}{783}$

3. Estimate to the nearest whole number:

   a) $59 \times \frac{1}{3}$ b) $24\frac{1}{4} \times 1\frac{2}{3}$.

4. *(Study the textbook!)* In Primary Math 5A, read pages 44 - 45, doing the problems in your textbook and studying the 3 methods on page 45. Note how these methods develop the useful principle *cancel first, then multiply*.

   a) Write the answers to Problems 2 and 3 on page 48 as a list of 6 fractions.

   b) Use Method 3 to find $48 \times \frac{23}{12}$ and $320 \times \frac{13}{80}$.

5. *(Study the textbook!)* Read pages 49 - 51 of Primary Math 5A, noting the area models and studying Method 1 and 2 on page 51. Then answer Problems $5 - 10$ of Practice 3E (no diagrams are necessary).

6. *(Study the workbook!)* Now open Workbook 5A.

   a) Write solutions to Problems 2a and 2b in Exercise 22 by drawing an appropriate area model.

   b) Give Teacher's Solutions to Problems 2, 3, and 4 of Exercise 23. Use area models for your illustrations.

7. Find the following products by drawing area models like those used in Section 4.2. *Hint:* Start with a rectangle representing a whole unit, then one representing $2\frac{1}{3}$.

   a) $2\frac{1}{3} \times 6$ b) $2\frac{1}{3} \times 6\frac{1}{2}$

   c) $2\frac{7}{8} \times 2\frac{3}{4}$.

8. Show that the distributive property holds for fractions by drawing a picture illustrating that

$$\frac{2}{3}\left(\frac{1}{2} + \frac{1}{3}\right) = \left(\frac{2}{3} \times \frac{1}{2}\right) + \left(\frac{2}{3} \times \frac{1}{3}\right).$$

9. Read the paragraph 'Anticipating, detecting and correcting errors' in the Preface of this book. One common student error is to write

$$2\frac{1}{4} \times 1\frac{1}{3} = 2\frac{1}{12}.$$

Give an area model and brief explanation which simultaneously shows both the error this student is making and what the correct solution is.

10. *(Study the textbook!)* Read and think about the problems on page $56 - 59$ of Primary Math 5A. Give Teacher's Solutions for Exercise 28 and Exercise 29 in Primary Math Workbook 5A by drawing the bar diagrams like on page 68.

11. Identify whether the following problems are using measurement division (MD) or partitive division (PD). (If in doubt, draw a picture!)

   a) If it takes a half-yard of material to make an apron, how many aprons can be made with 3 yards of material?

   b) How many half bushels are there in $2\frac{1}{4}$ bushels?

   c) The perimeter of a square flower bed is 32 feet. Find the length of each side.

   d) Mary poured 6 cups of juice equally into 8 glasses. How much was in each glass?

   e) How many laps around a 1/4 mile track make 6 miles?

   f) We drove 3240 miles from New York to Los Angles in 6 days. What was our average distance per day?

6.4 Division of Fractions

One might think that students who understand how to multiply fractions and how to divide whole numbers would be able to readily understand division of fractions on their own. That is not the case. Division is the most subtle — and the most enlightening — of the four operations on fractions. By studying it one learns new ways of using fractions. This study also solidifies understanding of division in general, provides a lead-in to the topic of ratios, and is important preparation for algebra.

To these ends, it is important that students learn both the mechanics and the interpretations of fraction division. How should one go about teaching these? As with previous topics, the teaching sequence is essentially dictated by the mathematics. In the remainder of this section we will go through the following four steps in detail.

1. Review of whole numbers ÷ whole numbers.

2. Fractions ÷ whole numbers.

3. Whole numbers ÷ fractions.

4. Fractions ÷ fractions.

It might not be clear why Step 2 should preceed the similar-looking Step 3. But try drawing the bar diagrams for the following two problems,

$$\frac{2}{3} \div 2 \quad \text{and} \quad 5 \div \frac{2}{3},$$

and you will understand. In fact, it is only in Step 3 that students encounter a fundamentally new idea. Pay particular attention to this transition as you read this section.

A Teaching Sequence

Step 1 — Dividing a whole number by a whole number. The first step in teaching fraction division is making students comfortable viewing fractions as expressions of division — seeing, for example, that $\frac{3}{4}$ is the answer to the division problem $3 \div 4$ (this is Rule 3 from Section 6.2).

EXAMPLE 4.1. *Two girls share 5 cookies equally. How much did each girl get?*

This is a partitive question asking us to find $5 \div 2$. It can be answered in two ways. Putting the cookies in a row and chopping the row in half shows that $5 \div 2 = 2\frac{1}{2}$.

Alternatively, we can chop each cookie in half and distribute the halves equally:

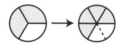

This approach solves the same problem, but leads to a different calculation:

$$5 \div 2 \; = \; 5 \text{ half cookies} \; = \; 5 \times \frac{1}{2} \; = \; \frac{5}{2} \text{ cookies.}$$

Of course the two answers are equal because $2\frac{1}{2}$ cookies = $\frac{5}{2}$ cookie. But the second approach directly connects the expressions $5 \div 2$ and $\frac{5}{2}$, and also shows that dividing by 2 is the same as multiplying by $\frac{1}{2}$, which is a simple instance of the "invert and multiply" rule.

Step 2 — Dividing a fraction by a whole number. Fractions can be partitioned into equal parts just as well as whole numbers.

EXAMPLE 4.2. *Four boys shared $\frac{2}{3}$ of a pie equally. What fraction did each receive?*

This is the partition division problem $\frac{2}{3} \div 4$. It can be illustrated using an area model

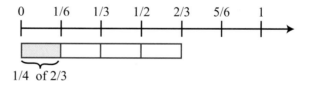

or a measurement model

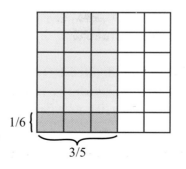

1/4 of 2/3

Interpreting *of* as multiplication, both models show that

$$\frac{2}{3} \div 4 \; = \; \frac{1}{4} \text{ of } \frac{2}{3} \; = \; \frac{1}{4} \times \frac{2}{3} \; = \; \frac{2}{3} \times \frac{1}{4}.$$

Therefore, without pictures, the question is answered by the calculation $\frac{2}{3} \div 4 = \frac{2}{3} \times \frac{1}{4} = \frac{1}{6}$.

EXAMPLE 4.3. *Illustrate $\frac{3}{5} \div 6$ with an area model.*

Rectangular arrays are once again useful because we can chop them in two directions. First, draw a rectangle representing the whole unit. Partition it into 5 equal columns and lightly shade 3. We then chop horizontally to make 6 equal rows.

1/6 {

3/5

This picture shows that

$$\frac{3}{5} \div 6 \;=\; \frac{1}{6} \text{ of } \frac{3}{5} \;=\; \frac{3}{5} \times \frac{1}{6},$$

which is $\frac{1}{10}$.

Step 3 — Whole number divided by a fraction. Dividing by a fraction is conceptually more difficult than dividing by a whole number. Most students find this an especially confusing topic. Here are two examples using different models.

EXAMPLE 4.4. *Jill bought 5 oranges. She cut each into half-oranges. How many pieces of oranges did she have?*

This is measurement division for $5 \div \frac{1}{2}$ (5 oranges is how many $\frac{1}{2}$ oranges?). The picture above makes clear that $5 \div \frac{1}{2}$ is $5 \times 2 = 10$.

Students frequently confuse "dividing by $\frac{1}{2}$" with "dividing in half." These are different statements! In Example 4.4 we divided 5 *by* $\frac{1}{2}$ and got 10, whereas in Example 4.1 we divided 5 *in* half and got $\frac{5}{2}$.

EXAMPLE 4.5. $\dfrac{3}{4}$ *of a number is 39. What is the number?*

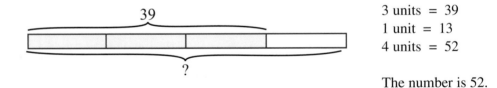

3 units = 39
1 unit = 13
4 units = 52

The number is 52.

Example 4.5 is a partitive division question asking us to find $39 \div \frac{3}{4}$. The two steps of the solution (take $\frac{1}{3}$ of 39, then multiply by 4) can be done as a single operation: multiply by $\frac{4}{3}$. Thus the above diagram shows that $39 \div \frac{3}{4} = 39 \times \frac{4}{3}$. Such diagrams are one way of illustrating and leading students to the "invert and multiply" rule.

Step 4 — Fraction divided by a fraction. The simplest examples of a fraction divided by a fraction are those in which two fractions have the same denominator. In this case, division of fractions looks much like its whole number counterpart.

EXAMPLE 4.6. *What is $\frac{6}{7} \div \frac{2}{7}$?*

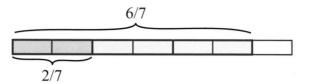

To answer using measurement division, draw bar diagram above. It is then evident that 3 segments of length $\frac{2}{7}$ make $\frac{6}{7}$, and therefore $\frac{6}{7} \div \frac{2}{7} = 3$. Notice that the denominator plays no role — we are really answering the question "What is $6 \div 2$?" So for fractions with the same denominator we define division in the following natural way:

$$\frac{6}{7} \div \frac{2}{7} = 6 \div 2 = 3.$$

EXAMPLE 4.7. *Illustrate $\frac{5}{3} \div \frac{2}{3}$ by measurement division.*

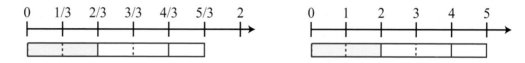

The measurement division question "$\frac{5}{3}$ is how many $\frac{2}{3}$'s?" is illustrated on the left (the answer is $2\frac{1}{2}$). Changing the scale — but not the diagram — gives the picture on the right, which is the diagram for $5 \div 2$. The fact that the diagrams are identical again shows that when dividing fractions with equal denominators, one can ignore the denominators:

$$\frac{5}{3} \div \frac{2}{3} = 5 \div 2 = \frac{5}{2}.$$

EXAMPLE 4.8. *$\frac{5}{6}$ of a gallon of gasoline filled only $\frac{3}{7}$ of a lawn tractor's gas tank. How many gallons of gas does the tractor's gas tank hold?*

While the words "how many" might suggest measurement division, the bar diagram makes clear that this is partitive division.

Of course, bar diagrams are not the only way to solve the problem. Here are three distinct Teacher Solutions. Read them carefully and spend some time thinking about the similarities and differences. Which solution is easiest to understand? Is algebra useful?

Teacher's Solution A.

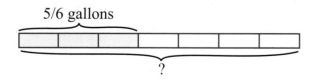

3 units $= \frac{5}{6}$ gallons
1 unit $= \frac{1}{3} \times \frac{5}{6} = \frac{5}{18}$ gallons
7 units $= \frac{5}{18} \times 7 = \frac{35}{18}$ gallons

The tank holds $\frac{35}{18}$ gallons (slightly less than 2 gallons).

Teacher's Solution B

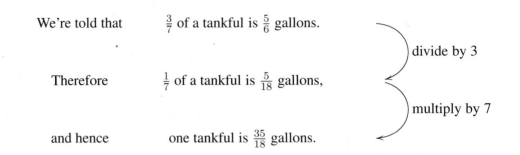

We're told that $\frac{3}{7}$ of a tankful is $\frac{5}{6}$ gallons.

Therefore $\frac{1}{7}$ of a tankful is $\frac{5}{18}$ gallons,

and hence one tankful is $\frac{35}{18}$ gallons.

divide by 3

multiply by 7

Teacher's Solution C (Grade 7 level). Let T be total number of gallons the tank holds. We're told that

$$\frac{3}{7}T = \frac{5}{6} \text{ gallons.}$$

Dividing both sides by 3 gives $\frac{1}{7}T = \frac{5}{18}$ gallons, and multiplying by 7 gives $T = \frac{35}{18}$ gallons.

Homework Set 27

1. *(Study the textbook!)* Read pages 53 and 54 in Primary Math 5A. Give Teacher's Solutions to Problems $4 - 9$ in Practice 3F (page 55).

2. Illustrate the following with a bar diagram and solve the problem.

   a) measurement division for $2 \div \frac{1}{3}$.

   b) measurement division for $\frac{3}{2} \div \frac{1}{6}$.

   c) partitive division for $14 \div 4$.

   d) partitive division for $\frac{2}{5} \div \frac{1}{3}$.

   e) measurement division for $\frac{7}{2} \div \frac{1}{4}$.

   f) partitive division for $5 \div \frac{7}{3}$.

   g) partitive division for $\frac{2}{3} \div 3$.

   h) partitive division for $\frac{5}{3} \div \frac{8}{3}$.

3. Reread Teacher's Solution A above. Give a similar solution to the following problems.

   a) After spending $\frac{4}{7}$ of her money on a jacket, Rita had $36 left. How much money did she have at first?

   b) While filling her backyard swimming pool, Anita watched the level rise from $\frac{1}{9}$ full to $\frac{1}{3}$ full in $\frac{2}{3}$ hour. What is the total time required to fill the pool?

4. Reread Teacher's Solution B above. Give a similar solution to the following problems.

   a) After reading 186 pages, Jennifer had read $\frac{3}{5}$ of her book. How many pages long was the book?

   b) A dump truck contains $\frac{2}{3}$ of a ton of dirt, but is only $\frac{3}{10}$ full. How many tons of dirt can the truck hold?

5. Give a Teacher's Solution using algebra:

   a) $\frac{3}{7}$ of the coins in a box are nickels. The rest are pennies. If there are 48 pennies, how many coins are there altogether?

   b) A farmer took $\frac{3}{4}$ hour to plow $\frac{2}{5}$ of his corn field. At that rate, how many hours will be needed to plow the entire field?

6. Give a Teacher's Solution to each of the following problems.

   a) Michelle spent $\frac{3}{5}$ of her money on a backpack. With the rest of her money she bought 3 CDs at $12 each. How much did the backpack cost?

   b) Whitney made a large batch of cookies. She sold $\frac{2}{3}$ of them and gave $\frac{1}{5}$ of the remainder to her friends. If she had 60 cookies left, how many cookies did she originally make?

   c) Tony spent $\frac{2}{5}$ of his money on a pair of running shoes. He also bought a coat which cost $6 less than the shoes. He then had $37 left. How much money did he have at first?

   d) A fish tank weighs 11.5 lbs when it is $\frac{1}{8}$ full of water and 34 lbs when it is $\frac{3}{4}$ full. How much does the empty tank weigh?

6.5 Division Word Problems

At this point you may be wondering why we are spending so much time on fraction division. Isn't it enough for students to simply learn to solve problems like $\frac{3}{4} \div \frac{2}{5}$ by the "invert and multiply" procedure? That will indeed enable them to calculate an answer. But students who know nothing but that mechanical procedure cannot relate it to interpretations of division. They will be unable to solve real-world division problems involving fractions! It is therefore especially important that division of fractions be developed *in the context of word problems*.

We begin this section by describing how the "invert and multiply" procedure emerges from the interpretations of fraction division. But our main focus is on word problems, including how to move back and forth between word problems and interpretative diagrams, and how to make up word problems of your own.

In the example $\frac{6}{7} \div \frac{2}{7}$ in the previous section we saw that the quotient of fractions with the same denominator is simply the quotient of their numerators: $\frac{6}{7} \div \frac{2}{7} = 6 \div 2 = 3$. We can summarize that observation as a rule.

Rule 5 (Fraction Division). $\quad \dfrac{a}{b} \div \dfrac{c}{b} = a \div c$ or equivalently $\dfrac{a}{b} \div \dfrac{c}{b} = \dfrac{a}{c}$.

As stated, Rule 5 explains how to divide fractions only when the denominators are the same. But any fraction division problem can be transformed into that case by using equivalent fractions.

EXAMPLE 5.1. *What is* $\dfrac{1}{4} \div \dfrac{2}{3}$?

To answer, we convert to twelfths and apply Rule 5: $\quad \dfrac{1}{4} \div \dfrac{2}{3} = \dfrac{3}{12} \div \dfrac{8}{12} = \dfrac{3}{8}$.

Example 5.1 can also be solved by replacing division by $\frac{2}{3}$ with multiplication by $\frac{3}{2}$. In your homework you will show how this "invert and multiply" procedure follows from Rule 5. Here is some background.

reciprocal

The *reciprocal* of a fraction is the fraction obtained by switching numerator and denominator. The reciprocal of $\frac{2}{3}$ is $\frac{3}{2}$ and the reciprocal of $\frac{1}{3}$ is 3 (0 has no reciprocal). The product of a fraction and its reciprocal is always 1; for example, $\frac{2}{3} \cdot \frac{3}{2} = 1$. For that reason, the reciprocal of a fraction is also called its *inverse*. We will say more about inverses in the next section.

inverse

The "invert and multiply rule" says that division by a fraction is the same as multiplication by its inverse. This is a fact about fraction arithmetic. But it is a general fact that holds for all fractions (except 0), so we must use letters to write it down. (We will not give this rule a number because it follows from Rule 5).

Invert and Multiply Rule. $\quad \dfrac{a}{b} \div \dfrac{c}{d} = \dfrac{a}{b} \times \dfrac{d}{c}$.

Many students first encounter the "invert and multiply" rule in algebra, where they are taught that the way to find $x \div \frac{3}{4}$ is to write

$$x \div \frac{3}{4} = x \times \frac{4}{3}$$

and proceed. But students should understand this method *before beginning algebra*. It is a fact about arithmetic, not a fact about algebra. Here are three additional classroom explanations for the arithmetic fact "$6 \div \frac{3}{4} = 6 \times \frac{4}{3}$."

- *Partitive Division Explanation:* The question "6 is $\frac{3}{4}$ of what number?" can be answered by reasoning "If $\frac{3}{4}$ of the number is 6, then $\frac{1}{4}$ of it is 2, so the number is 8". The answer is obtained by dividing by 3 and then multiplying by 4, that is, by multiplying 6 by $\frac{4}{3}$.

- *Measurement Division Explanation:* To answer "How many units of size $\frac{3}{4}$s make 6?" one can switch to *counting fourths*. Since 6 is 6×4 fourths, the question becomes "How many units of size 3 fourths make 24 fourths?" and the answer is $24 \div 3 = 8$. Thus the answer is $(6 \times 4) \div 3$, which again is $6 \times \frac{4}{3}$.

- *Prealgebra Explanation:* By the missing factor definition of division, $6 \div \frac{3}{4}$ is the number x which satisfies $\frac{3}{4}x = 6$. We can solve that equation by multiplying both sides by $\frac{4}{3}$:

$$\frac{4}{3} \times \frac{3}{4} x = \frac{4}{3} \times 6.$$

Noting that $\frac{4}{3} \times \frac{3}{4} = 1$ and using the commutative property then shows that $x = 6 \times \frac{4}{3}$.

The "invert and multiply" rule is simple and useful, and should be mastered by all students. But this is only part of the story. The main teaching goal is to develop skill at using fraction division to *solve practical problems*.

Creating word problems

Creating word problems is an advanced teaching skill that all teachers should attempt to learn. Ironically, experience at creating word problems is valuable because it will help you *read* word problems better. Designing and writing word problems also yields insights that will help you choose, classify, and order word problems — three tasks that teachers do every day. The examples below are guides to constructing word problems for fraction division.

There is a system for creating a division word problem. One proceeds in small steps: decide on an interpretation (measurement or partitive), draw a model, find the answer, choose a unit, and then — only then — think up a situation. You may have to try several different units and situations before you find one which is realistic with the given numbers.

EXAMPLE 5.2. *Write a word problem for* $109\frac{1}{3} \div 2\frac{2}{3}$.

1. Choose an interpretation. We will use the measurement interpretation and ask "$109\frac{1}{3}$ is how many $2\frac{2}{3}$'s?"

2. Draw the corresponding picture.

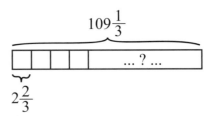

3. The answer is $109\frac{1}{3} \div 2\frac{2}{3} = \frac{328}{3} \div \frac{8}{3} = \frac{328}{8} = 41$.

4. Choose a unit. Recall that for measurement division the dividend and divisor must be the same whole unit. If we use centimeters (cm) for a unit, then $109\frac{1}{3}$ cm is a little over an arms length and $2\frac{2}{3}$ cm is about the thickness of a book, which suggests a situation.

5. Make up a word problem which would produce the model above using cm as the unit:

   A stack of math textbooks is $109\frac{1}{3}$ cm high. If each book is $2\frac{2}{3}$ cm thick, how many textbooks are in the stack?

   This word problem satisfies all the criteria of Section 2.3.

EXAMPLE 5.3. *Write a partitive word problem for $45 \div \frac{3}{5}$.*

1. The interpretive question "45 is $\frac{3}{5}$ of what size?" will be our guide.

2. Draw the corresponding picture (see Section 6.3).

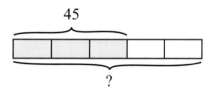

3. The answer is $45 \div \frac{3}{5} = 45 \times \frac{5}{3} = 75$.

4. Money units are often convenient for making word problems. Using dollars as the unit, we are looking for a situation where $\frac{3}{5}$ of some dollar amount is $45.

5. Spending money gives a "before and after" word problem. As a twist, we can make it a two-step problem by giving the amount *not* spent.

   After spending $\frac{2}{5}$ of his money on a shirt, Sam had $45 left. How much money did he have at first?

   This word problem compares the unit *his money* with another unit *dollars*.

   This method for producing word problems is versatile and flexible. For instance, to create two-step problems, just add another bar to the model you create.

EXAMPLE 5.4. *Make up a two–step problem involving $45 \div \frac{3}{5}$.*

Replace Step 2 above with the following model.

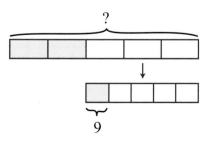

Creating a problem means making up a story around this model.

Sam spent $\frac{2}{5}$ of his money on a shirt and $\frac{1}{5}$ of the remainder on a tie. The tie cost $9. How much did he have to begin with?

The most interesting word problems cannot be classified as addition, subtraction, multiplication, or division word problems. They are multi-step problems which require several operations. Models can help teachers make up such word problems in a structured way.

EXAMPLE 5.5. *Make up a 2–step word problem with multiple operations.*

1. Be creative! Experiment with bar diagrams.

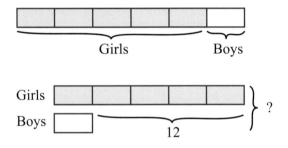

2. Answer the question. Since 4 units is 12, 1 unit is 3. Hence the total (6 units) must be 18.

3. Make up a story that corresponds to the bar diagram.

$\frac{5}{6}$ of a choir are girls. There are 12 more girls than boys. How many children are in the choir altogether?

This problem combines subtraction ($\frac{5}{6} - \frac{1}{6}$) with division ($12 \div \frac{4}{6}$).

Homework Set 28

1. The **common denominator method** involves rewriting the problem as a division of fractions with the same denominator and then noting that $\frac{a}{c} \div \frac{b}{c} = \frac{a}{b}$ (Rule 5). Use the common denominator method to find:

   a) $2 \div \dfrac{7}{16}$ b) $\dfrac{2}{7} \div 5$

   c) $\dfrac{3}{4} \div \dfrac{5}{6}$ d) $\dfrac{4}{5} \div \dfrac{5}{8}$

   e) $\dfrac{a}{b} \div \dfrac{c}{d}$

2. *(Mental Math)* Solve the following problems. Show your method.

   a) $32 \div 5\dfrac{1}{3}$ b) $\dfrac{18}{19} \div \dfrac{36}{57}$ c) $\dfrac{8}{15} \div \dfrac{13}{64}$

3. Below is the measurement division model for $6 \div \frac{4}{5} = 7\frac{1}{2}$. Note that $\frac{4}{5}$ goes into 6 seven times with 2 fractional units left over (circled). Those two fractional units give the $\frac{1}{2}$ in $7\frac{1}{2}$ because they represent (choose one):

   a) $\frac{1}{2}$ of the dividend (i.e., $\frac{1}{2}$ of 6),

   b) $\frac{1}{2}$ of the whole unit (i.e., $\frac{1}{2}$ of 1),

   c) $\frac{1}{2}$ of 4 fractional units (i.e., $\frac{1}{2}$ of $\frac{4}{5}$).

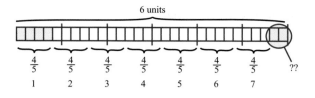

$\frac{4}{5}$ $\frac{4}{5}$ $\frac{4}{5}$ $\frac{4}{5}$ $\frac{4}{5}$ $\frac{4}{5}$ $\frac{4}{5}$??

1 2 3 4 5 6 7

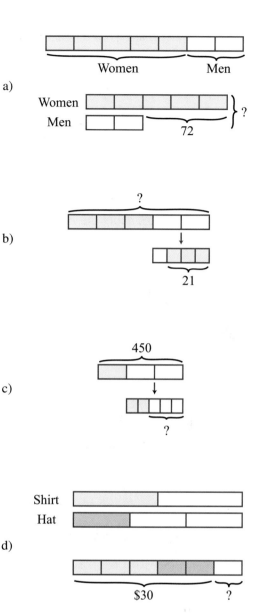

a)

b)

c)

d)

4. Make up a short word problem of the type specified.

   a) measurement division for $135 \div 5$.

   b) partitive division for $135 \div 5$.

   c) measurement division for $32 \div 3\frac{3}{4}$.

   d) partitive division for $72 \div \frac{3}{5}$.

   e) measurement division for $\frac{1}{2} \div \frac{1}{3}$.

   f) partitive division for $\frac{3}{5} \div 7$.

5. Give Teacher's Solutions for the following word problems.

   a) Alice spent $\frac{5}{11}$ of her money on a backpack. She had $42 left. How much was her backpack?

   b) Jenny made 56 candles. She sold $\frac{2}{7}$ of them and split the remaining candles evenly with her sister. How many candles did her sister get?

   c) A grocer received a shipment of 600 loaves of bread. He sold $\frac{1}{5}$ of the shipment on Monday and $\frac{1}{4}$ of shipment on Tuesday. How many loaves were left?

   d) Jerry had $240. He spent $\frac{5}{8}$ of it on a bike and $\frac{5}{6}$ of the remainder on a pair of inline skates. How much money did he have left?

   e) A pet shop sold $\frac{1}{4}$ of its puppies in the first week and $\frac{5}{6}$ of the remaining puppies in the second week. If the pet shop sold 28 puppies altogether in those two weeks, how many puppies did it start with?

   f) Julie used $\frac{4}{7}$ of a bag of flour to make 6 cupcakes and 30 cookies. With the rest of the flour she made 18 more cupcakes. What fraction of the flour did she use to make the cookies?

6. Make up a 2–step fraction word problem such that the bar diagram in the Teacher's Solution is the following.

7. Give Teacher's Solutions using algebra for the following word problems.

   a) 512 is $\frac{8}{9}$ of what number?

   b) In a chicken coop, $\frac{2}{7}$ of the chickens were roosters and the rest were hens. If there are 21 more hens than roosters in the coop, how many chickens are there altogether?

   c) Harold spent $\frac{1}{3}$ of his money on a T-shirt. He spent $\frac{3}{5}$ of the remainder on a pair of shorts. If he has $12 left, how much did the T-shirt cost?

8. Make up a short word problem of the type specified.

   a) partitive division for $\frac{3}{5} \div \frac{1}{3}$.

   b) partitive division for $21 \div \frac{7}{3}$.

6.6 Fractions as a Step Toward Algebra

In elementary school, fraction arithmetic is introduced using models and interpretations, as we have done in this chapter. That led to five fraction rules which completely describe how to add and subtract, multiply, and divide, and simplify fractions. Those rules, written below using letters, are the basis for all calculations done with fractions.

The next stage of teaching fractions involves building skill at fraction arithmetic. This requires a significant cognitive advance: the student moves to the more abstract level where one talks about the number $\frac{3}{4}$, rather than $\frac{3}{4}$ *of something*. This cognitive advance occurs naturally as students, in the course of doing hundreds of problems in grades 5–7, become comfortable doing increasingly complicated calculations with fractions. As we will see, such calculations are also essential preparation for algebra.

Review of:

all you need

Fraction Rules

Rule 1. $\dfrac{a}{b} = \dfrac{an}{bn}$ for all whole numbers $n \neq 0$.

Rule 2. $\dfrac{a}{b} \pm \dfrac{c}{b} = \dfrac{a \pm c}{b}$. After finding common denominators, this gives $\dfrac{a}{b} \pm \dfrac{c}{d} = \dfrac{ad \pm bc}{bd}$.

Rule 3. $a \div b = \dfrac{a}{b}$.

Rule 4. $\dfrac{a}{b} \cdot \dfrac{c}{d} = \dfrac{ac}{bd}$.

Rule 5. $\dfrac{a}{b} \div \dfrac{c}{b} = \dfrac{a}{c}$. After finding common denominators, this gives $\dfrac{a}{b} \div \dfrac{c}{d} = \dfrac{a}{b} \cdot \dfrac{d}{c}$.

This section describes two aspects of the development of fraction arithmetic. We start by describing the types of problems which help develop skill and understanding of fraction arithmetic. The rest of this section is "teacher level" mathematics which clarifies an important point: while fractions are introduced using models and word problems, *the arithmetic rules do not depend on models and interpretations.*

Before beginning, we make a comment on the above five rules. All five are evidently important. Rule 1 (equivalent fractions) and Rule 3 (how fractions arise from whole numbers) are aspects of the definition of fractions, and Rules 2, 4, and 5 show how fractions are added and subtracted, multiplied and divided. But why only these five rules? We could, after all, model additional rules, such as

$$\frac{a}{b} \cdot \frac{b}{a} = 1.$$

The answer is that there is no need: Rules 1–5 are *enough*. Once one understands Rules 1–5 and whole number arithmetic, all facts about fraction arithmetic follow automatically (we will give examples at the end of this section). The implication for teaching is that it is unnecessary to endlessly return to models.

Fraction arithmetic in the classroom. The development of fraction arithmetic in the classroom begins with simple problems such as

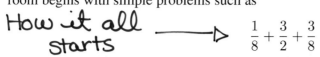

$$\frac{1}{8} + \frac{3}{2} + \frac{3}{8}$$

where using the arithmetic properties is helpful and natural (in this case, we can add in any order, and it is easiest to begin by adding $\frac{1}{8}$ and $\frac{3}{8}$). By grade 6 or 7 students have progressed to problems like the following.

EXERCISE 6.1. *a) Fill in the two missing fractions and the rule justifying the second step.*

$$\frac{1}{8} + \frac{3}{4}\left[\frac{1}{8} + \frac{1}{2}\right] = \frac{1}{8} + \left(\frac{3}{4} \cdot \frac{1}{8}\right) + \left(\frac{3}{4} \cdot \underline{}\right) \qquad \textit{Distributive property}$$

$$= \frac{1}{8} + \left(\frac{3}{32} + \frac{3}{8}\right) \qquad\qquad \underline{}$$

$$= \left(\frac{1}{8} + \frac{3}{8}\right) + \frac{3}{32} \qquad\qquad \textit{Any-order property}$$

$$= \underline{} + \frac{3}{32} \qquad\qquad\qquad \textit{Fraction addition rule}$$

$$= \frac{19}{32} \qquad\qquad\qquad\qquad \textit{Fraction addition rule.}$$

b) Simplify the same expression in an easier way, writing your solution in the same format.

Such calculations give students practice simplifying and manipulating numbers in exactly the ways that they will later be doing in algebra (see homework problems 1 and 2). In fact, problems like Exercise 6.1 have at least two features which can be used to help students prepare for algebra.

a) Such calculations can often be done in multiple ways. When students are given the opportunity to compare their approaches, they see that correct answers can be found in different ways, some easier than others.

b) Writing such calculations in detail calls attention to the principles at play. Students can be asked to write a calculation in detail, using a new line for each step, and to articulate their reasoning for each step.

Exercises of type b), done occasionally, emphasize that fraction arithmetic involves only the five rules and familiar arithmetic properties (those listed on page 96). Elementary students can explain these verbally, using phrases such as "We can add in either order" and "Multiplying by 1 does not change the number." Ultimately, the formal names of the properties should be learned before students start their first algebra course.

Fraction arithmetic — mathematics. Earlier, we asserted that the rules of fraction arithmetic do not depend on models and interpretations. In fact, from a logical viewpoint, one should start with fraction arithmetic, and then develop interpretations which illustrate it. The opposite order is used in elementary school for pedagogical reasons. But many curricula return to fractions in middle school and develop fraction arithmetic from scratch in a way that does not rely on interpretations. That is what we do next.

Start teaching Algebra Fract.

We start by assuming that we have a collection of numbers called "fractions." We also assume that there is

- *some* way to add and subtract fractions, and *some* way to multiply and divide fractions,
- addition and multiplication satisfy the Any-order, distributive, and identity properties, plus the following "multiplicative inverse property."

inverse of a fraction

Multiplicative Inverse Property. For each nonzero fraction x there is a unique fraction called the *inverse*, written $\frac{1}{x}$, which satisfies

$$x \cdot \frac{1}{x} = 1.$$

Starting with the whole numbers $1, 2, 3, 4, \ldots$ the multiplication inverse property tells us that there are fractions $\frac{1}{1}, \frac{1}{2}, \frac{1}{3}, \frac{1}{4}, \ldots$ (the "fractional units"). We then get all fractions by taking multiples of these fractional units. The following definition simultaneously defines fractions and explains the notation for fractions.

Demonstrate

DEFINITION 6.2. *Each fraction is a multiple of a fractional unit, specifically*

$$\frac{a}{b} = a \cdot \frac{1}{b}.$$

This is exactly how we defined a fraction at the beginning of this chapter — the denominator specifies a fractional unit and the numerator specifies how many of those units we have. As we will show in Theorem 6.4 below, these "bare-bones" assumptions are enough to figure out the formulas for adding and multiplying fractions, and to prove Rules 1–5. In fact, they completely determine fraction arithmetic (with no mention of models!).

Some immediate consequences of the Definition 6.2 and the arithmetic properties include

Slide

$$\frac{a}{a} = 1 \text{ for } a \neq 0 \qquad \frac{0}{a} = 0 \text{ for } a \neq 0, \qquad \text{and} \qquad \frac{a}{1} = a.$$

The last fact shows how every whole number can be thought of as a fraction (for instance, we can write 5 as $\frac{5}{1}$).

A less immediate consequence is the formula for multiplying fractional units. That formula was derived earlier (in Section 6.3) from an area model. But in fact it follows from the arithmetic properties alone, as follows.

LEMMA 6.3. *Assuming only the arithmetic properties, we have* $\dfrac{1}{a} \cdot \dfrac{1}{b} = \dfrac{1}{ab}$ *whenever a and b are nonzero.*

Proof. By the multiplicative inverse property, the number ab has an inverse $\dfrac{1}{ab}$. Then:

$$\frac{1}{a} \cdot \frac{1}{b} = \frac{1}{a} \cdot \frac{1}{b} \cdot 1 \qquad \text{Multiplicative identity property}$$

$$= \frac{1}{a} \cdot \frac{1}{b} \cdot (ab)\frac{1}{ab} \qquad \text{Multiplicative inverse property}$$

$$= \left(a \cdot \frac{1}{a}\right)\left(b \cdot \frac{1}{b}\right)\frac{1}{ab} \qquad \text{Any-order property}$$

$$= 1 \cdot 1 \cdot \frac{1}{ab} \qquad \text{Multiplicative inverse property}$$

$$= \frac{1}{ab} \qquad \text{Multiplicative identity property.} \qquad \square$$

THEOREM 6.4. *Rules 1–5 follow from the definition of fractions and the arithmetic properties.*

Proof. We will verify the rules one at a time. For some proofs you will be asked in your homework set to supply the reasoning for each equality as was done in Lemma 6.3.

Rule 1 (Equivalence of Fractions).

$$\frac{na}{nb} = na \cdot \frac{1}{nb} = na\left(\frac{1}{n} \cdot \frac{1}{b}\right) = \left(a \cdot \frac{1}{b}\right)\left(n \cdot \frac{1}{n}\right) = \frac{a}{b} \cdot 1 = \frac{a}{b}.$$

Rule 2 (Fraction Addition).

$$\frac{a}{b} + \frac{c}{b} = a \cdot \frac{1}{b} + c \cdot \frac{1}{b} = (a+c) \cdot \frac{1}{b} = \frac{a+c}{b}.$$

Thus the distributive property forces us to conclude that fractions must be added according to Rule 2. (The same reasoning shows Rule 2 for subtraction.)

Rule 3 (Fraction-Division Equivalence). By definition, $a \div b$ is the unknown number x which satisfies $a = b \cdot x$. Multiplying both sides of this equation by the inverse of b gives

$$a \cdot \frac{1}{b} = (b \cdot x)\frac{1}{b}$$

and applying the Any-order and multiplicative inverse property to the right hand side of the equation implies that x is $a \cdot \dfrac{1}{b}$, which is $\dfrac{a}{b}$ by Definition 6.2.

Rule 4 (Fraction Multiplication). You will prove this in your homework.

✳ **Rule 5 (Fraction Division).** By the definition of division, $\frac{a}{b} \div \frac{c}{d}$ is the number x which satisfies $\frac{a}{b} = \frac{c}{d} \cdot x$. To find x, multiply both sides of this equation by $\frac{d}{c}$:

$$\frac{a}{b} \cdot \frac{d}{c} = \left(\frac{c}{d} \cdot x\right) \cdot \frac{d}{c} \qquad \text{from above}$$

$$= \left(\frac{c}{d} \cdot \frac{d}{c}\right) \cdot x \qquad \text{Any-order property}$$

$$= \frac{cd}{cd} \cdot x \qquad \text{Rule 4 and the Any-order property}$$

$$= cd \cdot \frac{1}{cd} \cdot x \qquad \text{Definition of fractions (Def. 6.2)}$$

$$= 1 \cdot x \qquad \text{Multiplicative inverse property}$$

$$= x \qquad \text{Multiplicative identity property.}$$

Thus $x = \dfrac{a}{b} \cdot \dfrac{d}{c}$ as claimed.

□

A fraction whose numerator or denominator is itself a fraction is called a *complex fraction*. If you look back over this section, you will see that Rules 1–5 apply to complex fractions. Complex fractions can always be simplified using $\frac{a}{b} = a \div b$ — which holds when a and b are fractions — and the "invert and multiply" rule. For instance,

complex fraction

$$\frac{\frac{3}{5}}{\frac{7}{8}} = \frac{3}{5} \div \frac{7}{8} = \frac{3}{5} \cdot \frac{8}{7} = \frac{24}{35}.$$

Similarly, the fact that Rule 3 applies to fractions implies that the inverse of a fraction is its reciprocal:

$$\frac{1}{\frac{c}{d}} \underset{\text{Rule 3}}{=} 1 \div \frac{c}{d} \underset{\text{Rule 5}}{=} 1 \cdot \frac{d}{c} \underset{\text{Mult. Id.}}{=} \frac{d}{c},$$

Reciprocals are inverses

$$\implies \frac{1}{\frac{c}{d}} = \frac{d}{c}.$$

In this chapter we have covered fractions at two levels. We first introduced the idea of a fraction and used models and word problems to interpret addition, subtraction, multiplication, and division for fractions. Those interpretations led to rules for fraction arithmetic. Then, in this section, we started over (as is often done in middle school curricula), deriving the rules directly from the definition of fractions and the arithmetic properties. Along the way we saw two facts.

- The interpretations of addition, subtraction, multiplication, and division, originally learned for whole numbers, extend to fractions in a way that is consistent with the arithmetic properties.

- The arithmetic of fractions (which includes Rules 1–5) does not depend on models and interpretations — it is forced upon us by the definition of fractions and the arithmetic properties (Theorem 6.4).

Classroom teaching should respect this logic. Fraction arithmetic should not be presented as set of formulas handed down by a greater authority. Instead, concrete interpretations and models can be used to show how fraction arithmetic is natural and inevitable. Then, as soon as they are ready, students should begin computations which develop their skill and convince them fraction arithmetic is consistent with the interpretations and with whole number arithmetic. Instruction should be aimed at showing how fractions make sense!

Homework Set 29

1. *(Algebra preparation)* Simplify using fraction arithmetic as in Exercise 6.1. Be sure to give the reason for each equality by citing the rule or property used.

a) $\left(\left(\dfrac{2}{7}+\dfrac{2}{5}\right)\div\dfrac{1}{2}\right)\cdot\dfrac{5}{6}$

b) $\dfrac{3}{8}\left(\left(\dfrac{5}{6}-\dfrac{1}{2}\right)\cdot\dfrac{2}{5}\right)$

c) $\dfrac{4}{5}-2\left(\dfrac{3}{4}-\dfrac{2}{3}\right)$

d) $\left(\dfrac{5}{9}\div\dfrac{5}{6}\right)-\left(\dfrac{4}{5}\cdot\dfrac{3}{4}\right)$

2. *(Algebra preparation)* Do the computations, leaving your answer as a fraction in simplest form.

a) $\left(5+\dfrac{7}{9}\right)\cdot\dfrac{3}{4}\div 3$

b) $5-\left(\dfrac{1}{6}\div\left(\dfrac{1}{3}-\dfrac{1}{5}\right)\right)$

c) $4\div\left(\left(12\cdot\dfrac{2}{3}\right)\div\dfrac{7}{4}\right)$

d) $\left[\left(\dfrac{1}{4}\cdot\dfrac{3}{4}\right)+\left(\dfrac{2}{3}\div\dfrac{4}{3}\right)\right]\div\dfrac{11}{12}$

e) $x\left(\dfrac{y}{x}+z\right)-zx$

f) $y\left(x^2\div z\right)+z\div\dfrac{y}{3}$

3. Prove that $\dfrac{a}{a}=1$ for $a\neq 0$ using Definition 6.2 and the multiplicative inverse property.

4. Prove $b\cdot\dfrac{a}{b}=a$ for $b\neq 0$ using Definition 6.2 and arithmetic properties.

5. Kyle was unable to complete the problem he started:

$$\dfrac{20}{21}\times\dfrac{27}{5}\div\dfrac{18}{35}=\dfrac{20\times 27\times 35}{21\times 5\times 18}$$

a) What caused his difficulty?

b) Write a Teacher's Solution for Kyle's problem (begin by copying the problem, then write a succession of small, clear steps linked by equal signs).

6. Simplify the following complex fractions (use your Mental Math skills to make the calculations easier by factoring and cancelling).

a) $\dfrac{1}{\frac{13}{88}}$

b) $\dfrac{\frac{34}{40}}{17}$

c) $\dfrac{\frac{9}{16}}{\frac{3}{4}}$

d) $\dfrac{\frac{132}{256}}{\frac{11}{16}}$

e) $\dfrac{\frac{\frac{3}{2}}{\frac{5}{6}}}{\frac{7}{8}}$

f) $\dfrac{\frac{2^8\cdot 3^3\cdot 5^3}{6^3\cdot 4^3}}{\frac{10^2\cdot 6^2}{15^1\cdot 3^2 2^2}}$

g) $\dfrac{\frac{3}{4}+\frac{3}{8}}{\frac{3}{4}-\frac{3}{8}}$

h) $\dfrac{\frac{7}{4}+\frac{9}{5}}{71}$

i) $\dfrac{5\frac{1}{2}-2\frac{1}{3}+1\frac{5}{6}}{6\frac{3}{8}-2\frac{5}{6}-2\frac{1}{4}}$

j) $\dfrac{5\frac{8}{9}-\left(15\frac{13}{18}-12\frac{5}{6}\right)}{12\frac{5}{6}+\left(5\frac{8}{9}-9\frac{13}{18}\right)}$

7. Look back at the proof of Theorem 6.4 in this section.

    a) Give the reasons for each equality in the proof of Rule 1.

    b) Give the reasons for each equality in the proof of Rule 2.

8. Prove Rule 4 using the definition of fractions, Lemma 6.3, and the Any-order property.

9. *(Cross multiplication)*   Prove that if a, b, c, d are whole numbers with $b \neq 0$ and $d \neq 0$, then

$$\frac{a}{b} = \frac{c}{d} \iff ad = bc.$$

10. Why do arithmetic properties involve addition and multiplication only? The fraction rules show why we do not need additional properties for division — such rules would be redundant. For instance, the "distributive property for division,"

$$(a + b) \div c = (a \div c) + (b \div c),$$

follows from Rule 3 and the distributive property:

$$
\begin{aligned}
(a + b) \div c &= (a + b) \cdot \frac{1}{c} \\
&= a \cdot \frac{1}{c} + b \cdot \frac{1}{c} \\
&= \frac{a}{c} + \frac{b}{c} \\
&= (a \div c) + (b \div c).
\end{aligned}
$$

Show that the following "division properties" follow from Rules 1–5 and the arithmetic properties:

    a) $(a \div b) \div c = a \div (b \cdot c)$

    b) $a \div (b \div c) = (ac) \div b$

    c) $(a \div b) \cdot c = (ac) \div b.$

Notice that these properties, written in fraction notation, are ways to simplify complex fractions.

11.   a) Prove that $\dfrac{a}{b} \div \dfrac{c}{d} = \dfrac{a \div c}{b \div d}$ whenever b, c, and d are not zero.

    b) Use the rule you just proved to calculate $\dfrac{6}{25} \div \dfrac{3}{5}$.

    c) Now use it to calculate $\dfrac{3}{7} \div \dfrac{2}{3}$. Do you see that sometimes it is easier to use this rule, and other times it is not?

CHAPTER 7

Ratios, Percentages, and Rates

We deal with mathematical information every day, mostly in the form of ratios, percentages, and rates. What is the chance of rain today? What is the interest rate for a loan? What is the price of gasoline? What grade did you get on the last math test? How large a tip should you leave at a restaurant? We use ratios in cooking and chemistry, and to describe batting averages. Polling data, nutritional facts, and sale prices are expressed in percentages. We pay fixed rates for water, phone calls, electricity and taxes.

Ratios, percents, and rates are useful because they are intuitive. Of course, that intuition has to be *learned*. In this chapter we study how the Primary Mathematics curriculum cultivates this intuition through the use of bar diagrams and simple logic. We begin all three topics by asking, *"What is the unit of measurement?"*

7.1 Ratios and Proportions

quantity

Measurements make sense only when a unit is specified. One can say "the book weighs 5 pounds," but the statement "the book weighs 5" is meaningless until we are told which unit of weight has been used. Measurements yield *quantities* — numbers with units — such as 5 pounds, $2\frac{1}{3}$ cups, or 8.21 seconds.

Nevertheless, one can *compare* measurements without specifying a unit. For example, suppose Carla is twice as tall as her little brother. It does not matter whether their heights are measured in inches, centimeters, or pencil lengths. Twice as tall is twice as tall. Any unit can be used provided that *the same unit is used for both measurements*. That simple observation explains what ratios are and why they are useful.

> **SCHOOL DEFINITION 1.1.** *We say that the **ratio** between two quantities is $A : B$ if there is a unit so that the first quantity measures A units and the second measures B units. (In writing the ratio one does not specify the unit.)*

Determining a ratio is very easy: we simply make measurements using some unit and record the result, taking care to specify the order of the measurements, but deliberately leaving out all information about the unit of measurement. A beautiful introduction to this process is given on pages 71 − 74 of Primary Math 5A. Have a look!

EXAMPLE 1.2. *If orange juice is made by mixing 5 cans of water with 1 can of concentrate, then the water-to-concentrate ratio is* 5 : 1.

Notice that the ratio tells us nothing about the size of the can (which was the unit of measurement). Also notice the importance of specifying the order: while the water-to-concentrate ratio is 5 : 1, the concentrate-to-water ratio is 1 : 5. We would not want to confuse the two!

It is sometimes useful to consider ratios of three quantities.

EXAMPLE 1.3. *The crowd at a basketball game consisted of 400 men, 200 women, and 300 children. Thinking in units of 100 people, the ratio of men to women to children was* 4 : 2 : 3.

In any measurement we are free to choose the units. In the above example we took "100 people" as the unit. But we could equally well have taken the unit to be one person and said the ratio is 400 : 200 : 300. This second ratio describes exactly the same physical situation; each of the numbers is 100 times larger simply because we have switched the unit of measurement. That observation leads to the notion of equivalent ratios.

DEFINITION 1.4. *Two ratios are* **equivalent** *(are "equal ratios") if one is obtained from the other by multiplying or dividing all of the measurements by the same (nonzero) number.*

ratio in
simplest form

Thus the ratio 6 : 10 is equivalent to 18 : 30 (multiplying by 3) and also equivalent to 3 : 5 (dividing by 2). Of these, the ratio 3 : 5 is in "simplest form" because the numbers 3 and 5 have no common factor.

EXERCISE 1.5. *Read pages 71-76 of Primary Math 5A. These pages introduce ratios. Notice the rapid transition from concrete to pictorial to abstract.*

a) *On page 75, how are boxes used to illustrate how changing the size of the units creates an equivalent ratio?*

b) *On page 76, the idea of the simplest form is explained. The student helpers in the margins show how to find the simplest form of a ratio by dividing both numbers by* _____ .

The process of writing down a ratio cannot be reversed: knowing the ratio is not, by itself, enough to determine the actual measurements. The ratio gives only partial information.

The key to using ratios is seeing how to combine the ratio with other information *to determine a unit*. Once you know the unit, everything else follows.

EXAMPLE 1.6. *The ratio of boys to girls in the class is 5 : 3. There are 6 more boys than girls. How many students are there in the class?*

The ratio 5 : 3 was obtained by measuring using the same unit. To solve the problem we draw a diagram and determine that unit.

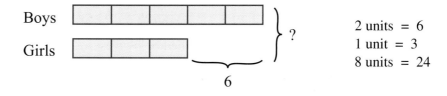

2 units = 6
1 unit = 3
8 units = 24

There are 24 children.

EXAMPLE 1.7. *The ratio of Jim's money to Peter's money was 4:7 at first. After Jim spent $\frac{1}{2}$ of his money and Peter spent \$60, Peter had twice as much money as Jim. How much money did Jim have at first?*

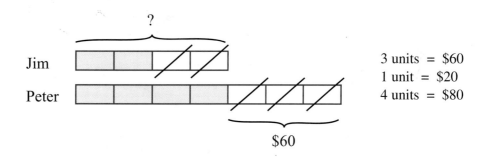

3 units = \$60
1 unit = \$20
4 units = \$80

Jim started with \$80.

Proportions

A blueprint of a house allows us to visualize the shape and relative size of the rooms. The blueprint is a scale drawing — the measurements in the blueprint are in a fixed ratio to the actual measurements. Knowing that ratio, we can use the blueprint to determine the size of each room.

scale

For example, if an inch on the blueprint corresponds to 60 actual inches, we say the *scale* is the ratio 1 : 60. If a wall is 2 inches long on the blueprint, the length of the actual wall (in inches) is found by solving the problem

$$1 : 60 = 2 : \underline{\qquad}.$$

Such an equation is called a proportion.

DEFINITION 1.8. *A proportion is a statement that two ratios are equal.*

EXAMPLE 1.9. *The ratio of girls to boys in a class is 4:5. If there are 12 girls in the class, how many boys are there?*

This question can be written as

$$4 : 5 = 12 : \underline{\quad}.$$

Recall what it means for these ratios to be equal: there is some number which when multiplied by 4 gives 12 and when multiplied by 5 gives ___. To get from 4 to 12 we multiply by 3, so the unknown number is $5 \times 3 = 15$. There are 15 boys in the class.

EXERCISE 1.10. *The ratio of Isabel's money to Rosalind's money is* $8 : 3$*. If Isabel has $24, how much money do the two girls have together?*

Here are three different Teacher's Solutions to Exercise 1.10.

- *Using proportions.* If Rosalind has R dollars, then the statement of the problem implies $8 : 3 = 24 : R$. As you will show in Homework Problem 6, the proportion $8 : 3 = 24 : R$ is equivalent to

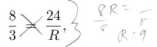

$$\frac{8}{3} \times \frac{24}{R},$$

or $8R = 3 \times 24$. Solving shows that Rosalind has $R = 9$ dollars, so Isabel and Rosalind together have $24 + $9 = 33.

- *Using a bar diagram.*

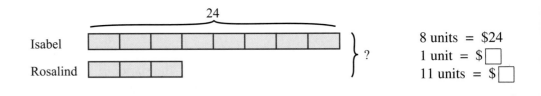

They have $\square$ altogether.

- *Using algebra.* The bar diagram also shows how to solve the problem using algebra. Let x stand for the amount of money in 1 unit in the bar diagram above. Then Isabel has $8x$ dollars and Rosalind has $3x$ dollars. The solution using algebra then goes as follows.

Solution: By the definition of ratio, there is a number x so that Isabel's money is $8x$ and Rosalind's money is $3x$. Hence

$$
\begin{aligned}
8x &= 24 \\
x &= 3 \\
\text{Total: } 11x &= 11 \cdot 3 = 33
\end{aligned}
$$

They have $33 altogether.

Thus far, bar diagrams have been our main tool for solving word problems. Yet two of the three solutions above use prealgebra methods. In fact, after using bar diagrams to familiarize students with the idea of ratios, the Primary Mathematics curriculum moves on to an algebraic approach to ratios in 7th grade. There are two reasons for this shift. First, the topic of ratios occurs at that point in the curriculum (the end of elementary school) where the mathematical content switches from an emphasis on arithmetic to an emphasis on algebra. Second, bar diagrams are not always the best approach for solving ratio problems, as the following example shows.

EXAMPLE 1.11. *Two numbers are in the ratio 3:5. After subtracting 11 from each, the new ratio is 2:7. What are the two numbers?*

This problem appears to be simple. But you will have trouble creating a bar diagram for it (try!). An algebraic solution is easier.

Teacher's Solution using algebra:

Since the ratio is $3:5$, there is a number x such that first number is $3x$ and the second is $5x$. After subtracting 11, the ratio becomes $(3x-11):(5x-11)$. Since that is equal to $2:7$, we get the proportion

$$\frac{3x-11}{5x-11} = \frac{2}{7}.$$

Now solve:

$$21x - 77 = 10x - 22,$$
$$11x = 55,$$
$$x = 5.$$

The first number is $3x = 15$ and the second is $5x = 25$.

Ratios and fractions

Ratios are not numbers — one cannot add, subtract, multiply or divide ratios. For instance, how would you multiply the following? Is there even a plausible interpretation for doing so?

$$(3:2:7) \times (8:4:5) = ?$$

Nevertheless, ratios can often be usefully converted into fractions *if one is careful to specify the whole unit*. In any given situation that can be done in several ways.

EXERCISE 1.12. *Read Problem 6 on page 24 of Primary Math 6A. In that problem the ratio $2:5$ is converted into four different fractions depending upon the choice of a whole unit. Observe:*

- *In part c) the ratio $2:5$ is converted into the fraction statement "The length of A is $\frac{2}{7}$ of the total length." The whole unit is the total length.*

- *In part e) the ratio $2:5$ is converted into the fraction statement "The length of A is $\frac{2}{5}$ of the length of B." The whole unit is the length of B.*

- *In part f), what choice of whole unit leads to the fraction $\frac{5}{2}$?*

It is also sometimes useful to regard fractions as ratios.

EXERCISE 1.13. *Read and answer Problem 12 on page 26 of Primary Math 6A.*

Regarding ratios as numbers can lead to trouble, as the following example shows.

EXAMPLE 1.14. *A bag contains 6 white and 10 red marbles. Then 4 white marbles and 20 red marbles are added to the bag. What is the new ratio of white to red marbles?*

Diana, Kevin, and Mary came up with the following different solutions.

- Diana reasoned that the initial ratio was 6 : 10, or 3 : 5, and the added marbles had a ratio of 4 : 20 or 1 : 5. She then "added ratios," writing

$$3 : 5 + 1 : 5 = 4 : 10.$$

  After simplifying, she concluded that the new ratio was 2 : 5.

- Kevin converted the information "6 white and 10 red marbles" to the fraction $\frac{6}{10} = \frac{3}{5}$ and the information "4 white and 20 red marbles" to the fraction $\frac{4}{20} = \frac{1}{5}$. He then wrote

$$\frac{3}{5} + \frac{1}{5} = \frac{4}{5}$$

  and concluded that the new ratio was 4 : 5.

- Mary simply counted marbles: in the end there were $6 + 4 = 10$ white and $10 + 20 = 30$ red marbles, so the new ratio was 10 : 30 or 1 : 3.

Who is right? And what did the other two do incorrectly? (See Homework Problem 7.)

Homework Set 30

1. (*Study the textbook!*)   Read pages $71 - 78$ of Primary Math 5A, doing the problems mentally as you read. In Practice 5A, answer Problems $1 - 4$ and give Teacher's Solutions for Problems $5 - 7$.

2. (*Study the textbook!*)   Read pages $79 - 81$ of Primary Math 5A, doing the problems mentally as you read. In Practice 5B, answer Problems $4 - 7$ and give Teacher's Solutions for Problems 8 and 9.

3. Draw a picture illustrating why the ratios 12:16, 6:8 and 3:4 are equal (see page 75 of Primary Math 5A).

4. In **Workbook 5A**, read and answer problems on pages $82 - 90$ by filling in the answers in the workbook (do not copy onto your homework paper).

5. (*Study the textbook!*)   Read pages $21 - 33$ of Primary Math 6A, doing the problems mentally as you read. Give

Teacher's Solutions for Problems $6 - 8$ of Practice 3A and Problems $6 - 9$ of Practice 3B.

6. If $a : b = c : d$, prove that a) $\dfrac{a}{b} = \dfrac{c}{d}$ and b) $ad = bc$.

   Hint: By Definition 1.4, if the ratios $a : b$ and $c : d$ are equivalent then there is a (nonzero) number x so that $a = cx$ and $b = dx$.

7. Reread the three student solutions in Example 1.14 above. Who is right, and what did the other two do incorrectly? (*Hint:* it will help to be very clear about units. Diana's ratio 3 : 5 is a count using what unit? Her ratio 1 : 5 is a count using what unit? Kevin's $\frac{3}{5}$ means $\frac{3}{5}$ of what unit?)

8. A class is presented with the following problem.

In a bag of marbles, the ratio of white marbles to red marbles is 2 : 3 and the ratio of red to black marbles is 6 : 11. What is the ratio of white to black marbles?

Conner, who likes using fractions, writes $\frac{2}{3} \times \frac{6}{11} = \frac{4}{11}$ and announces, without explanation, that the ratio of white to black marbles is 4 : 11. Explain why he is right. (*Hint:* taking the number of black marbles to be the whole unit, what fraction are red, and then what fraction are white?)

7.2 Changing Ratios and Percentages

We begin this section by considering problems involving changing ratios. We then start the next topic: percentage. Bar diagrams are valuable aids for both types of problems.

In a "changing ratio" problem one is presented with a before-and-after situation. The problem is to relate the measurements and ratios before the change to measurements and ratios after the change. Such problems can be illustrated by drawing separate before and after bar diagrams.

EXAMPLE 2.1. *The ratio of the number of Jason's marbles to Tom's is 3 : 5. Jason has 42 marbles. If Jason buys another 8 marbles, what will be the new ratio of Jason's marbles to Tom's?*

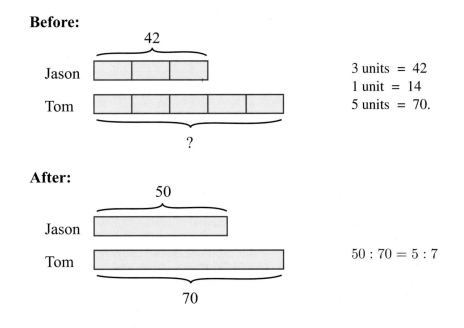

Before:

42

Jason

Tom

?

3 units = 42
1 unit = 14
5 units = 70.

After:

50

Jason

Tom

70

50 : 70 = 5 : 7

The new ratio of Jason's marbles to Tom's is 5:7.

EXERCISE 2.2. *Before proceeding, read pages 34–37 of Primary Math 6A, noting how the bar diagram is constructed in each example.*

In the next problem it becomes important to record the amount removed. This helps to determine the unit, which is the key to solving the problem.

EXAMPLE 2.3. *Jill had the same amount of money as Karen. After Jill spent $34 and Karen spent $16, the ratio of Jill's money to Karen's is 1 : 4. How much money did each girl have at first?*

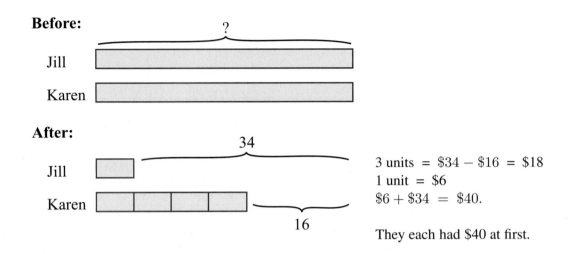

3 units = $34 − $16 = $18
1 unit = $6
$6 + $34 = $40.

They each had $40 at first.

EXAMPLE 2.4. *Sam has $\frac{3}{7}$ as many stamps as Lisa. If Sam gives $\frac{1}{6}$ of his stamps to Lisa, what will be the ratio of the number of Sam's stamps to Lisa's?*

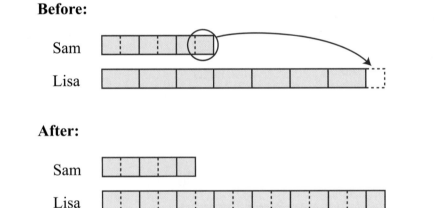

The ratio of Sam's stamps to Lisa's is 5 : 15 or 1 : 3.

Percentage

A percent is a specific type of fraction— one whose denominator is 100. One percent (written 1%) is the same as the fraction $\frac{1}{100}$. We can therefore move between fractions, percents, and decimals simply by multiplying or dividing by 100:

$$\frac{27}{100} = 27\% = 0.27.$$

percent

To speak of a percentage, we choose a whole unit, divide it into 100 equal parts, and count the parts. (The word percent comes from the Latin phrase *per centum*, which means "out of a hundred"). That can be visualized by drawing a "percent ruler."

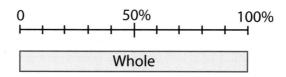

Percents are an especially useful and intuitive way of speaking about parts of a whole. They are used often: grades, sports statistics, interest rates, and survey results are just a few things that are reported as percentages.

Since percents are a special type of fraction, the idea is readily understood by students *who already understand fractions*. The introduction to percents on pages 47–52 of Primary Math 6A shows one path a classroom teacher might follow. Take a look, noticing the various ways percents are represented and how percents are linked to fractions.

Once students understand the basic idea of percents, there are many interesting real-world problems to challenge them. Thus the rest of this section and all of the next section is devoted to word problems involving percents. As you will see, word problems develop practical skills.

One quantity as a percentage of another. Working with percents is easy once one learns *to identify the whole unit*, that is, the quantity corresponding to 100%. But this can be tricky! In fact, identifying the whole unit is a major difficulty for many students; it is a skill that must be specifically developed.

The key to identifying the whole unit in word problems is to become attuned to the following common English phrases.

Phrase	Whole Unit (100%)
1. "Jeremy has 20 sticks of bubble gum. 30% **of the sticks** are ..."	20 sticks
2. "Carla's saving is 125% **of Adam's savings**."	Adam's money
3. "Carla's saving is 25% more **than Adam's**."	Adam's money
4. "How many percent fewer boys **than girls** ..."	Number of girls
5. "The **number of tickets** was increased by 20% ..."	Number of tickets before the increase

EXERCISE 2.5. *Read problems 3-10 on page 60 of Primary Math 6A. Identify the whole unit for each problem. (For instance, in Problem 3 the whole unit is the length of B).*

To see how the whole unit enters a bar diagram, think about drawing the bar diagram for the phrase "Carla's saving is 125% of Adam's savings" (the second phrase in the above chart). Since Adam's money is the whole unit, we draw a bar representing his money and label it *Adam* (short for "Adam's money"). We then draw a "percent ruler" to show that Adam's money corresponds to 100%.

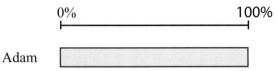

Carla's saving is 125% of Adam's savings. After extending the ruler to show 125%, we can draw another bar to represent Carla's money.

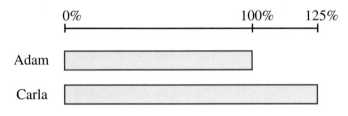

That's it! Note that this bar diagram also illustrates the third phrase, showing that the second phrase and third phrase have the same meaning. As you read the following problem, think about the order in which you would construct the bar diagram.

EXAMPLE 2.6. *David saves $600 and Justin saves $720. Express Justin's savings as a percentage of David's.*

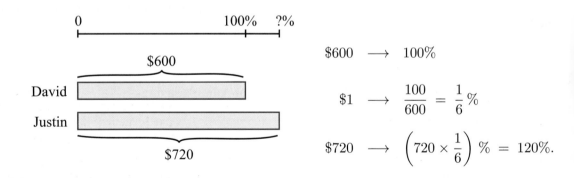

Justin's savings is 120% of David's.

Notice how the logic proceeds once the diagram is drawn. The first line of the solution can be read directly off the diagram: "$600 corresponds to 100%." This is written $600 \longrightarrow 100\%$ where the direction of the arrow indicates that, in this problem, we are converting dollars into percents. We can also get part of the last line from the question: we want to know what percent corresponds to $720, so we can write "$720 \longrightarrow$ ____ %" in the third line.

Now notice that we can get from $600 to $720 by dividing by 600 and then multiplying by 720. Doing the same with the percentages solves the problem.

EXERCISE 2.7. *A baker made 350 cookies. 100 of them were chocolate chip and the rest were sugar cookies. How many percent fewer chocolate chip cookies were there than sugar cookies?*

The whole unit in this problem is the number of sugar cookies. Fill in the blanks in the solution below. As you do so, think about the order in which you would construct the diagram and what explanations you might use to guide students through this solution.

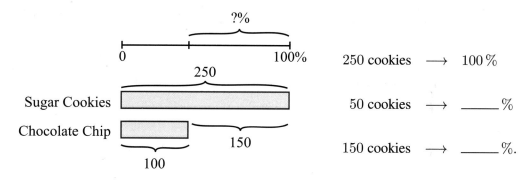

$$250 \text{ cookies} \longrightarrow 100\,\%$$

$$50 \text{ cookies} \longrightarrow \underline{\quad}\%$$

$$150 \text{ cookies} \longrightarrow \underline{\quad}\%.$$

There are ___ % fewer chocolate chip cookies than sugar cookies.

Notice the shortcut we took in the solution. To get from 250 cookies to 150 cookies we could have divided by 250 and then multiplied by 150 (following the method of Example 2.6). But since 50 is a common factor of 250 and 150, it is easier divide by 5 and then multiply by 3. Look for such shortcuts as you do your homework.

34 problems

Homework Set 31

1. *(Study the textbook!)* Read pages 34 − 38 of Primary Math 6A doing the problems mentally as you read. Give Teacher's Solutions for problems 1, 2, 4, 6, 7, 8 in Practice 3C.

2. Give Teacher's Solutions for Problems 26 − 29 of Review A in Primary Math 6A.

3. Give Teacher's Solutions for Problems 26 − 31 of Review B in Primary Math 6A.

4. Give a Teacher's Solution *using algebra* for the problem solved in Example 2.3 of this section. *Hint:* For a) Let x be the number of dollars each had at first (so x corresponds to the '?' in the bar diagram).

5. Give a Teacher's Solution using algebra for the problem solved in Example 2.4 of this section.

6. Give a Teacher's Solution *using algebra* for the following problem: A truck contains 1000 pounds of sand and concrete in the ratio 2 : 3. After x pounds of sand is added, the ratio of the sand and concrete becomes 4 : 5. Find x.

7. *(Study the textbook!)* Read pages 47–52 of Primary Math 6A, doing the problems mentally as you read. Answer all problems in Practice 4A. For Problems 6 − 10, also state what the 'whole unit' is in the problem.

8. *(Study the textbook!)* Read pages 55–59 of Primary Math 6A. Then answer all problems in Practice 4C. For Problems 5 − 10, state what the 'whole unit' is and give Teacher's Solutions to Problems 9 and 10.

7.3 Solving Percent Problems by the Unitary Method

In this section we continue looking at percentage problems. The examples will illustrate how to solve percentage problems using the so-called "unitary method." Along the way we will explore a few common fallacies about percents, including some that are exploited in advertisements.

unitary method

Recall that percentages specify parts of a whole. We are often given information about the part and want to determine the size of the whole, or of some other part. The *unitary method* is an approach to solving such problems. It simply says: find the whole unit (what corresponds to 100%). With that information, you can answer many questions.

This simple idea is very powerful! To illustrate its use, consider the following problem involving a sale price.

EXAMPLE 3.1. *The price of a shirt was marked down 35% to $26. What was the original price?*

In this situation, the whole unit is the original price of the shirt. A 35% reduction means the new price is 65% of the original. We can illustrate this using a comparison diagram.

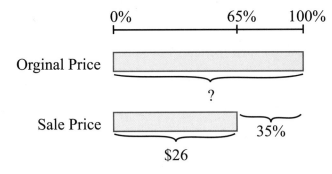

We must convert percents to dollars, so we begin by writing the given information as "65% ⟶ $26" and the question as "100% ⟶ $?" Then notice that 65% and 100% are both multiples of 5%, and we can get from one to the other by dividing by 13 and multiplying by 20:

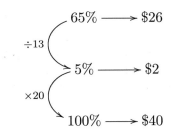

Thus the original price of the shirt was $40.

EXERCISE 3.2. *a) Draw a simpler version of the above diagram which has only one bar. Observe that your diagram asks the partitive question "$26 is 65% of what?"*

b) Rewrite 65% as 65/100 and solve the problem by division of fractions.

The next several problems point out some common confusions about percents. We will solve each one using the unitary method.

One common fallacy is that equal percents mean equal amounts. You can use that principle to immediately guess an answer to the following problem. Compare your guess to the result of the actual computations.

EXAMPLE 3.3. *A salesman sold 2 refrigerators for $600 each. The first was sold at a 25% profit while the second was sold at a 25% loss. Find his net profit or loss.*

a) Profit on the first refrigerator.

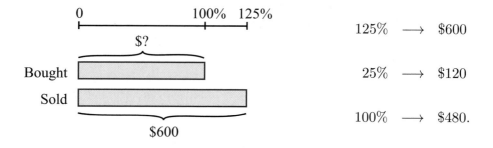

The profit was $120 on the first refrigerator.

b) Loss on the second refrigerator.

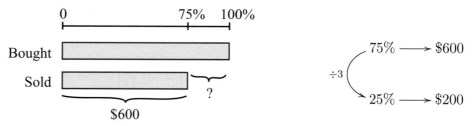

The salesman lost $200 on the second refrigerator.

c) The salesman had a net loss of $200 − $120 = $80.

There is a lesson to be learned from Example 3.3: *equal percents do not necessarily mean equal amounts!* The meaning of a percent, like that of a fraction, depends on the whole unit. In Example 3.3, the whole unit for the profit (the cost of the first refrigerator) is different than the whole unit for the loss (the cost of the second refrigerator), and consequently the 25% profit and the 25% loss represent different dollar amounts.

Here is a situation that you can undoubtedly identify with. You enter a store and see a sticker announcing an additional 10% off a sweater which is already marked down 20%. Does that mean you will get 30% off the original price?

EXAMPLE 3.4. *A $40 sweater was reduced 20% in a sale. Later the sales price was reduced 10%. What was the price then?*

This problem is simple enough to do without a bar diagram. The initial sale price of the shirt was 80% of $40, which is

$$\$40 \times \frac{80}{100} = \frac{\$4 \times 8 \times 100}{100} = \$32.$$

Taking 10% off that sale price makes the final price

$$\$32 \times \frac{90}{100} = \frac{\$32 \times 9}{10} = \$28.80.$$

Thus the final cost of the shirt was $28.80.

On the other hand, a 30% reduction for the original price of the shirt would make the cost

$$\$40 \times \frac{70}{100} = \frac{\$4 \times 7 \times 100}{100} = \$28,$$

which is less than the price the store is charging. The lesson to be learned from this example is that *percent reductions do not add*. A percent reduction off of a previous reduction is not quite as good a deal as it sounds!

EXERCISE 3.5. *If a price is reduced by 20%, and then the sale price is reduced by 30%, what percent is the overall reduction?*

Here is a similar phenomenon. If the price of a $100 stereo is increased by 10%, then reduced by 10%, *it does not return to the original price*:

$$\$100 \xrightarrow{\text{10\% increase}} \$110 \xrightarrow{\text{10\% reduction}} \$99.$$

Again, the point is that the whole unit for the increase is different from the whole unit for the reduction.

Our final example concerns the common fallacy that a doubling is a 200% increase.

EXAMPLE 3.6. *The value of an $18 stock rises by 200%. What is its value then?*

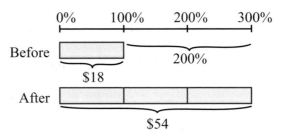

The stock rose to $54. An increase of 200% does not mean that the price doubled — a 200% increase is a *tripling*.

Homework Set 32

1. In Primary Math 6A, answer Problems 1 − 4 of Practice 4B. Then give Teacher's Solutions for Problems 5 − 10 of Practice 4B.

2. Give a Teacher's Solution with algebra for the problem of Example 3.1.

3. *(Study the textbook!)* Read pages 61 − 66 of Primary Math 6A, doing the problems mentally as you read. Then answer problems 7–10 in Practice 4D, identifying the whole unit and giving a Teacher's Solution for each.

4. a) Write your solution to Exercise 3.5 in this section.

   b) Give similar solutions to Problems 1, 4, 5, and 6 in Practice 4D of Primary Math 6A.

5. Give clear solutions to each of the problems in Practice 4E in Primary Math 6A. There is no need to include a di-agram with each, but each solution should include a few words of explanation to make the reasoning clear. (Problem 6 is tricky; the answer is not 20%).

6. Consider the following problem:

   In the spring Woody Woodchuck lost 25% of his weight. Then he gained 20% in the summer and lost 10% in the fall. In the winter he again gained 20%. Did he lose or gain weight that year?

   a) Give a clearly written solution starting with "Using a unit of weight so that Woody's initial weight is 100 units, …"

   b) Give a clearly written solution starting with "If Woody initially weighed x lbs, then …"

7.4 Rates, Speed, and Arithmetic with Units

We can compare two quantities measured with the same unit by dividing to find the ratio. We can also compare quantities measured with different units by dividing; the quotient is then called a *rate*. The procedure is the same, but for rates it is essential to specify the units used.

> **DEFINITION 4.1.** *A rate is the quotient of two quantities with different specified units.*

The most familiar example is speed. To calculate speed we choose a unit of distance, say miles, and a unit of time, say hours. We then watch a moving object, record how far it goes and how long it takes, and divide. That yields a measurement of speed such as

$$60 \, \frac{\text{miles}}{\text{hour}}.$$

The same procedure is used in many contexts.

EXAMPLE 4.2. *If Jodi earned $72 in 8 hours, at what rate was she earning money?*

Dividing both numbers and units, we get

$$\text{rate: } \frac{72 \text{ dollars}}{8 \text{ hours}} = 9 \frac{\text{dollars}}{\text{hour}},$$

so she was earning $9 per hour.

EXAMPLE 4.3. *A jug which holds 1.8 liters can be filled from a faucet in 12 seconds. At what rate does the water flow from the faucet?*

Dividing, we get

$$\frac{1.8 \text{ liters}}{12 \text{ seconds}} = 0.15 \frac{\text{liters}}{\text{second}},$$

so the water is flowing from the faucet at 0.15 liters per second.

Note that both the numbers and the units are divided. The answer — the rate — is not just a number, it is a number with a specified unit. In fact, because we divide, we end up forming a new unit equal to the unit of the first measurement divided by the unit of the second measurement. Such quotients of units are read aloud using the word 'per.'

EXAMPLE 4.4. *A cookie recipe makes 30 cookies and requires 2 eggs. Find the rate of eggs per cookie.*

Dividing, we get

$$\frac{1}{15} \frac{\text{egg}}{\text{cookie}},$$

so the recipe uses eggs at a rate of $\frac{1}{15}$ egg per cookie.

It might seem strange to use the word 'rate' in this context. But that is a useful way of thinking if one wants to scale the recipe to find, for example, how many eggs are needed to make 150 cookies.

Rates can be multiplied and divided — one multiplies and divides both the numbers and the units. One of the most useful applications of this idea is *unit conversion*, in which one converts a measurement expressed in one unit to a different unit by multiplying by a "conversion rate".

- To convert 38 dollars to yen, multiply by the exchange rate 120 yen per dollar:

$$38 \text{ dollars } \times 120 \frac{\text{yen}}{\text{dollar}} = (38 \times 120) \text{ dollars} \times \frac{\text{yen}}{\text{dollar}} = 4560 \text{ yen}.$$

- To convert 17 inches to centimeters, use the rate 2.54 cm per inch:

$$17 \text{ inches } \times 2.54 \frac{\text{cm}}{\text{inch}} = (17 \times 2.54) \text{ inches } \times \frac{\text{cm}}{\text{inch}} \approx 43 \text{ cm}.$$

Notice how neatly the units cancel! In the first calculation, dollars in the numerator cancelled with dollars in the denominator, leaving the correct unit (yen) for the answer. In the second example, inches in the numerator similarly cancelled with inches in the denominator.

In calculations with rates, there is often confusion about whether one should be multiplying or dividing. But if one includes units in each step of a rate calculation and looks for cancellations, the units serve as guides and checks on the calculation. In that sense *units are your friends*.

EXAMPLE 4.5. *54 miles per hour is how many meters per second? (A mile is about 1600 meters)*

Write down the rate and substitute 1 mile $\approx$ 1600 m and 1 hour = 60 minutes = 3600 seconds:

$$54 \, \frac{\text{miles}}{\text{hour}} \approx 54 \times \frac{1600 \text{ m}}{3600 \text{ sec}} = 54 \times \frac{4}{9} \, \frac{\text{m}}{\text{sec}} = 24 \, \frac{\text{m}}{\text{sec}}.$$

For problems involving adding and subtracting rates, the units again tell us what to do.

EXAMPLE 4.6. *Linus takes 6 hours to mow his neighbor's lawn with a self-propelled mower, while it takes Charlie only 3 hours with a tractor mower. If Linus and Charlie work together, how long will it take to mow the lawn?*

Linus's Rate: $\dfrac{1}{6} \, \dfrac{\text{lawns}}{\text{hour}}$,

Charlie's Rate: $\dfrac{1}{3} \, \dfrac{\text{lawns}}{\text{hour}}$.

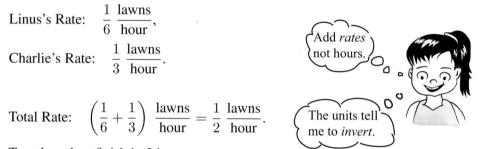

Total Rate: $\left(\dfrac{1}{6} + \dfrac{1}{3}\right) \dfrac{\text{lawns}}{\text{hour}} = \dfrac{1}{2} \, \dfrac{\text{lawns}}{\text{hour}}$.

Together, they finish in 2 hours.

As the girl observes, the last step is very easy if one pays attention to the units. The total rate is expressed in lawns per hour, while the question asks how many hours per lawn. All we have to do is invert: $\frac{1}{2} \, \frac{\text{lawns}}{\text{hour}}$ becomes $2 \, \frac{\text{hours}}{\text{lawn}}$, so the whole lawn takes 2 hours to mow.

We conclude with a more challenging multi-step problem of the same type.

EXAMPLE 4.7.

a) *Larry, Moe, and Curley can finish a job in $7\frac{1}{2}$, 6, and 10 hours respectively. If they work together, how long will it take for them to complete the job?*

b) *After they have worked for 1 hour, Curley gets hit on the head and has to go to the hospital. How long would it take Larry and Moe to complete the work?*

To solve a), note that Larry works at a rate of $\frac{15}{2}$ hours per job, so does $\frac{2}{15}$ jobs per hour. Similarly, Moe does $\frac{1}{6}$ and Curley does $\frac{1}{10}$ jobs per hour. Together, the three stooges do

$$\left(\frac{2}{15} + \frac{1}{6} + \frac{1}{10}\right) \frac{\text{jobs}}{\text{hour}} = \frac{8 + 10 + 6}{60} \, \frac{\text{jobs}}{\text{hour}} = \frac{2}{5} \, \frac{\text{jobs}}{\text{hour}}.$$

After inverting, that becomes $\frac{5}{2}$ hours per job, so the job takes $2\frac{1}{2}$ hours.

To solve b), note that they have worked for 1 hour at the rate found in part a) and have finished $\frac{2}{5}$ of the job, so $\frac{3}{5}$ of the job remains. Larry and Moe work at a combined rate of

$$\left(\frac{1}{6} + \frac{1}{10}\right) \frac{\text{jobs}}{\text{hour}} = \frac{8}{30} \frac{\text{jobs}}{\text{hour}} = \frac{4}{15} \frac{\text{jobs}}{\text{hour}},$$

or $\frac{15}{4}$ hours per job. They can therefore complete the work in

$$\frac{15}{4} \frac{\text{hours}}{\text{job}} \times \frac{3}{5} \text{ job} = \frac{9}{4} \text{ hours} = 2\frac{1}{4} \text{ hours}.$$

Homework Set 33

1. **(Do this problem only if you have Primary Math 5B)** Read pages 44–50 of Primary Math 5B calculating each problem mentally as you read. Give Teacher Solution's for the problems in Practice 4A.

2. Read pages 74–80 of Primary Math 6A, doing each problem mentally as you read. Answer all problems in Practice 5A.

3. Answer all problems in Practice 5B of Primary Math 6A.

4. Water flows from a hose at a rate of 1.9 liters per second. How many gallons per minute is that? (1 gal ≈ 3.8 ℓ).

5. Water evaporates from a pond at a rate of 0.3 liters per square meter per day. If the pond has a surface area of 6000 square meters, how much water evaporates per week?

6. A car travels from City A to City B at an average speed of 60 mph. The car returns via the same route at an average speed of 40 mph. The average speed of the car for the entire trip is:
   a) 52 mph   b) 50 mph
   c) 48 mph   d) Cannot be determined.

7. One hose can fill a swimming pool in 30 hours, while the other hose fills the swimming pool in 70 hours. How long would it take to fill up the swimming pool using both hoses together?

8. It takes one corn mill 6 minutes to grind a 50 pound bag of corn into cornmeal, while it takes a slower mill 9 minutes to grind a bag of corn. If both mills are working at the same time, how long would it take to grind 1500 pounds of corn?

9. A machine shop polishes small metal parts using three polishing machines. Machine A and Machine B, working together, take $1\frac{1}{2}$ hours to polish a ton of parts. Machine A and Machine C take 1 hour to polish a ton of parts, while Machine B and Machine C require only $\frac{3}{4}$ hour to polish a ton of parts. Find each machine's working rate in tons per hour.

   Hint: Start by defining Machine A's rate to be a ton/hour, Machine B's rate to be b ton/hour, and Machine C's rate to be c ton/hour. Then find a, b, and c.

10. Look through the problems in Review D of Primary Math 6A (pages 83-86). Like all Reviews in the Primary Math books, this is designed to evaluate and consolidate learning. Try part of it yourself. First answer the question: what division is asked for in Problem 10? Then solve Problems $20 - 37$.

CHAPTER 8

Negative Numbers and Integers

Historically, negative numbers entered mathematics only after the invention of algebra. Arabic scholars, who invented algebra in the middle ages, would encounter problems like $4 + x = 1$, but label these "absurd" since they have no whole number or fractional solution. Later, around 1300 A.D, it was realized that it is useful to rewrite this equation as $x = 1 - 4 = -3$ and accept -3 as a number. Mathematicians began using negative numbers routinely and discovered that algebra became more consistent, more powerful, and simpler.

That's right — negative numbers make algebra *simpler*. In fact, algebra would be a mess without negative numbers! Here's why. In algebra we often encounter expressions like $(7 - x) + 3$, which we simplify to $10 - x$. But if we don't allow negative numbers, we can't make this simplification when $x > 7$ (because then $7 - x$, being less than zero, is "absurd"). We would have to separate the two cases, as the early Arabs did, and write

$$(7 - x) + 3 \text{ is equal to } 10 - x \text{ when } x \leq 7, \text{ but is absurd when } x > 7.$$

More complicated expressions lead to three, four, or more cases. Attempts at simplification result in a proliferation of cases!

Remarkably, these difficulties disappear when one allows negative numbers. One simply applies the usual rules of arithmetic and everything works neatly. We can apply the Any-Order Property to rewrite $(7 - x) + 3$ as $(7 + 3) - x = 10 - x$ *without any thought about the value of* x. That makes algebra enormously easier, and more than makes up for whatever discomfort we might feel adjusting to the idea of using negative numbers.

For these reasons the arithmetic of negative numbers enters most curricula at the same time as algebra, and the two are developed together. Of course, the goal of teaching is to "keep things simple." That requires preliminary instruction, separate from algebra, on the arithmetic of negative numbers with the aim of making students comfortable and familiar with negative numbers. The key is to build on the students' knowledge of arithmetic and to make clear that the arithmetic of negative numbers is a minor extension of what they already know.

The first two sections of this chapter describe some simple ways of introducing arithmetic with negative numbers. The last section brings in the connection with algebra by showing how the rules for negative number arithmetic are consequences of the Any-order, distributive, and additive identity properties.

8.1 Negative Numbers

Negative numbers are most simply introduced by extending the number line.

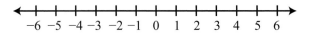

DEFINITION 1.1. *The **integers** are the numbers*

$$\ldots, -3, -2, -1, 0, 1, 2, 3, \ldots.$$

*The numbers greater than zero are called **positive** and those less than zero are called **negative**.*

The notation for negative numbers may initially confuse students. The numeral -3 is made from two symbols, yet it represent a single number, just as 17 is two symbols representing a single number, and just as $2/3$ represents a single number. In particular, the minus sign in the numeral -3 does not refer to subtraction (although we will make a connection to subtraction later).

The full number line appears naturally in measurements. One nice application is the thermometer, where one sees the need for negative numbers. Other applications include elevation (feet above sea level), timelines (marked in units of time before and after a chosen "time zero"), and bank accounts (dollars of credit or debit). In each of these applications we are making measurements in which "less than zero" is a realistic possibility. These applications can help students see the utility of negative numbers.

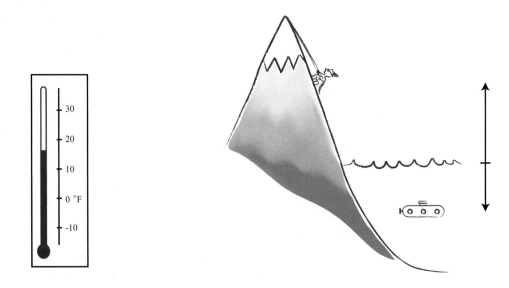

The number line model beautifully illustrates three important concepts about the integers.

less than

- The integers are ordered: We say "a is less than b" and write $a < b$ whenever b is to the right of a on the number line.

absolute value

- The *absolute value* of an integer a, written $|a|$, is the distance between a and zero on the number line. Thus $|6| = 6$ and $|-6| = 6$.

opposite

- Each integer a has an *opposite*, namely the integer, denoted $-a$, with the same absolute value on the opposite side of zero. The operation "take the opposite" can be visualized by putting a pin in the number line at 0 and rotating by $180°$. The opposite of a positive number is negative, the opposite of a negative number is positive, and zero is its own opposite.

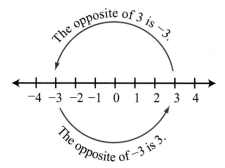

Notice that rotating $180°$ twice returns each number to where it started. That illustrates the general principle "the opposite of the opposite is the original number." This principle, written using letters, is our first rule about integers:

Rule 1: $-(-a) = a$ for any integer a.

The words "for any integer number a" should be emphasized. Rule 1 works for negative numbers as well as positive numbers: starting from -5 and taking the opposite twice brings you back to -5. Unfortunately, many students develop a bad habit of assuming that letters always stand for positive numbers; they understand that the letter a in Rule 1 might be 1, 3, or 945, but do not realize that it can also be -5 or -389. Algebra teachers should guard against accidentally promoting this bad habit by offering frequent examples and problems in which letters represent negative numbers.

One should also be cautious about reading too much into Rule 1. Because it looks like the statement that $(-1) \cdot (-1) = 1$, it is tempting to use Rule 1 to explain the fact that "a negative times a negative is a positive" to students. But that is not correct because we have not yet linked "take the opposite" to multiplication by -1 (we will do that in the next section).

Integer Addition

Addition of integers is usually introduced using models with the goal of building intuition and making students comfortable with negative numbers. Whichever model is used, the teaching of addition requires considering four cases. Two cases use the interpretations of addition already familiar to the students, while the other two cases require a new idea. We will illustrate the four cases using the number line model.

- **Positive + Positive.** In this case we can use the familiar "counting on" interpretation of addition, visualized as steps on a number line:

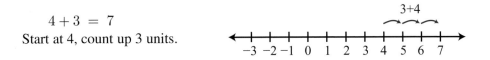

$4 + 3 = 7$
Start at 4, count up 3 units.

This corresponds to situations like "We had \$4 and earned \$3 more" or "The elevator started on the 4th floor and went up 3 more floors."

- **Negative + Positive.** Even though this involves a negative number, the "counting on" interpretation still applies:

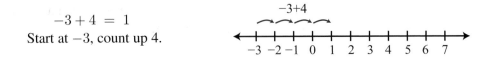

$-3 + 4 = 1$
Start at -3, count up 4.

Some motivational word problems are "The outside temperature started at $-3°$ and rose $4°$. What was the temperature then?" and "Jimmy owed a friend \$3. After he earned \$4, how much money was his to spend?"

- **Positive + Negative.** This is the key case. The "counting on" interpretation suggests that the way to find $4 + (-3)$ is to

$$\text{Start at } 4 \text{ and count up } -3.$$

But what does "count up -3" mean? Our old interpretation of addition is inadequate for this case, and must be extended to apply to negative numbers. We can make such an interpretation using the words "opposite of":

Interpretation: "count up -3" is the opposite of "count up 3," so means "count *down* 3."

With that agreed, the model is simple:

$4 + (-3) = 1$
Start at 4, count down 3.

This can be motivated with word problems like, "If I have \$4 and I acquire a debt of \$3, how much money is mine to spend?"

Note that this interpretation is consistent with the commutative property since the interpretation implies that $-3 + 4$ and $4 + (-3)$ are equal. As we will see later, consistency with the arithmetic properties is the key to making valid interpretations.

- **Negative + Negative.** Using the same interpretation, $-4 + (-3)$ is found by starting at -4 and counting down 3, arriving at -7.

Notice that both $4 + (-3)$ and $4 - 3$ are interpreted as, "Start at 4 and count down 3," so $4 + (-3) = 4 - 3$. Thus, this interpretation motivates a second general rule of integers.

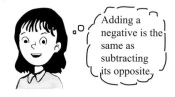

Rule 2: $a + (-b) = a - b$ for any two integers a, b.

Adding a negative is the same as subtracting its opposite.

Unfortunately, not all word problem situations work well for the last two cases. For example, the situation "Starting on the 4th floor, the elevator went up -3 floors" is not realistic (no one would say "the elevator went up -3 floors") and not helpful because it does not lead one to conclude that "count up -3" should mean "subtract 3."

Three models are frequently used to illustrate negative numbers. The first is just a neater version of the counting up/down used above.

Vector Model — Each number a corresponds to an arrow (a 'vector') along the number line with length $|a|$; positive numbers correspond to right-pointing arrows, negative numbers to left-pointing arrows. Addition is illustrated by starting at zero and laying arrows end-to-end.

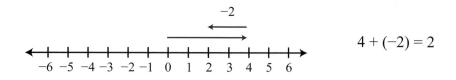

$$4 + (-2) = 2$$

What about set models? Negative numbers can't be modelled with sets — there cannot be -5 apples on the table. (This is why negative numbers are not intuitive!) To illustrate negative numbers it is necessary to use an "extended set model."

Chip Model — This extends the set model by including "negative" chips in addition to "positive" chips. The chips are round plastic disks, some black and some red (or white). It is agreed that (i) each black chip represents $+1$, each red chip represents -1, and (ii) red/black pairs cancel. Addition is illustrated by combining piles of chips and removing cancelling pairs.

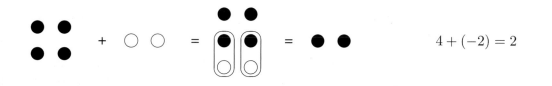

$$4 + (-2) = 2$$

problems with the chip model

The chip model can lead to problems in the classroom. It is hard to remember that black is positive and red is negative because this is a arbitrary social convention (in accounting "red ink" is debt). Similarly, there is nothing about the chips that suggests that black/red pairs should cancel; this also seems arbitrary. That can defeat the purpose, which is to show students that the rules for negative numbers are forced upon us.

Money Model — Here one uses paper money together with 'Bank debts' with negative denominations. Addition is modelled exactly as with chips, but now the connection with numbers is clear and the cancellation rule (a $1 bill cancels a $1 debt) is intuitive and easily remembered.

10		10
	10 Dollars	
10		10

-10	I owe the	-10
	Classroom Bank	
-10	10 Dollars	-10

As always, manipulatives should be used cautiously and efficiently. Before bringing out manipulatives, teachers should know exactly what concept they intend to convey, and should make the goal clear to the class. Manipulatives should then be used briefly, with the focus on the mathematics and with the class quickly returning to numbers. Manipulatives should never become a self-contained game.

In fact, *using manipulatives to teach negative numbers may be counterproductive.* The students are already familiar and comfortable with whole number operations; understanding of integer arithmetic should be built on that knowledge. Making a big production out of manipulatives risks giving students the impression that negative numbers are a difficult new concept — which isn't true.

Homework Set 34

1. Illustrate the following sums using a (i) vector model, (ii) money model, (iii) chip model:
   a) $7 + (-3)$
   b) $-8 + (-9)$.

2. *(Mental Math)* Compute the following mentally and write down your answer in a way that shows your thinking:
   a) $-984 + (537 + 984)$
   b) $136 + (-97) + (-76)$.

3. Are the following statements true or false? Give an example to illustrate your answer.

   a) Every integer is a whole number.
   b) The sum of two negative numbers is always negative.
   c) A negative number plus a positive number is always negative.
   d) A positive number plus a negative number is always negative.
   e) To add two negative numbers, we find the sum of their absolute values and take the negative sign for the answer.

4. What are the three ways the symbol "−" is used in integer arithmetic?

5. Create word problems as described:
   a) $-13 + 32$ using the vector model,
   b) $343 + (-44)$ using the money model,
   c) $-78 + (-22)$ using the vector model,
   d) $-35 + (-189)$ using the money model.

6. a) Find the absolute values: $|0|$, $|13 - 8|$, and $|8 - 13|$.
   b) For which numbers a is $-a$ positive? For which is $-|a|$ positive?
   c) A student claims that $|a| = -a$ is true only for $a = 0$. Explain why the student is wrong. What misconception does the student have about $-a$?

7. The most important facts about the absolute value are that $|a| \geq 0$ for any number a, and $|a| = 0$ only when $a = 0$. Why are these facts clear from the definition?

8. Use the vector model to verify the following identities.
   a) $a + (-a) = 0$ (draw one picture for $a > 0$, another for $a < 0$).
   b) $-(a + b) = -a - b$ (draw one picture for $a > 0, b > 0$, another for $a > 0, b < 0$ with $|b| < a$).

8.2 Arithmetic with Integers

As noted in the introduction to this chapter, teaching negative number arithmetic presents a paradox. The needed rules and their justifications are algebraic, but algebra makes sense only after one understands negative numbers. For that reason, most curricula develop negative numbers in two stages:

1. The rules of arithmetic with negative numbers are introduced using models and patterns. Students become comfortable using those rules after practicing with written problems and Mental Math.

2. As algebra is developed, it is shown that the previously learned rules (such as "negative times negative is positive") are the only rules possible if the arithmetic properties (commutative, associative, and distributive) are to hold for integers.

The previous section covered Stage 1 for addition. There we extended the interpretation of addition to the integers and wrote down convenient rules which we deduced from that interpretation. In this section we similarly extend the interpretations of subtraction, multiplication, and division. One approach to Stage 2 is described in the next section.

How does one subtract a negative number? The teaching sequence for subtraction is the same as for addition: there are the same four cases with the new interpretation again appearing in the third case. In fact, the reasoning for the third case (pos. - neg.) parallels the thinking we used for addition. We start with the "counting down" interpretation of subtraction, as in

$$7 - (-5) = \boxed{} \qquad \text{start at 7 and count down } -5.$$

But counting down -5, being the opposite of counting down 5, should be interpreted as counting *up* 5. Thus

$7 - (-5) = \boxed{}$
Start at 7, count down -5, *meaning*
Start at 7, count up 5

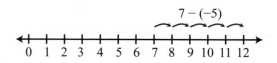

We can reach the same conclusion using the first two rules since Rule 2 (with $a = 7$ and $b = -5$) tells us that $7 - (-5) = 7 + -(-5)$, and that is the same as $7 + 5$ by Rule 1. Either way, we conclude that *subtracting a negative number is the same as adding its opposite*. That fact, written in algebraic form, is the following identity (we will not consider this a new rule because it is a consequence of Rules 1 and 2).

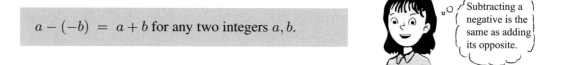

$$a - (-b) = a + b \text{ for any two integers } a, b.$$

Subtracting a negative is the same as adding its opposite.

There are other ways to help explain subtraction with negative numbers. We can use the part-whole interpretation, a pattern, a missing addend interpretation, and the arithmetic of integers to help explain why $5 - (-3) = 8$.

- Recall from Section 1.4 that in the "part-whole interpretation" subtraction is seen as the distance between points on the number line. Using it, one answers the question:

If the outside temperature falls from $5°C$ to $2°C$, what was the temperature drop?

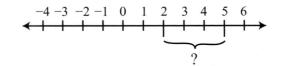

by noting that the temperature drop is the distance from 5 to 2, which is $5 - 2 = 3$. Similarly, when the subtrahend is negative we can ask:

If it falls from $5°C$ to $-3°C$, what was the temperature drop?

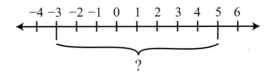

The temperature drop is still the distance on the number line, this time between -3 and 5 on the number line. Hence $5 - (-3) = 8$.

- Appeal to the pattern:

$$
\begin{aligned}
5 - 2 &= 3 \\
5 - 1 &= 4 \\
5 - 0 &= 5 \\
5 - (-1) &= \underline{} \\
5 - (-2) &= \underline{} \\
5 - (-3) &= \underline{}.
\end{aligned}
$$

- By the Missing Addend definition of subtraction, $5 - (-3)$ is the number that fills in $-3 + \underline{} = 5$. Looking at the number line, this is clearly 8.
- Since any number minus itself is zero, we can start with $(-3) - (-3) = 0$ and add 8 to both sides.

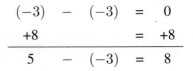

The last two approaches are, in fact, algebraic proofs (see Homework Problem 1).

Teaching comment. First or second-graders who have understood the basics of subtraction may ask, "What is $5 - 7$?" Such insightful questions can be answered by extending the number line, labeling the negative numbers, answering the question, and mentioning that negative numbers will be discussed in later grades. There is no reason for withholding this information. (On the other hand, if this question arises before subtraction is understood, it is best deferred and answered later.)

Multiplication of integers

Extending multiplication to the integers also requires considering cases. The order and the logic parallels what was done above for addition and subtraction. In the last two cases we encounter the familiar principles that "positive times negative is negative" and "negative times negative is positive."

• **Positive × Negative.** Repeated addition still works:

$$3 \times (-4) = 3 \text{ groups of } -4 = (-4) + (-4) + (-4) = -12.$$

This can be illustrated using the vector model.

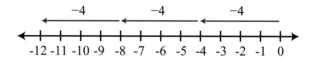

• **Negative × Positive.** The familiar interpretations of multiplication break down in this case. One cannot define -4×3 to be "-4 groups of 3." That phrase has no clear meaning. However, in the vector model there is a simple interpretation of multiplication by -4.

Interpretation: To obtain the vector corresponding to -4×3, start with the vector corresponding to 3, reverse its direction, and make it 4 times as long.

The vector corresponding to $-(4 \times 3)$ is obtained similarly: start with the vector corresponding to 3, make it 4 times as long, and then reverse its direction. These two processes obviously give the same vector. That means that $-4 \times 3 = -(4 \times 3)$, and in general

Rule 3: $-a \cdot b = -(a \cdot b)$ for any two integers a, b.

Notice that, with this interpretation, $-4 \times 3 = -12$ is the same as $3 \times (-4) = -12$. That indicates that Rule 3 is compatible with the commutative property.

In the classroom, Rule 3 can also be introduced by having students guess that -4×3 is -12, and then verifying their guess using the distributive property. That can be done by checking whether -4×3 plus 12 is zero. The check is done by writing 12 as 4×3 and using distributive property:

$$(-4 \times 3) + 12 = (-4 \times 3) + (4 \times 3) = (-4 + 4) \times 3 = 0 \times 3 = 0.$$

• **Negative** $\times$ **Negative.** The previous interpretation still works. Using it we have

$$
\begin{aligned}
-3 \times (-4) &= -(3 \times (-4)) && \text{Rule 3} \\
&= -(-12) && \text{Positive} \times \text{negative case} \\
&= 12 && \text{Rule 1.}
\end{aligned}
$$

In general:

$-a \cdot -b = a \cdot b$ for any two integers a, b.

This rule shows that "negative times negative is positive" and in particular $(-1)(-1) = 1$. We have not given it a number because it is a consequence of Rules 1 and 3.

EXERCISE 2.1. *Show that this rule follows from Rule 3, Rule 1, and the Commutative property.*

Students can also be led to these rules by an appeal to patterns, as by filling in the chart below.

$\times$	3	2	1	0	-1	-2	-3
3	9	6	3	0	_	_	_
2	6	4	2	0	_	_	_
1	3	2	1	0	_	_	_
0	0	0	0	0	_	_	_
-1	_	_	_	_	_	_	_
-2	_	_	_	_	_	_	_
-3	_	_	_	_	_	_	_

Unfortunately, models for integer multiplication are less satisfactory than for addition and subtraction. One can incorporate multiplication into the vector model by agreeing that multiplication by, say, 5 makes a vector 5 times as long, and multiplication by -5 makes it 5 times as long *and reverses its direction.*

Word problems are also not very satisfactory. Here is one approach.

$4 \cdot 3 = 12$	Getting \$3 four times is getting 12 dollars.
$4 \cdot (-3) = -12$	Paying a \$3 penalty four times is a 12 dollar penalty.
$(-4) \cdot 3 = -12$	Not getting \$3 four times is not getting 12 dollars.
$(-4) \cdot (-3) = 12$	Not paying a \$3 penalty four times is getting 12 dollars.

The interpretations in the last two cases are strained. Do you think you could explain these to a class? The fact is that relying solely on models and "real world" interpretations to explain multiplication of negative numbers makes the concept more confusing than it need be.

Division

Division is the last operation to cover. The rules for division follow easily from the rules for multiplication by using the missing factors approach. For instance, using measurement division for $-6 \div -2$ we ask "-6 is how many groups of -2?"

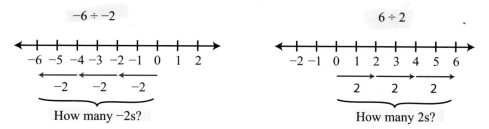

The interpretive model is the same as $6 \div 2$ (6 is how many groups of 2?) with the arrows in the opposite direction. Thus $-6 \div (-2) = 6 \div 2$ or, in fraction notation, $\frac{-6}{-2} = \frac{6}{2}$. That suggests another general rule.

Rule 4: $\quad \dfrac{-a}{-b} = \dfrac{a}{b}$ for any two integers a, b.

Continuing with fraction notation, we can combine Rules 1 and 4 to find that

$$\frac{-6}{2} = \frac{-6}{-(-2)} = \frac{6}{-2}.$$

We can also write $\frac{6}{2}$ as $6 \times \frac{1}{2}$ and apply Rule 3 to obtain

$$-\left(\frac{6}{2}\right) = -\left(6 \times \frac{1}{2}\right) = (-6) \times \frac{1}{2} = \frac{-6}{2}.$$

Putting those two equations together gives our final rule.

Rule 5: $\quad -\dfrac{a}{b} = \dfrac{-a}{b} = \dfrac{a}{-b}$ for any two integers a, b.

Algebra preparation

Once the principles of integer arithmetic are familiar, students should get plenty of practice simplifying expressions like

$$[46 + 3 \cdot (-14)] \times (45 - (-8) - 13).$$

This is algebra, done with numbers only. Students who are adept at such numerical problems will be well prepared for both the concepts and computations they will encounter in beginning algebra (see Homework Problem 3 below).

Homework Set 35

1. Show the identity $a - (-b) = a + b$ is true for any integers a and b in the following three ways.

    a) By applying Rule 2 to the expression $a - (-b)$.

    b) By the missing factor approach, the subtraction $a - (-b)$ is the number which fits into the equation $\underline{\quad} + -b = a$.

    c) By starting with $(-b) - (-b) = 0$ and adding $a + b$ to both sides.

2. Which of the models described in Section 8.1 makes it clear that $5 + (-7) + 3$ can be added in any order (with the same answer)?

    Comment. The Any-order property does not hold for subtraction since, for instance, $5 - (7 + 3) \neq (5 - 7) + 3$. However, we can always rewrite subtractions as additions using Rule 2, and then the Any-order property *does* hold. That makes algebra easier!

3. (*Mental Math*) Simplify the following expressions mentally, then check your answer by writing down a step-by-step simplification. (These are "algebra preparation" exercises.)

    a) $(23 + 26 + (-13)) \cdot 25$

    b) $(6 + (-17)) + (34 + (-13))$

    c) $(4 + 2 \cdot (113 - (-7))) \div 4$

    d) $-6 \cdot (8 - 20) \cdot 15$

    e) $268 - (4 \cdot (-15)) - (-130)$

    f) $((-84 + 76) \cdot 50) - 94$

    g) $(-97 + 113) \div (18 + (-14))$

    h) $(52 - ((9 - 22) \cdot 2)) \cdot 4$

    i) $5z + (-2z) - (2z (62 + (-57)))$

    j) $\left(x^3 - \left(3x^2 + (-2x)\right) x\right) + 2x^3$

    k) $x^2 - (-y) + (-x)\left(x + (-y^2)\right)$

    l) $((x - y)(y + x)) - (-y^2 + x^2)$

4. Suppose a is a positive number and b is a negative number (so neither is zero). State whether the following are positive or negative.

    a) ab

    b) $-ab$

    c) $-a^2 b^2$

    d) $(ab)^2$

    e) $-a \div b$

    f) $-|a - b|$

    g) b^n if n is even

    h) b^n if n is odd

    Remember, when dealing with constants, you can pick numbers for a and b mentally to help with your intuition!

5. Prove that $-a \times b = a \times -b$ for integers a, b. *Hint:* Use the following ideas in order: Rule 3, the commutative property, Rule 3 (backwards), the commutative property.

6. We can extend the usual definition of exponents to include negative exponents by setting $4^{-3} = \frac{1}{4^3}$. This is consistent with the integer and power rules:

    $$4^{-3} = 4^{0-3} = \frac{4^0}{4^3} = \frac{1}{4^3}.$$

    a) Simplify $2^{12} \cdot 12^{-5} \cdot 15^8$ until it has the form $2^a \cdot 3^b \cdot 5^c$ for whole numbers a, b, c.

    b) Similarly simplify into a fraction such that each exponent is positive:

    $$\frac{8^3 \cdot 3^{-3} \cdot 24^3 \cdot 18^5}{4^2 \cdot 9^7 \cdot 156^0}$$

    c) Do the same for $15^6 \cdot 20^{-2} \cdot 12^{-4}$.

7. a) Show that $\dfrac{1}{10^{-n}} = 10^n$.

    b) Simplify the following into a fraction with all exponents positive.

    i) $\dfrac{6^3 \cdot 3^6 \cdot 8^{-2}}{10^{-3} \cdot 15^4}$

    ii) $\dfrac{36^4 \cdot 6^{-4} \cdot 96^{-3}}{48^{-2} \cdot 15^2 \cdot 256}.$

8.3 Integers as a Step Towards Algebra

We began this chapter by introducing the integers as points on the number line. We then found interpretations of addition, subtraction, multiplication and division by looking at the models and summarized those interpretations in the five conceptual rules below. That process is probably convincing, but how do we know the models and our interpretations are correct? Is it possible that other books or other cultures have used different interpretations and been led to different rules? Is it possible to *prove* the rules?

Rule 1: $-(-a) = a$

Rule 2: $a - b = a + (-b)$

Rule 3: $-a \cdot b = -(a \cdot b)$

Rule 4: $\dfrac{-a}{-b} = \dfrac{a}{b}$

Rule 5: $-\dfrac{a}{b} = \dfrac{-a}{b} = \dfrac{a}{-b}$

A related question concerns how we simplify and rearrange expressions involving integers. We have been assuming, as in Problem 2 and 3 of the previous homework, that we can manipulate integers *exactly* as we manipulate whole numbers using the familiar properties (which we review below). Why is that correct?

Both questions have a single answer: if we want the usual properties of arithmetic to be true for integers, then the above rules *must* hold. Once we accept the arithmetic properties, we can *prove* that the five rules hold. Thus integer arithmetic can be developed by the path

Arithmetic properties $\implies$ Rules 1–5 $\implies$ Familiar integer arithmetic.

This approach is the second stage of teaching negative numbers in algebra; it uses algebraic reasoning instead of models and interpretations. This section gives some of the details.

In Chapter 4 we singled out and named the basic properties of whole number arithmetic:

1. Commutative: $a + b = b + a$, $ab = ba$,

2. Associative: $a + (b + c) = (a + b) + c$, $a(bc) = (ab)c$,

3. Distributive: $a(b + c) = ab + ac$,

4. Identities: $a + 0 = a$, $a \cdot 1 = a$.

We now add one more, an additive version of the Multiplicative Inverse Property of Section 6.6. This did not appear previously because it involves negative numbers, in fact it is essentially the algebraic definition of negative numbers:

> **Additive Inverse Property.** For each integer a there exists a unique integer called the *opposite of* a, denoted by $-a$, which satisfies
>
> $$a + (-a) = 0.$$

This clever wording is actually making two statements. It defines the opposite of a to be any integer b satisfying $a + b = 0$ and asserts that (i) such a number b always exists, and (ii) there is only one such b. Statement (ii) can be useful; it means that whenever we have an integer b with $a + b = 0$ we can conclude that $b = -a$.

EXERCISE 3.1. *Illustrate the Additive Inverse Property using a) the vector model and b) the chip model.*

With this list of properties in hand, we can give a set of theorems which show that the arithmetic properties imply the rules.

THEOREM 3.2 (Rule 1). $-(-a) = a$ *for a an integer.*

Proof.

$$
\begin{aligned}
-(-a) &= 0 + -(-a) && \text{Additive identity property}\\
&= [a + -a] + -(-a) && \text{Additive inverse property}\\
&= a + [-a + -(-a)] && \text{Associative property}\\
&= a + 0 && \text{Additive inverse property}\\
&= a && \text{Additive identity property.} \qquad \square
\end{aligned}
$$

Look at the proof above. The main idea is in the first two steps, where we add zero and replace it with $a + (-a)$. After manipulating the expression, we get a (what we want) plus another 0. This is a common proof technique called "adding an appropriate zero proof." This idea is simple, but certainly not obvious. We will use this same technique in the proofs of the next two rules.

THEOREM 3.3 (Rule 2). $a + (-b) = a - b$ *for all integers a and b.*

Proof. Using the additive identity and inverse properties, we see that

$$a = a + 0 = a + [(-b) + b] = [a + (-b)] + b.$$

Thus the number $a + (-b)$ fits in the blank in the equation $a = \underline{\quad} + b$. But according to the missing factors definition of subtraction (see page 19), the number that fits in the blank is $a - b$. Therefore $a + (-b) = a - b$. $\square$

THEOREM 3.4 (Rule 3). $-a \cdot b = -(a \cdot b)$ *for any integers a, b.*

Proof.

$$
\begin{aligned}
-a \cdot b &= -a \cdot b + 0 && \text{Why?}\\
&= -a \cdot b + [a \cdot b + -(a \cdot b)] && \text{Additive inverse property}\\
&= (-a \cdot b + a \cdot b) + -(a \cdot b) && \text{Associative property}\\
&= (-a + a)b + -(a \cdot b) && \text{Distributive property}\\
&= 0 + -(a \cdot b) && \text{Additive inverse property}\\
&= -(a \cdot b) && \text{Additive identity property.} \qquad \square
\end{aligned}
$$

The proofs of Rules 4 and 5 are homework problems. Use the justification in Section 8.2 as a guide for their proofs (replace the numbers 6 and 2 by letters a and b).

To summarize, Rules 1–5 are really forced upon us by the arithmetic properties and not the models — a distinctly algebra concept. We teach it backwards by using models and interpretations first because deriving the rules from the properties is too abstract for students until after they are comfortable with the computations. Showing that the rules are derived from the arithmetic properties is still important; students need to understand that these are the only interpretations possible and are not the arbitrary whim of their mathematics teacher.

In algebra one uses the arithmetic properties and the rules to derive many other identities. We conclude this section with some examples of such reasoning which involve inequalities. Recall that we ordered the integers in Section 8.1 by agreeing to write $a \leq b$ if a is equal to b or is to the left of b on the number line. The following properties are evident from that definition and our interpretations of addition and multiplication.

Order Properties

1. For any two numbers a and b one and only one of the statements $a < b$, $a = b$, or $a > b$ is true.

2. (Transitive property) If $a < b$ and $b < c$ then $a < c$.

3. Adding a constant to both sides does not change an inequality: if $a < b$ then $a + c < b + c$ for any c.

4. Multiplying by a positive number preserves inequalities: if $c > 0$ and $a < b$ then $ac < bc$.

One can use these Order Properties, along with the previous properties and rules, to prove other facts about inequalities. We will give two examples, and you will do similar proofs in your homework. The first is a useful fact that is clear from the number line picture.

LEMMA 3.5. *If c is a positive integer then $-c$ is negative.*

Proof.

$0 < c$	Given
$0 + (-c) < c + (-c)$	Order property 3
$-c < c + (-c)$	Additive identity property
$-c < 0$	Additive inverse property. $\qquad\square$

That was easy! In your homework you will prove the converse statement: if c is a negative integer then $-c$ is positive.

Let's try another example. Order Property 4 has a familiar companion fact: multiplying by a negative number *reverses* inequalities. Here is a proof.

THEOREM 3.6. *Suppose a, b, c are integers with $c < 0$ and $a < b$. Then $ac > bc$.*

Proof. Since $c < 0$ we have $-c > 0$ (that is the converse of Lemma 3.5 just mentioned). Hence

$a < b$	Given
$a(-c) < b(-c)$	Order property 4
$-ac < -bc$	Rule 3
$-ac + (ac + bc) < -bc + (ac + bc)$	Order property 3
$bc < ac.$	

In the last step we "cancelled opposites." That is correct because it is done using the familiar properties of arithmetic. But to see that the last step follows from the properties we must erase it and replace it with several steps:

$bc + (ac + -ac) < ac + (bc + -bc)$	Comm. and Assoc. Properties
$bc + 0 < ac + 0$	Additive Inverse Property
$bc < ac$	Additive Identity Property. $\qquad\square$

Homework Set 36

1. Prove that $-(-7) = 7$ by mimicking the proof of Theorem 3.2.

2. Prove that $-7 \cdot 5 = -35$ by mimicking the proof of Theorem 3.4.

3. Prove that $-6 \cdot -7 = 42$. Justify each step by citing one of the rules or properties stated on the first page of this section.

4. Using only the arithmetic properties, prove that $\dfrac{-a}{-b} = \dfrac{a}{b}$ for any integers a, b.

5. Using only the arithmetic properties, prove that $-\dfrac{a}{b} = \dfrac{-a}{b}$ for any integers a, b.

6. Using only the arithmetic properties, prove that $\dfrac{-a}{b} = \dfrac{a}{-b}$ for any integers a, b.

7. Prove that $(-1)a = -a$ for every integer a.

8. Insert one of the symbols $<$ or $>$ to make the following statements true.

   a) If $x > 5$, then $x + 8$ ___ 13.

   b) If $x > -3$, then $-5x + 18$ ___ 33.

9. If possible, find a pair of integers a and b which satisfies each of the following statements.

   a) $|a + b| = |a| + |b|$

   b) $|a + b| < |a| + |b|$

   c) $|a + b| > |a| + |b|$

   d) $|a + b| \le |a| + |b|$.

   Which statements a) – d) hold for all integers?

10. If $a < b$ does it follow that $a^2 < b^2$? Prove or give a counterexample.

11. If $a < b$ does it follow that $c - b < c - a$ for each integer c? Prove or give a counterexample.

12. Adapt the proof of Lemma 3.5 to prove: if c is a negative integer then $-c > 0$.

13. Prove that if two integers a and b satisfy $a < b$ then $-b < -a$.

14. Prove that $x^2 > 0$ for every integer $x \ne 0$.

    Hint: Consider the cases $x > 0$ and $x < 0$ separately. For $x > 0$ we use Order Property 4 with the appropriate choice of a, b, and c. For $x < 0$ use Lemma 3.5 and the fact that $(-x)^2 = x^2$ by Exercise 2.1 of Section 8.2.

CHAPTER 9

Decimals, Rational and Real Numbers

What exactly is "the set of numbers?" We actually have two different answers to that question. Ever since Section 1.1 we have used the number line model in which numbers are points on the number line. That geometric viewpoint makes the ordering, relative size, and closeness of numbers apparent.

It is then reasonable to say that *every* point on the line specifies a number. The numbers which arise in this way are called "real numbers."

DEFINITION 1. *A **real number** is a point on the number line.*

But numbers are more than just geometric points — they can be added, subtracted, multiplied, and divided. In previous chapters we introduced those operations in the order they are developed in elementary school, defining them first for whole numbers and then extending them first to fractions and then to negative numbers. The resulting set of numbers are called "rational numbers."

DEFINITION 2. *A **rational number** is a fraction or the negative of a fraction, i.e., a number that can be written as $\frac{a}{b}$ where a and b are integers with $b \neq 0$.*

At this point we know how to add, subtract, multiply, and divide rational numbers:

$$\frac{3}{4} - \frac{1}{2} = \frac{1}{4}, \qquad \frac{4}{9} \div \frac{2}{3} = \frac{2}{3}, \qquad \text{and} \qquad \frac{3}{5} \times \left(-\frac{4}{7}\right) = -\frac{12}{35}.$$

Thus we have two distinct descriptions of numbers: a geometric one describing real numbers as points on the number line, and an "algebraic" one describing the four operations on rational numbers. In this chapter we will explore the interesting story of how these two approaches are related, and how both are related to decimals.

9.1 Decimals

Decimals specify points on the number line by repeatedly subdividing intervals into tenths ("deci" means tenth). Just as a mailing address locates someone by specifying a state, a city in that state, a street in that city and a house on that street, a decimal number gives the "address" of a point on the number line — the digits give successively more accurate information which, together, precisely locate a single point.

decimals

This process is an extension of place value notation. Whole numbers are written as a string of digits that specify multiples of the "denominations" $1, 10, 100, 1000$, etc. according to their position. *Decimals* are numbers written with the same logical notation, but including place value positions corresponding to the denominations $\frac{1}{10}, \frac{1}{100}$, etc. obtained by dividing 1 by powers of 10. Thus each decimal has an expanded form, such as

$$8.264 \;=\; \left(8 \times 1\right) \;+\; \left(2 \times \frac{1}{10}\right) \;+\; \left(6 \times \frac{1}{100}\right) \;+\; \left(4 \times \frac{1}{1000}\right).$$

decimal point

Notice the role of the decimal point: it identifies the ones digit (the digit immediately to its left). That determines the place values of all the digits and allows us to distinguish the numbers 8.264, 82.64, 826.4 and 8264. Because a decimal point at the beginning of a number is hard to spot, one usually inserts an initial 0, for example writing 0.37 instead of $.37$.

The decimal 8.264 can be thought of as directions for walking along the number line starting at 0: take 8 steps of size 1, then 2 steps of size $\frac{1}{10}$, 6 steps of size $\frac{1}{100}$, and 4 steps of size $\frac{1}{1000}$. Because the increments shrink rapidly, only a few decimal places are needed to locate a point on the number line with great precision. The system is remarkably simple and efficient.

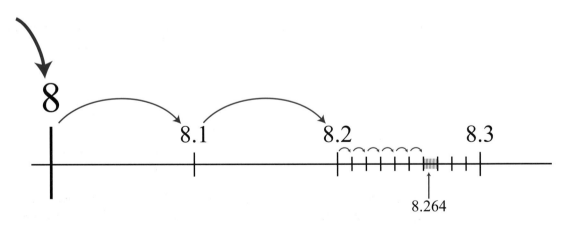

Like other place value ideas, decimals are more difficult for children than one might think. The historical record also suggests that the idea is not obvious — decimals and the decimal point were not introduced until the year 1610! Clearly, teaching decimals requires a renewed emphasis on place value notions.

The Primary Mathematics curriculum introduces decimals in the fourth grade. At that point students are familiar with addition and subtraction of fractions with like denominators (but have not yet seen multiplication and division of fractions). The students' knowledge of fractions is used to launch the topic of decimal numbers. Decimals are introduced as a new way to write tenths:

$$\frac{8}{10} \text{ cm} \quad \text{ and } \quad 0.8 \text{ cm}$$

are two ways of writing the same number. Similarly the fraction $\frac{67}{100}$ can be written as 0.67.

Decimals can be illustrated using measurement models with metric measurements and set models using chips and coins (a penny is $0.01 and a dime is $0.1 dollars).

The central idea behind decimals — that we repeatedly subdivide into ten equal parts — can be illustrated by a measurement model

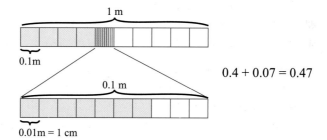

$$0.4 + 0.07 = 0.47$$

and by the area model called the *hundreds square*. Each column or row of the hundreds square represents 0.1 and each small square represents 0.01, and the appropriate area is shaded.

hundreds square

0.28

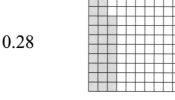

Students sometimes mistakenly depict 0.2 by shading two small squares of a hundreds square. That error can be exposed and corrected by first illustrating 2 tenths and then overlaying a hundreds square.

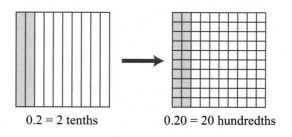

0.2 = 2 tenths   0.20 = 20 hundredths

EXERCISE 1.1. *Here are some problems that help students convert between fractions and decimals and understand the use of place value concepts for decimals. (Fill in the blanks as you read.)*

- 0.2 *cm is* $\dfrac{2}{\boxed{}}$ *of 1 centimeter.*

- $\dfrac{12}{10} = \boxed{}$ *tenths* $=$ *10 tenths* $+$ $\boxed{}$ *tenths* $= 1 + 0.2 =$ _____.

- $0.01 = \dfrac{1}{100} = $ *1 hundredth.*

- $0.37 = \dfrac{3}{10} + \dfrac{7}{\boxed{}} = 0.3 +$ _____.

- $\$0.43 = 43$ *cents* $= \dfrac{43}{\boxed{}}$ *of a dollar* $=$ *4 dimes and 3 pennies.*

Operations with Decimals

The basic place value principle of whole number addition — "add the ones, tens, and hundreds separately, regrouping when necessary" — carries over to decimals. Chip models make that clear.

EXAMPLE 1.2. *Find* $3.62 + 5.8$.

$$
\begin{array}{r}
1 \\
3.62 \\
+\ 5.8 \\
\hline
9.42
\end{array}
$$

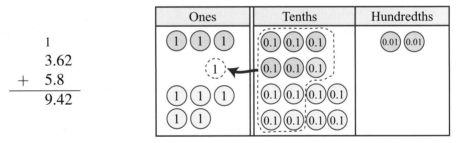

Notice that aligning the decimal point automatically aligns the ones, tenths, and hundredths columns. Once that is understood, the chip model is no longer needed.

EXAMPLE 1.3. *Find* $4.4 - 2.28$.

In the chip model, this subtraction involves decomposing one tenth into 10 hundredths. To clarify that in the algorithm it is helpful to rewrite 4.4 as 4.40. The problem is then the same as $440 - 228$ when we count in hundredths.

$$
\begin{array}{r}
{}^{3}{}^{10} \\
4.\cancel{4}\,\cancel{0} \\
-2.2\,8 \\
\hline
2.1\,2
\end{array}
$$

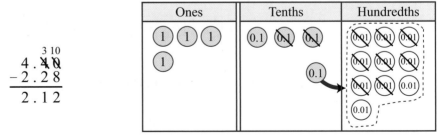

We can multiply a decimal by a whole number by a similar approach: convert a whole number multiplication problem by counting in tenths, hundredths, or thousandths. Multiplication by a small whole number can again be illustrated by a chip model.

EXAMPLE 1.4. *Find* 1.42×3.

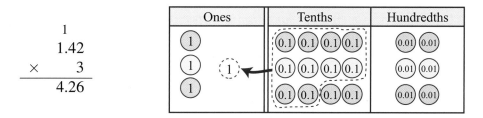

$$
\begin{array}{r}
1 \\
1.42 \\
\times \quad 3 \\
\hline
4.26
\end{array}
$$

The two approaches to long division described in Section 3.4 also carry over to decimal division (we will give examples below). All four algorithms for decimals are covered at the beginning of Primary Math 4B; that placement provides an opportunity for students to review the algorithms in a new context.

Multiplying and Dividing by 10

One fact about decimals is especially important: one can multiply and divide by 10 simply by shifting the decimal point. This is another fact about place value which *must be taught explicitly*. The idea can be introduced using money and chip models. Given a pile of pennies and dimes, we can create a pile of coins worth ten times as much by replacing each penny with a dime, and each dime with a dollar. When that replacement is recorded in a place-value chart it appears as a shift to the left, or equivalently a shift of the decimal point.

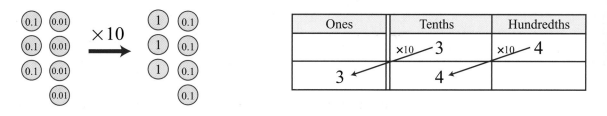

$$0.34 \times 10 = 3.4$$

Similar pictures show that one divides by 10 by shifting the decimal point one place to the left.

This shift in the decimal point can also be explained using fractions:

$$0.234 \times 10 \ = \ \frac{234}{1000} \times 10 \ = \ \frac{234}{100} \ = \ 2.34.$$

EXERCISE 1.5. *Calculate* $5.7 \div 100$ *by converting to fractions, dividing, and converting back to decimals.*

These examples demonstrate the very useful *shifting procedure:*

- To multiply a decimal number by 10, shift the decimal point 1 place to the right. To multiply by 100, shift the decimal point 2 places to the right, etc.

- To divide by 10, 100, etc., similarly shift the decimal point to the left.

Multi-digit decimal multiplication and division

Teaching students how to multiply and divide decimals does not require returning to first principles and using chip models. It is much more efficient to build on students' knowledge of whole number and fraction arithmetic. In fact, it is easy to multiply decimals by converting to fractions, multiplying the fractions, and converting back to decimal notation. For example,

$$2.17 \times 3.4 = \frac{\square}{100} \times \frac{34}{10} = \frac{217 \times 34}{1000} = \frac{7378}{1000} = 7.378.$$

In the numerators of this calculation we see the whole number multiplication $217 \times 34 = 7378$. The denominators show that the number of decimal places in the answer (namely 3) is the sum of the number of decimal places in 1.02 and 2.3 (2 in the first, 1 in the second). That observation leads to a general procedure for decimal multiplication.

---

1. Erase the decimal points and multiply the factors as if they were whole numbers.

2. Insert a decimal point in the product so that the total number of decimal places is the same on the two sides of the equation.

There are two alternative ways to locate the decimal point.

2'. By estimating. In the example above, the estimate $2.17 \times 3.4 \approx 2 \times 3 = 6$ shows where to insert the decimal point in the digits 7378.

2". By shifting decimal points. Using compensation we can multiply one factor by 10 or 100 and divide the other factor by the same amount without changing the answer. This is done by shifting the decimal point in opposite directions on the two factors.

$$0.08 \times 206 = 8 \times 2.06 \approx 8 \times 2 = 16$$

The same principles apply to division. Compensation now says that the shifts should be in the *same* direction; that allows us to convert any decimal division to a division problem involving only whole numbers. For example,

$$162.800 \div 0.037 = 162800 \div 37.$$

This is obvious in fraction form: multiplying numerator and denominator by 1000 shows that

$$162.8 \div 0.037 = \frac{162.8}{0.037} = \frac{162800}{37}.$$

EXAMPLE 1.6. *Estimate* $0.52 \div 2.9$, *then find the value to 2 decimal places.*

Rounding, we see that $0.52 \div 2.9 \approx 0.5 \div 3$, which is between 0.1 and 0.2. For better accuracy, we can convert $0.52 \div 2.9$ to the whole number division $5.2 \div 29$ and use long division:

```
         0 . 1  7  9
   29 |  5 . 2
       - 2 . 9
         2 . 3  0
       - 2 . 0  3
           2  7  0
         - 2  6  1
                 9
```

$\implies$ $\boxed{0.52 \div 2.9 \approx 0.18}$

Such examples lead to a general procedure for dividing a decimal by another decimal:

1. Shift the decimal point of the divisor to make it a whole number and then shift the decimal point of the dividend the same number of places.

2. Find the quotient by long division, aligning the decimal points of the quotient and the dividend.

Homework Set 37

1. Write each of the following in decimal form.

   a) $4 \times 10 + 3 \times 1 + 2 \times \dfrac{1}{10} + 8 \times \dfrac{1}{100}$

   b) $7 \times \left(\dfrac{1}{10}\right)^2 + 3 + 5 \times \left(\dfrac{1}{10}\right)^7$

   c) $18 \times \left(\dfrac{1}{10}\right)^5$

2. *(Mental Math)* Calculate mentally and show how you did it.

   a) $17.32 - 9.97$

   b) $3.2 \times 5.3 + 1.1 \times 3.2$

   c) $3.7 + 33.8 + 6.3$

   d) 1.7×1.7

   e) 1.6×1.8

   f) $12 \times 10,010$

   g) $32 \div 16000$

   h) $52,000,000 \div 130,000$

   i) 0.032×0.0010001

3. *(Mental Math)* Estimate using Simple Estimation (see Section 3.5).

   a) $48.2 \div 2.8$ b) 0.21×125.2

   c) $13,345 \div 652$ d) 0.49×0.0057

   e) $0.035 \div 0.0068$ f) 14.2×16.3

4. Round off the following.

   a) What is 0.01739 to the nearest thousandth? To the nearest ten thousandth?
   b) What is 0.0495 to the nearest hundredth? To the nearest thousandth?

5. Daniel writes $0.4 < 0.13$ "because 4 is less than 13." Explain the correct reasoning

   a) by drawing hundredths charts,
   b) by a number line picture, and
   c) by converting to fractions.
   d) For which of your explanations does it help to write 0.4 as 0.40?

6. Illustrate the following problems using chip models as in Chapter 3.

   a) $5.73 + 1.67$ b) $5.3 - 1.72$

   c) $6.002 - .324$ d) 3.85×3

7. Create a teaching sequence for decimal addition, that is, write down a sequence of 4–6 problems that lead students from the easiest decimal addition to the hardest decimal addition (see Section 3.1).

8. Find $56.4 \div 3$ by long division and label the steps using the partitive interpretation as in Examples 4.2 and 4.4 of Section 3.4.

9. Find $5.75 \div 0.25$ by long division and label the steps using a measurement interpretation as in Section 3.4.

10. Without doing division, put the following three numbers in order beginning with the smallest.

$$1.78 \div 0.0047 \qquad 17.8 \div 0.47 \qquad 17.8 \div 4.7$$

11. Use long division to find (a) $0.01378 \div 2.6$ and (b) $0.07296 \div 0.24$.

9.2 Rational Numbers and Decimals

As we saw in the last section, decimals can be written as fractions. Everyone should know a few such equivalences, including

$$0.5 = \frac{1}{2}, \qquad 0.25 = \frac{1}{4}, \qquad 0.75 = \frac{3}{4}, \quad \text{and} \quad 0.1 = \frac{1}{10}.$$

In this section we will investigate the relationship between fractions and decimals in general.

It is always easy to convert decimals into fractions: 0.38 is 38 hundredths, or $\frac{38}{100}$. That is the whole story, except that we may want to express the fractions in simplest form, as in

$$0.2572 = \frac{2572}{10000} = \frac{1286}{5000} = \frac{643}{2500} \quad \text{and} \quad 3.5 = 35 \text{ tenths} = \frac{35}{\Box} = \frac{\Box}{2}.$$

The denominators which occur in these fractions are special. Before simplifying, the denominator is a power of 10, so has the form $10^n = (2 \cdot 5)^n = 2^n \cdot 5^n$. When we simplify, some of these factors of 2 and 5 may cancel with factors in the numerator. But after cancellation, the denominator of the fraction is still a product of 2's and 5's.

In the other direction, some fractions are easily converted into decimals. One method is to multiply by 1 in the form $\frac{2}{2}$ or $\frac{5}{5}$ until the denominator is a product of an *equal number* of number of 2's and 5's, so is a power of 10.

EXAMPLE 2.1.

a) $\dfrac{71}{100} = 0.71$ *Simple!*

b) $\dfrac{3}{5} = \dfrac{3}{5} \cdot \dfrac{2}{2} = \dfrac{6}{10} = 0.6$ *Introduce a factor of 2 to make the denominator 10.*

c) $\dfrac{3}{25} = \dfrac{3}{5 \cdot 5} \cdot \dfrac{2 \cdot 2}{2 \cdot 2} = \dfrac{12}{100} = 0.12$ *Introduce 2's to make the denominator a product of an equal numbers of 2's and 5's.*

d) $\dfrac{7}{250} = \dfrac{7}{2 \cdot 5 \cdot 5 \cdot 5} =$ *You try it!*

Fractions can also be converted to decimals by noting that $\frac{a}{b}$ is $a \div b$, which we can find by long division. For example, one sees that $\frac{7}{16} = 0.4375$ by using long division to find $7 \div 16$:

$$
\begin{array}{r}
0.\,4\ \ 3\ \ 7\ \ 5 \\
16\,\overline{)\,7.\,0\ \ 0\ \ 0\ \ 0} \\
\underline{-6\ \ 4} \\
6\ \ 0 \\
\underline{-4\ \ 8} \\
1\ \ 2\ \ 0 \\
\underline{-1\ \ 1\ \ 2} \\
8\ \ 0 \\
\underline{-8\ \ 0}
\end{array}
$$

This division can also be done on a calculator. However, as we will explain shortly, students who do not learn to convert fractions to decimals by long division will be unable to see an important aspect of the relation between fractions and decimals.

finite decimals

The above examples are all *finite decimals* — decimals which can be written with a finite number of digits. But some fractions cannot be written as finite decimals. For example, long division as above for $1 \div 3$ shows that $\frac{1}{3} = 0.33333\ldots$ and similarly

$$\frac{1}{6} = 0.166666\ldots \qquad \text{and} \qquad \frac{1}{12} = 0.0833333\ldots$$

with digits repeating without end. Thus some fractions correspond to *repeating decimals*.

repeating decimals

When students are first learning to convert fractions to decimals, it is important to avoid repeating decimals. The following fact is a way for teachers to quickly recognize whether a fraction is a finite decimal or not. Notice that it applies only when the fraction is *in simplest form*.

Rational-Decimal Fact 1. *A rational number, given as $\frac{a}{b}$ in simplest form can be written as a finite decimal if and only if the denominator b is a product of 2's and 5's only.*

Proof. We have already mentioned that any finite decimal can be written

$$\frac{\text{integer}}{10^n} = \frac{\text{integer}}{2^n \cdot 5^n}.$$

There may be cancellation, as in the example

$$0.884 = \frac{884}{10^3} = \frac{884}{2^3 \cdot 5^3} = \frac{\cancel{2} \cdot 442}{\cancel{2} \cdot 2^2 \cdot 5^3} = \frac{\cancel{2} \cdot 221}{\cancel{2} \cdot 2 \cdot 5^3} = \frac{\square}{\square},$$

but the denominator is still a product of 2's and 5's.

How about the other way? Why can a rational number whose denominator is a product of 2's and 5's be written as a finite decimal? Such a number can be written as $\dfrac{N}{2^n \cdot 5^m}$ where N is an integer and n, m are whole numbers. We can then multiply by factors of $\frac{2}{2}$ or $\frac{5}{5}$, as we did in Examples 2.1c and 2.1d above, until the powers of 2 and 5 in the denominator pair up to form a power of 10. For instance,

$$\frac{78}{2^2 \cdot 5^6} = \frac{78}{2^2 \cdot 5^6} \cdot \frac{2}{2} \cdot \frac{2}{2} \cdot \frac{2}{2} \cdot \frac{2}{2}$$

$$= \frac{78 \cdot 2 \cdot 2 \cdot 2 \cdot 2}{2^6 \cdot 5^6}$$

$$= \frac{78 \cdot 16}{(2 \cdot 5)^6}$$

$$= \frac{1248}{1,000,000} = 0.001248.$$

This method works whenever the denominator is a product of 2's and 5's only. □

EXERCISE 2.2. *Four of the following numbers can be written as finite decimals.*

$$\frac{3}{25} \quad \frac{2}{33} \quad \frac{7}{40} \quad \frac{9}{128} \quad \frac{50}{62} \quad \frac{9}{75}$$

Which four? Remember to reduce to simplest form first!

Now suppose we are given a fraction which does not meet the criterion of Rational-Decimal Fact 1, that is, a fraction in simplest form whose denominator has a factor other than 2 or 5 in its prime factorization. We can still find its decimal equivalent by long division. Here is an example.

EXAMPLE 2.3. $\dfrac{14}{33} = 0.424242\ldots$.

After two steps, the calculation repeats. That is not a coincidence. Here is another example.

EXAMPLE 2.4. $\dfrac{23}{66} = 0.3484848\ldots.$

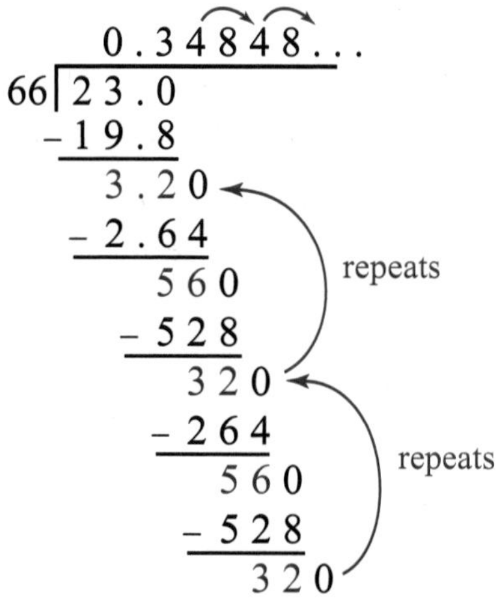

$$
\begin{array}{r}
0.34848\ldots \\
66\overline{\smash)23.0} \\
-19.8 \\
\hline
3.20 \\
-2.64 \\
\hline
560 \\
-528 \\
\hline
320 \\
-264 \\
\hline
560 \\
-528 \\
\hline
320
\end{array}
$$

repeats

repeats

repetend

Notice the remainders (shown in blue). Whenever a remainder repeats, the calculations between the repeating remainders also repeat, which means the digits in the quotient also repeat. We call the shortest sequence of repeating digits in the quotient the *repetend* and identify it by writing a bar over the repeating digits. In the above example, the repetend in $0.34848484\ldots$ is 48 and so we write it as $0.3\overline{48}$.

EXAMPLE 2.5. $\dfrac{1}{7} = 0.\overline{142857}.$

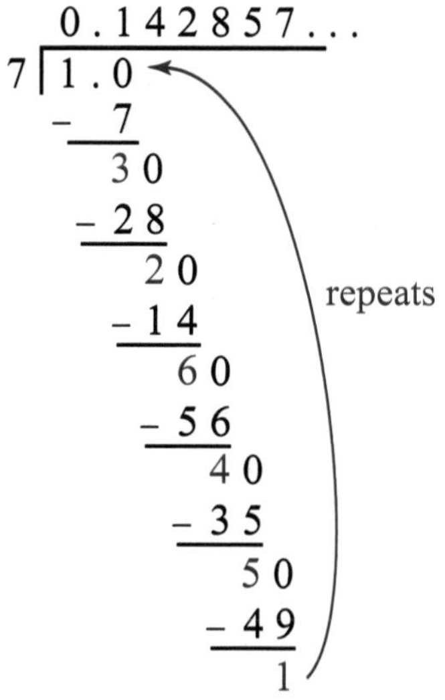

$$
\begin{array}{r}
0.142857\ldots \\
7\overline{\smash)1.0} \\
-7 \\
\hline
30 \\
-28 \\
\hline
20 \\
-14 \\
\hline
60 \\
-56 \\
\hline
40 \\
-35 \\
\hline
50 \\
-49 \\
\hline
1
\end{array}
$$

repeats

period

The number of digits in the repetend is called the *period*. The period of $0.\overline{42}$ is 2 and the period of $0.\overline{142857}$ is 6.

Rational-Decimal Fact 2. *Every rational number can be written as a finite or repeating decimal.*

Proof. To convert $\frac{a}{b}$ to a decimal we calculate $a \div b$ by long division. At each step in the long division the remainder r is a whole number with $0 \leq r < b$.

If $r = 0$, then the long division algorithm stops and the fraction can be represented by a finite decimal.

If $r \neq 0$, then the remainder must be a number from the following list: $1, 2, 3, \cdots, b - 1$. For instance, looking at the calculation $1 \div 7$ for $\frac{1}{7}$ the remainders are (in the ordered calculated) $3, 2, 6, 4, 5, 1$; each is greater than 0 and less than 7. Since there are only 6 possible remainders, one must repeat by the seventh step. In general, there are only $b - 1$ possibilities for the remainder r, hence a remainder must repeat after at most b steps. But as we noted after Example 2.4, once a remainder repeats, the entire long division repeats and therefore digits in the quotient repeat. $\square$

EXAMPLE 2.6. *Convert $\dfrac{1}{17}$ into a repeating decimal. (To speed such calculations, it helps to first make a table of multiples like the one on the left.)*

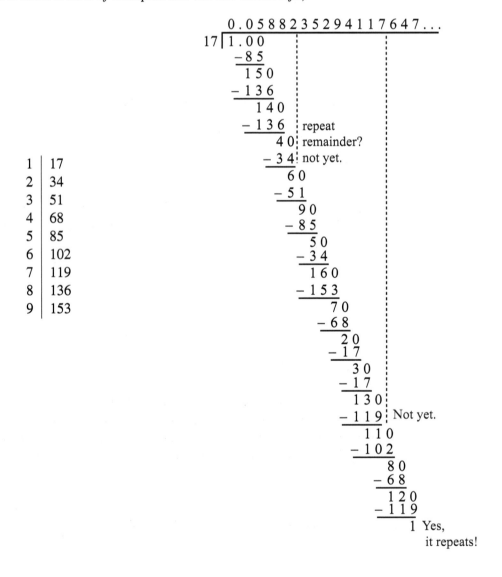

Notice that a calculator does not show that $\frac{1}{17}$ repeats! The main mathematical concept of this section — that fractions can be represented as finite or repeating decimals – can only be understood by students who know the long division algorithm.

There are two things to keep in mind when calculating a repetend. First, the period of the repetend is not always one less than the denominator as in the previous two examples ($\frac{1}{7}$ has period 6, $\frac{1}{17}$ has period 16). For instance, $\frac{1}{13} = 0.\overline{076923}$ has period 6, not 12. Second, *look for repeating remainders, not repeating digits in the quotient.* For example, while calculating $0.34\overline{83782}$ some students will stop after they find the second 8 and assume that the repetend is 837.

Our last rational-decimal fact states that we can convert repeating decimals to fractions.

Rational-Decimal Fact 3. *Every repeating decimal is a rational number.*

This is true because there is a specific algorithm for converting a repeating decimal to a fraction. We will explain that algorithm using a series of examples.

EXAMPLE 2.7. *Write $0.\overline{17}$ as a fraction.*

Let $x = 0.\overline{17}$. Multiply by 100 and subtract:

$$
\begin{array}{rcl}
100x &=& 17.171717\ldots \\
-\quad x &=& 0.171717\ldots \\
\hline
99x &=& 17
\end{array}
$$

Solving this equation shows that the repeating decimal $0.\overline{17}$ is $\frac{17}{99}$. This procedure works because multiplying by 100 shifts the digits so that the infinite repeating parts are aligned, so cancel when we subtract. This technique always works, with shifts coming from multiplying by *some* power of 10.

EXAMPLE 2.8. *Written as a fraction $0.\overline{361}$ is $\frac{361}{999}$.*

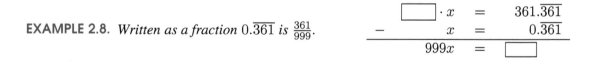

$$
\begin{array}{rcl}
\boxed{} \cdot x &=& 361.\overline{361} \\
-\qquad x &=& 0.\overline{361} \\
\hline
999x &=& \boxed{}
\end{array}
$$

After seeing a few such examples, students often suggest a way of instantly writing down a repeating decimal as a fraction: divide the repetend by the number obtained by replacing each digit of the repetend by a 9. Thus, for example, $0.\overline{1456} = \frac{1456}{9999}$. That is correct, but this "rule" works only for special repeating decimals. It does not work for the next example.

EXAMPLE 2.9. *Written as a fraction $0.11\overline{32}$ is $\frac{1121}{9900}$.*

$$
\begin{array}{rcl}
10\,000x &=& 1132.\overline{32} \\
-\quad 100x &=& 11.\overline{32} \\
\hline
9900x &=& \boxed{}
\end{array}
$$

In general, the method is to multiply by two different powers of 10 and subtract, choosing the powers of 10 to align the infinite repeating part. Subtraction then gives an equation of the form

$$(\text{whole number}) \cdot x = (\text{whole number}).$$

Solving for x then gives x as a fraction.

The discussion of this section can be neatly summarized as a single theorem.

THEOREM 2.10 (Rational-Decimal Correspondence).

1. *Every rational number can be written as a finite or repeating decimal, and vice versa.*

2. *The decimal is finite $\Longleftrightarrow$ in simplest form the denominator is a product of 2's and 5's only. Otherwise, the decimal repeats with period less than the denominator.*

Homework Set 38

1. Express the following as fractions in simplest form.

   a) 0.125   b) 0.0875

   c) 0.525   d) 0.28125

2. Can the fraction be written as a finite decimal? If so, use the method of Exercise 2.1 in this section to convert to decimal form.

   a) $\dfrac{137}{625}$ b) $\dfrac{221}{1500}$

   (c) $\dfrac{27}{180}$ d) $\dfrac{123}{184}$

   e) $\dfrac{44}{260}$ f) $\dfrac{84}{350}$

3. *(No calculator!)*   Write the following fractions as finite or repeating decimals (the last one is a challenge).

   a) $\dfrac{3}{8}$ b) $\dfrac{23}{20}$

   c) $\dfrac{11}{21}$ d) $\dfrac{24}{9}$

   e) $\dfrac{3}{13}$ f) $\dfrac{36}{60}$

   g) $\dfrac{17}{22}$ h) $\dfrac{3}{29}$

4. Write the following as fractions in simplest form.

   a) $0.\overline{1}$ b) $0.\overline{01}$

   c) $0.\overline{001}$ d) $0.234\overline{0}$

   e) $0.\overline{189}$ f) $0.5\overline{05}$

   g) $8.1\overline{23}$ h) $2.31\overline{56}$

   i) $3.\overline{3890129}$ j) $1.23\overline{451}$

5. a) Use the method of Examples 2.7, 2.8, and 2.9 to find $0.\overline{9}$ in simplest form.
    b) What is $4329.\overline{9}$?

6. a) Make a table of the multiples of 19 up to 9×19 and use long division to find the decimal expansion of $1/19$. What is its period?

b) Without doing any further division, find the decimal expansion of 3/19. Explain your reasoning.

c) Compute 1/19 on your calculator. Does it appear to repeat?

7. *(Mental Math)* Use the facts $0.\overline{01} = \frac{1}{99}$ and $0.\overline{001} = \frac{1}{999}$ to mentally convert these decimals to fractions.

a) $0.\overline{03}$

b) $0.\overline{324}$

c) $5.\overline{32}$

d) $0.\overline{983}$

8. Finding patterns is a useful way to guess an answer, but it can be misleading.

a) Fill in the blanks

$$\frac{1}{11} + \frac{1}{2} = \frac{13}{22},$$

$$\frac{1}{11} + \frac{101}{200} = \frac{}{2200},$$

$$\frac{1}{11} + \frac{10101}{20000} = \frac{}{220000},$$

$$\frac{1}{11} + \frac{101010101}{200000000} = \underline{}$$

b) Use a calculator to write the last fraction above as a decimal. Guess the repetend.

c) Next, write $\dfrac{1}{11}$ as a repeating decimal.

d) Write $\dfrac{1}{2}$, $\dfrac{101}{200}$, $\dfrac{10101}{20000}$, and $\dfrac{101010101}{200000000}$ as finite decimals.

e) Add your answers to (c) and (d) to find the decimal expression for the last fraction in part (a). What is the repetend? Was you guess in (b) correct?

9.3 Real Numbers and Decimals

Every rational number is a point on the number line (see the introduction to Chapter 6), and is therefore a real number. But is every point on the number line a rational number? This question is trickier than it might seem. Pick a point P on the number line at random.

Is P a rational number? How can you even tell? One way is to write P as a decimal and check whether the decimal repeats. If it does then, as we have seen, P is a rational number. But how does one write P as a decimal? That question can be answered by repeatedly subdividing the number line into tenths.

Procedure for associating a decimal expansion to a point. Suppose we are given a point P between 3 and 4 on the number line and asked to write it as a decimal. Here is a systematic way of doing that.

What is the decimal expansion of P?

First, subdivide the interval between 3 and 4 into tenths. If P happens to be one of the finite decimals 3.1, 3.2, ..., 3.9 then we're done. Otherwise, P lies in one of the 10 smaller intervals: 3 to 3.1, 3.1 to 3.2, etc.

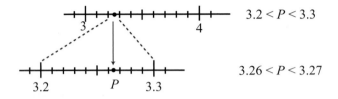

$3.2 < P < 3.3$

In the example shown, P lies between 3.2 and 3.3. Subdivide this interval into hundredths. Again, if P happens to be one of the finite decimals 3.21, 3.22, ..., 3.29 then we have finished out task.

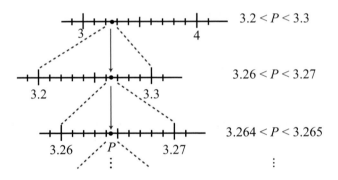

$3.2 < P < 3.3$

$3.26 < P < 3.27$

However, in this example P lies in the interval between 3.26 and 3.27, so we repeat the procedure, subdividing the interval from 3.26 to 3.27 into ten intervals of equal length.

$3.2 < P < 3.3$

$3.26 < P < 3.27$

$3.264 < P < 3.265$

Each time we subdivide an interval into tenths, we check if P is one of the nine new end-points. If not, we locate the interval P lies in, subdivide that interval into ten equal length intervals, and repeat.

decimal expansion This procedure generates a list of digits called the *decimal expansion* of the number P. If the procedure stops after a finite number of steps, then P is a finite decimal. Otherwise the procedure generates an infinite list of digits, so P has an infinite decimal expansion. Of course, we cannot write down infinitely many digits; we simply write

$$P = 3.264\ldots$$

where the dots indicate whatever additional digits are produced by the procedure.

EXAMPLE 3.1. *(a) Thinking of $\frac{3}{4}$ as a point on the number line, the procedure above generates the decimal expansion 0.75.*

(b) Thinking of $\frac{1}{3}$ as a point on the number line, the procedure above generates the infinite decimal expansion $0.\overline{3} = 0.333\ldots$.

There is one subtlety: the above procedure does not produce every possible list of digits. For example, $0.9999\ldots$ never arises. To understand this, consider the following alternative way of associating a decimal expansion to each point on the number line.

Alternative Procedure. Given a point P between 3 and 4 we proceed as before. In fact, if P is not a finite decimal we proceed exactly as before and obtain the same infinite decimal expansion for P. But if P is a finite decimal — say 3.2 — then at some stage in the procedure P is the point separating two adjacent subintervals. At that stage *we make a choice*, either considering P to be the endpoint of the interval from 3.19 to 3.20, or the beginning point of the interval from 3.20 to 3.21. Once that decision is made there are no further choices. We continue subdividing intervals into tenths and recording which subinterval P lies in, now regarding the endpoints as part of the subintervals. As the picture shows, we end up with two infinite decimal expansions for P, namely

$$3.1999\ldots \quad \text{and} \quad 3.2000\ldots$$

(the finite decimal 3.2 is *not* one of the possibilities). We again call these decimal expansions of P.

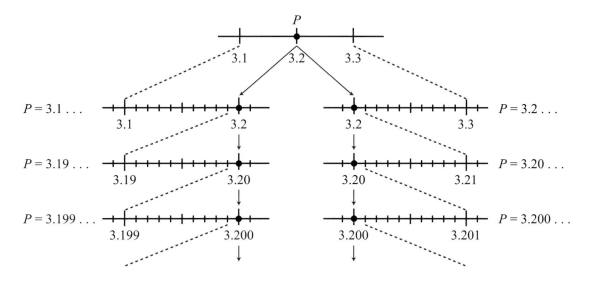

Comparing the two procedures, we see that each finite decimal has several decimal expansions. This is related to Problem 5 of Homework Set 38, where you showed that

$$1 = 0.999\ldots.$$

In general, each finite decimal (except 0) can be rewritten as an infinite decimal in two ways: by appending an infinite tail of zeros, or by reducing its last nonzero digit by 1 and appending repeating nines. For example,

$$26 = \begin{cases} 26.000\ldots \\ 25.999\ldots \end{cases} \qquad 140 = \begin{cases} 140.000\ldots \\ 139.999\ldots \end{cases} \qquad 7.28 = \begin{cases} 7.28000\ldots \\ 7.27999\ldots. \end{cases}$$

The Alternative Procedure produces all possible infinite lists of digits. In other words, every infinite list of digits is the "address" (in the sense of the Alternative Procedure) of some real number P. For example, given an infinite list of digits starting with $5.3964\ldots$ one can look at the interval from 5 to 6, then the interval from 5.3 to 5.4, then the interval from 5.39 to 5.40, etc. This produces an infinite list of nested intervals, each 1/10 the size of the previous one. It is a fundamental fact about the number line that there is one and only one point P which is simultaneously in *all* these intervals (this fact must actually be included as part of the definition of the number line). The given infinite list of digits is one of the decimal expansions of that point P.

Of course, there is no point in regarding 0.3, 0.30, 0.300, and $0.3\overline{0}$ as different decimal expansions. Thus we agree to drop all finite or infinite strings of zeros at the end of any decimal expansion. With that agreed, our conclusions about the decimal expansions of real numbers are summarized as follows.

THEOREM 3.2 (Real-Decimal Correspondence).

1. *Every real number P has a decimal expansion. That decimal expansion is unique (if we ignore ending zeros as above) unless P is a non-zero finite decimal, in which case P has exactly two decimal expansions, one finite, and one ending in an infinite tail of nines.*

2. *Conversely, every decimal expansion specifies a real number.*

At the beginning of this section we posed the question of whether every real number is rational. We can now answer that question. By Theorem 3.2 every real number has a decimal expansion. On the other hand, we know from the previous section that the decimal expansions of rational numbers are either finite or repeating. Thus decimal expansions which are infinite and non-repeating specify real numbers which are not rational. It is not hard to create such decimal expansions.

EXAMPLE 3.3. *Consider the infinite decimal expansion which starts with 0.101 and continues with two 0's and a 1, three 0's and a 1, four 0's and a 1, etc.*

constructing
irrational numbers

$$0.101001000100001\ldots.$$

This expansion is neither finite nor repeating, so the corresponding real number is not rational.

It is easy to modify this example to produce a great many infinite, non-repeating decimal expansions. These real numbers are called irrational.

DEFINITION 3.4. *An **irrational number** is a real number which is not rational (that is, one that cannot be written as $\frac{a}{b}$ for integers a and b).*

This is quite a discovery — a new type of number! This discovery broadens our understanding of the number line. On the number line there are two types of numbers. Each number is either rational or irrational (but not both). Most familiar are the rational numbers, which have finite or repeating decimal expansions. But there are also irrational numbers, which have infinite non-repeating decimal expansions. At this point we know little else about irrational numbers. We will take a close look at some particular irrational numbers in the next section.

Approximating real numbers

Imagine marking all the rational numbers on a number line. One approach is to mark all the multiples of $\frac{1}{2}$ (including negative multiples), then all the multiples of $\frac{1}{3}$, then of $\frac{1}{4}$, etc. Doing this, one quickly discovers that the rational numbers are dispersed along the entire number line and that there are rational numbers in any interval — however small — on the number line. As a result, we can approximate any real number by rational numbers.

approximation

To talk about approximations, we must be clear about (i) what kind of numbers are allowable as approximations, and (ii) how accurate an approximation is desired. In the following discussion our approximations will be rational numbers — in fact finite decimals. We will specify the desired accuracy by requiring that the approximation be within $\pm.01$, or $\pm.001$, or $\pm.0001$, etc., of the given number.

EXAMPLE 3.5. *From the decimal expansion $\frac{1}{7} = 0.142857\ldots$ we see that*

- 0.14 *is an approximation of $\frac{1}{7}$ with an accuracy of $\pm.01$,*
- 0.143 *is an approximation of $\frac{1}{7}$ with an accuracy of $\pm.001$.*

A more familiar example is approximations of π. Recall that π is a real number with a geometric definition (for any circle, the length of the circumference divided by the length of the diameter is a number, called π).

EXAMPLE 3.6. *From the decimal expansion $\pi = 3.14159265\ldots$ we see that*

- 3.14 *is an approximation of π with an accuracy of $\pm.01$,*
- 3.1416 *is an approximation of π with an accuracy of $\pm.00001$.*

Each of these approximations is obtained by truncating the decimal expansion, or by truncating and rounding off. We can use the same method to approximate any real number. We will state that observation as a theorem, using the term "any desired accuracy" to mean "within $\pm.01$, $\pm.001$, $\pm.0001$, etc. — whichever one you specify."

THEOREM 3.7. *Any real number can be approximated to any desired accuracy by a rational number.*

Proof. Each real number x has a decimal expansion. To approximate x to within $\pm 10^{-n}$ we simply truncate that expansion after the nth decimal place. The result is a finite decimal, so is a rational number, and by subtraction we see that the difference is less than 10^{-n}. □

Theorem 3.7 is a testimony to the amazing usefulness of decimal notation, which we first discussed in Section 1.1 in the context of preschool mathematics, and which continues to prove itself to be an extremely convenient and efficient way of writing numbers. As an application of Theorems 3.2 and 3.7 we will next see how to define addition, subtraction, multiplication, and division of real numbers.

Operations on real numbers

In earlier chapters we carefully developed arithmetic for whole numbers, fractions, and negative numbers. But those previous definitions do not tell us how to add, subtract, multiply, and divide real numbers. What, for example, is $\frac{2}{3} \div \pi$? Since real numbers are specified by their decimal expansions that is the same as asking "What is the decimal expansion of $\frac{2}{3} \div \pi$?" To answer, we approximate $\frac{2}{3}$ and π by truncating their decimal expansions and dividing. We then repeat using better and better approximations. Since $\frac{2}{3} = 0.6666\ldots$ and $\pi = 3.14159\ldots$ we can begin with

$$
\begin{aligned}
0.66 \div 3.14 &= \mathbf{0.21}01910828025477\ldots \\
0.66666 \div 3.14159 &= \mathbf{0.2122}046479648840\ldots \\
0.66666666 \div 3.14159265 &= \mathbf{0.2122065}889096092\ldots \\
0.666666666666 \div 3.14159265358979 &= \mathbf{0.2122065907}889817\ldots.
\end{aligned}
$$

In each step we are dividing finite decimals, which we already know how to do. Looking at the boldface digits, it is clear in this example – and it can be proved in general — that this process yields better and better approximations to a single decimal expansion, in this case

$$
\frac{2}{3} \div \pi = 0.212206590789193781025\ldots.
$$

That decimal expansion specifies a real number, which we *define* to be the quotient $\frac{2}{3} \div \pi$.

All four operations — addition, subtraction, multiplication and division — can be defined for real numbers in a similar way. Notice that at each stage we are working with rational numbers, so the arithmetic properties (commutative, associative, etc.) hold. It follows that *all of the properties and rules listed in Sections 6.6 and 8.3 hold for real numbers, and those of Section 6.6 apply to "fractions" $\frac{a}{b}$ where a and b are themselves real numbers (such as $3\pi/4$).* In school mathematics that fundamental fact is always tacitly assumed, but the reasoning described above is seldom given.

arithmetic properties for real numbers

We began this section by noting that real numbers are points on the number line. We saw that each real number is specified by its decimal expansion(s). For finite decimals, the decimal expansion specifies the number precisely. Otherwise, the decimal expansion is, in effect, a list of better and better approximations to the real number.

Decimal expansions are not the only way to specify real numbers. Certain real numbers arise in geometry (such as the number π), and others arise in algebra (such as the solutions $\pm\sqrt{2}$ of the equation $x^2 = 2$). It is often best to give these numbers names and work with them directly, calculating their decimal expansions only in the end, if needed. Beginning in middle school, students learn to routinely work with such "named numbers" and describe them by a variety of notations such as $\sqrt[3]{7}$, $8^{2/5}$, $\log 5$, and $\sin 43°$. Thus it is important that students learn about real numbers in grade 6 or 7, and that they fully understand how real numbers are related to decimal expansions.

Homework Set 39

1. Arrange the following real numbers in increasing order.

   a) 0.45

   b) $0.\overline{45}$

   c) $0.4\overline{55}$

   d) $0.454454445\ldots$

   e) $0.\overline{455}$

   f) $0.45545554\ldots$

   g) $0.454455444555\ldots$

2. Find a rational number between $\frac{3}{8}$ and $\frac{5}{9}$, one between $\frac{4}{13}$ and $\frac{5}{13}$, and one between 1.729999 and 1.73.

3. *(Calculator)* Find a rational number between $\frac{\sqrt{2}}{7}$ and $\frac{\sqrt{2}}{9}$.

4. Use the trick of Example 3.3 to find an irrational number between $\frac{1}{2}$ and $\frac{5}{9}$.

5. Find two irrational numbers whose sum is rational.

6. For the real numbers $\sqrt{5} = 2.23606797749\ldots$ and $\pi = 3.14159265358\ldots$, calculate the following *without a calculator* (show your work).

   a) Find $\sqrt{5} + \pi$ to an accuracy of $\pm 10^{-8}$.

   b) Find $\sqrt{5} \times \pi$ to an accuracy of $\pm .001$.

7. Suppose x is an irrational number.

   a) Prove that $\frac{3}{7}x$ is also irrational. (*Hint:* Suppose that $\frac{3}{7}x = \frac{a}{b}$ for some integers a and b, solve for x and contradict the fact that x is irrational.)

   b) Prove that
   $$\frac{p}{q}x + \frac{c}{d}$$
   is irrational whenever $p, q, c,$ and d are integers.

9.4 Newton's Method and $\sqrt{2}$

We have learned that some real numbers are not rational. At this point, though, it looks like irrational numbers are just theoretical — we cannot write down their decimal form (each has infinitely many digits!), so they seem to be of little consequence. But in fact, irrational numbers occur naturally and are used often. In this section we will describe a method for calculating square roots to any desired accuracy. We will also prove that the frequently used numbers $\sqrt{2}$ and $\sqrt{3}$ are irrational.

We begin by investigating $\sqrt{2}$ in detail. First, $\sqrt{2}$ is a real number because it corresponds to a point on the number line, constructed as follows. Create a right triangle which has both shorter sides of length 1. By the Pythagorean Theorem the length of the hypotenuse is $\sqrt{1^2 + 1^2} = \sqrt{2}$. Using a compass, we can then locate $\sqrt{2}$ as in the diagram below.

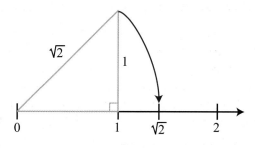

This shows that $\sqrt{2}$ is a specific real number. But it does not explain how to write down $\sqrt{2}$ as a decimal.

The following exercise shows an elementary way to find the first few digits of $\sqrt{2}$. It uses only one fact: a number x is smaller than $\sqrt{2}$ if $x^2 < 2$, and is bigger than $\sqrt{2}$ if $x^2 > 2$.

EXERCISE 4.1. *(Calculator) Square the numbers and fill in the blanks to find the interval that contains* $\sqrt{2}$.

(a)
$$1^2 = \underline{\quad}$$
$$(1.1)^2 = \underline{\quad}$$
$$(1.2)^2 = \underline{\quad}$$
$$(1.3)^2 = \underline{\quad}$$
$$(1.4)^2 = \underline{\quad}$$
$$(1.5)^2 = \underline{\quad}$$
$$(1.6)^2 = \underline{\quad}$$

Therefore $\underline{\quad} < \sqrt{2} < \underline{\quad}$

(b)
$$(1.4)^2 = \underline{\quad\quad}$$
$$(1.41)^2 = \underline{\quad\quad}$$
$$(1.42)^2 = \underline{\quad\quad}$$
$$(1.43)^2 = \underline{\quad\quad}$$
$$(1.44)^2 = \underline{\quad\quad}$$
$$(1.45)^2 = \underline{\quad\quad}$$

Therefore $\underline{\quad} < \sqrt{2} < \underline{\quad}$

(c) Find the next digit in the same way. In principle that involves squaring ten numbers, but you should be able to zero in on the interval containing $\sqrt{2}$ *more quickly. Write down only the squares of the two numbers which define that interval.*

There are other algorithms for finding $\sqrt{2}$ which are much more efficient. We will next use a picture and some simple algebra to derive a very efficient algorithm called "Newton's Method." To start, consider a square with sides of length $\sqrt{2}$; its area is $\sqrt{2} \times \sqrt{2} = 2$. Take an approximation to $\sqrt{2}$, say $A = 1.4$ ('A' for 'Approximation'). We can use this approximation to break up the square into four smaller rectangles.

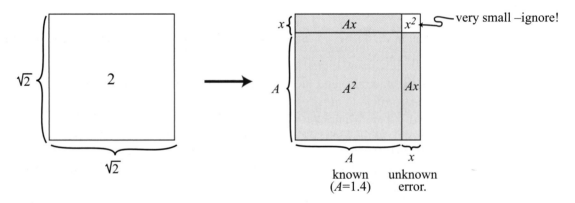

The only number we do not know is x; let's see if we can approximate it. The shaded region has area $A^2 + 2Ax$. That is almost the same area of as the entire square, which is 2. Thus

$$A^2 + 2Ax \approx 2.$$

Temporarily assuming this is an equality we can solve for x to get

$$2Ax \approx 2 - A^2 \quad \Longrightarrow \quad x \approx \frac{2 - A^2}{2A} = \frac{2}{2A} - \frac{A^2}{2A} = \frac{1}{A} - \frac{A}{2}.$$

(If you want, you can replace each letter 'A' in this calculation with its numerical value 1.4, but that makes the calculation harder to read!) We now have an approximated value for x in terms of A. That can be substituted into the original expression $\sqrt{2} = A + x$, giving

$$\sqrt{2} \approx A + \left(\frac{1}{A} - \frac{A}{2}\right) = \frac{A}{2} + \frac{1}{A}.$$

What have we learned? Starting with an approximation A for the $\sqrt{2}$ we found a new approximation

$$A_{new} = \frac{A}{2} + \frac{1}{A}.$$

This number A_{new} is a better approximation of the $\sqrt{2}$ than A. For instance, starting from $A = 1.4$,

$$A_{new} = \frac{1.4}{2} + \frac{1}{1.4} = \frac{7}{10} + \frac{5}{7} = \frac{99}{70}.$$

The decimal expansion of $\frac{99}{70} = 1.414\ldots$ is a better approximation of $\sqrt{2}$ than 1.4! Applying the boxed formula to *that* number gives an even better approximation. We can repeat as many times as we like, obtaining better and better approximations to $\sqrt{2}$ — in fact, the number of correct digits *doubles* with each iteration! Here are the first three iterations starting with $A = \frac{7}{5}$:

A	A_{new}			Decimal Expansion
$\frac{7}{5}$	$\longrightarrow$	$\frac{7}{10} + \frac{5}{7} = \frac{99}{70}$		$1.414\ldots$
$\frac{99}{70}$	$\longrightarrow$	$\frac{99}{140} + \frac{70}{90} = \frac{19601}{13860}$		$1.4142135\ldots$
$\frac{19601}{13860}$	$\longrightarrow$	$\frac{19601}{27720} + \frac{13860}{19601} = \frac{768398401}{543339720}$		$1.41421356237309504999\ldots.$

This last approximation gives the $\sqrt{2}$ to 17 correct decimal places — compare it to the correct value to 20 decimal places, which is

$$\sqrt{2} = 1.41421356237309504880\ldots.$$

This iterative procedure becomes an algorithm once we specify a stopping point. We can do that by comparing two successive approximations. For example, to find $\sqrt{2}$ to 10 correct decimal places we continue until A_{new} and A agree to 10 decimal places, then stop and take A_{new} as our answer. In fact, that is the algorithm simple calculators use to approximate the value of $\sqrt{2}$.

The logic underlying these calculations bears emphasis. First, $\sqrt{2}$ is a real number, so has a *specific* decimal expansion ($\sqrt{2}$ is not 1.414 followed by an infinite number of random digits, as some students mistakenly believe). We can use the above algorithm to calculate that decimal expansion to any accuracy. The algorithm produces a list of *rational* numbers (the fractions in the center column of the above chart) which are better and better approximations to $\sqrt{2}$. As we proceed, we uncover more and more digits of the decimal expansion of $\sqrt{2}$. We stop when the desired accuracy is achieved.

This algorithm is easily modified to calculate other square roots. A geometric construction like the one at the beginning of this section shows that each whole number N has a positive square root, that is, there is a real number x such that $x^2 = N$ (See Homework Problem 1). If we go back through our derivation, replacing 2 with the positive number N, we get an algorithm for approximating the $\sqrt{N}$.

Newton's Method for Approximating $\sqrt{N}$:

Start with an initial approximation A (which can be any positive number) and repeatedly apply the formula

$$A_{new} = \frac{A}{2} + \frac{N}{2A}.$$

Note that when $N = 2$ this agrees with the formula for approximating the $\sqrt{2}$. The term "Newton's Method" refers to a general method of this type described by Sir Isaac Newton around 1669 (See Homework Problems 9 and 10).

EXAMPLE 4.2. *Approximate $\sqrt{3}$ by using three iterations of Newton's Method starting with $A = \frac{3}{2}$.*

A	A_{new}		Decimal Expansion
$\dfrac{3}{2}$	$\longrightarrow$	$\dfrac{3}{4} + \dfrac{3}{2} \cdot \dfrac{2}{3} = \dfrac{7}{4}$	**1.75**.
$\dfrac{7}{4}$	$\longrightarrow$	$\dfrac{7}{8} + \dfrac{3}{2} \cdot \dfrac{4}{7} = \dfrac{97}{56}$	**1.732**142...
$\dfrac{97}{56}$	$\longrightarrow$	$\dfrac{97}{112} + \dfrac{3}{2} \cdot \dfrac{56}{97} = \dfrac{18817}{10864}$	**1.7320508**1001...

(The boldface digits are correct.)

Square Roots as Irrational Numbers

Is $\sqrt{2}$ rational? Calculating the decimal expansion, even to a million digits, does not help answer this question. No amount of calculation can tell us whether $\sqrt{2}$ is rational or irrational. Yet the answer was known to Pythagoras 2500 years ago! The key is to use deductive reasoning — to use logic instead of calculations. The remainder of this section presents one version of Pythagoras' reasoning (there are many).

We begin with an explanation suitable for elementary or middle school students. Suppose that $\sqrt{2}$ could be written as a fraction in simplest form, say as

$$\sqrt{2} = \frac{22}{15}.$$

Squaring both sides, we find that

$$2 = \left(\frac{22}{15}\right)^2 = \left(\frac{2 \cdot 11}{3 \cdot 5}\right)^2 = \frac{2 \cdot 2 \cdot 11 \cdot 11}{3 \cdot 3 \cdot 5 \cdot 5}.$$

But the righthand side is a fraction in simplest form (there are no cancellations!), so it cannot be a whole number.

EXERCISE 4.3. *Repeat this to show that $\sqrt{2}$ cannot be $\frac{35}{24}$, and cannot be $\frac{75}{53}$.*

In every case the reasoning is the same: if the original fraction is in simplest form, so is its square, and hence the square cannot equal 2. Thus no fraction is equal to $\sqrt{2}$, which means that $\sqrt{2}$ is irrational.

Some students might notice that the same reasoning shows that $\sqrt{3}$ and $\sqrt{5}$ are irrational; in fact it seems to show that $\sqrt{N}$ is irrational for any whole number N. But be careful: it is *not true* that square roots are always irrational. Some, such as $\sqrt{1}$, $\sqrt{4}$, and $\sqrt{9}$, are obviously rational — they are whole numbers. Theorem 4.4 below clarifies this point.

To make a precise proof, we simply repeat the "elementary school reasoning" described above, using letters to denote "any fraction." We first clarify a simple fact used in the above argument.

Simple fact. A fraction in simplest form is a whole number only if its denominator is 1.

This is evident to students who are experienced in simplifying fractions. Yet it is something that perhaps becomes less clear the more you think about it. Here is a "teacher knowledge" proof.

Proof. Suppose that a fraction $\frac{a}{b}$ is equal to a whole number N. Multiplying $\frac{a}{b} = N$ by b gives $a = Nb$. Therefore b is a factor of a, so the fraction can be simplified (by cancelling a factor of b) unless $b = 1$. □

We can now prove that $\sqrt{2}$ is irrational. The following proof uses the above "simple fact," and is easy enough for middle school students.

THEOREM 4.4. $\sqrt{2}$ *is irrational. In fact,* $\sqrt{N}$ *is irrational for every whole number N which is not a square ($N \neq 0, 1, 4, 9, 16, \ldots$).*

Proof. Suppose that $\sqrt{N}$ can be written as a fraction $\frac{a}{b}$ in simplest form. Writing out the prime factorizations of a and b, we have

$$\sqrt{N} = \frac{a}{b} = \frac{p_1 \cdot p_2 \cdots p_k}{q_1 \cdot q_2 \cdots q_\ell}$$

with no cancellations, that is, none of the primes in the denominator appears in the numerator. Squaring gives a fraction

$$N = \left(\frac{a}{b}\right)^2 = \frac{p_1^2 \cdot p_2^2 \cdots p_k^2}{q_1^2 \cdot q_2^2 \cdots q_\ell^2}$$

which also has no cancellations, so cannot be a whole number unless the denominator is 1. That occurs only when $N = (a/1)^2 = a^2$ is the square of a whole number (namely the number a). Thus $\sqrt{N}$ can be written as a fraction only when N is a square. □

There are dozens of other proofs that $\sqrt{2}$ is irrational, including many that can be understood — and enjoyed — by able middle school students.

Homework Set 40

1. The picture at the beginning of this section can be extended to the picture below. (a) What is the number x in this extended picture? How was it constructed in this extended picture? (b) Draw a similar picture which constructs $\sqrt{5}$, $\sqrt{6}$, and $\sqrt{7}$.

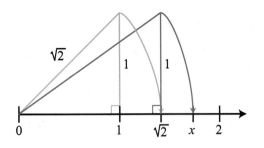

2. *(Calculator)* Use Newton's Method to approximate $\sqrt{2}$ by applying Newton's formula 3 times, taking your first approximation to be

   a) 1   b) $\frac{2}{3}$

   c) 5   d) -1.

3. After the first picture in this section, we did a calculation that lead to a formula for approximating $\sqrt{2}$. Use the same calculation (but replacing some of the 2's with n) to find Newton's formula for approximating $\sqrt{n}$.

4. a) *(Calculator)* Approximate $\sqrt{11}$ by applying Newton's formula in the previous exercise two times starting with $A = 3$.

   b) If one uses Newton's formula to find the $\sqrt{100}$ starting from $A = 10$, what is your next approximation A_{new}?

5. The "elementary student reasoning" given above Exercise 4.3 shows that $\sqrt{2}$ is irrational, but obviously cannot show that $\sqrt{9}$ is irrational. Give a one sentence explanation of why that reasoning fails for $\sqrt{9}$.

6. Use the fact that $\sqrt{2}$ is irrational to prove that $\sqrt{\sqrt{2}}$ is irrational.

7. Prove that $\sqrt[3]{2}$ is irrational by adapting the proof of Theorem 4.4 ($\sqrt[3]{2}$ is the real number x such that $x^3 = 2$.)

8. A student conjectures that $\sqrt{a+b} = \sqrt{a} + \sqrt{b}$. Using an instructional counterexample, how would you respond?

9. "Newton's Method" is a general method to approximate the roots of polynomial equations. Newton illustrated it with the example $z^3 - 2z - 5 = 0$. As the graph shows, there is a single value of z which solves this equation; that solution (the "root") is near $z = 2$. To find it, Newton started with the approximation 2, wrote the root as $z = 2 + x$, and tried to solve for the correction x.

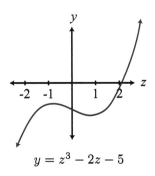

$$y = z^3 - 2z - 5$$

   a) By substituting $z = 2 + x$ into $z^3 - 2z - 5 = 0$ and simplifying, show that x satisfies $x^3 + 6x^2 + 10x - 1 = 0$. Since x is small, the x^2 and x^3 terms are very small. Newton therefore simplified this equation for x to $10x - 1 \approx 0$. The solution is $x \approx 0.1$ and so the root is $z \approx 2.1$.

   b) Find the next approximation by writing $z = 2.1 + x$ and repeating the procedure.

10. a) Use the algebraic method of the previous problem to derive Newton's Method for approximating $\sqrt{n}$, namely $A_{new} = \frac{A}{2} + \frac{n}{2A}$. *Hint*: $\sqrt{n}$ is a root of the equation $z^2 - n = 0$. Starting with an approximation A, write $z = A + x$, substitute and omit the x^2 term, and solve for x.

   b) Do the same to find Newton's Method for approximating $\sqrt[3]{n}$.

   c) *(Calculator)* Approximate $\sqrt[3]{10}$ by starting at $A = 2$ and applying Newton's Method twice. Find the answer first as a fraction then convert to decimals, and compare with your calculator's answer for $\sqrt[3]{10}$. How many correct digits did you get?

Bibliography

[1]   Adler, David (1987). *Roman Numerals*. HarperCollins.

[2]   American Council on Education. (1999). *To touch the future: Transforming the way teachers are taught*. Washington, DC: American Council on Education.

[3]   Anderson, J.R. (2000). *Learning and Memory, Second Edition*. New York: Wiley.

[4]   Anderson, J.R. (2000). *Cognitive Psychology and its Implications, Fifth Edition*. New York: Worth Publishing.

[5]   Anderson, J.R., Reder, L.M., and Simon, H.A. (1996). Situated learning and education. *Educational Researcher*, **25**, 5–11.

[6]   Anderson, J.R., Reder, L.M., and Simon, H. (1998). Radical constructivism and cognitive psychology. In D. Ravitch (Ed.), *Brookings papers on education policy 1998*. Washington, D.C.: Brookings.

[7]   Anderson, J.R., Simon, H.A., and Reder, L.M. (non-published). Applications and misapplications of cognitive psychology to mathematics education.

[8]   Anderson, J.R., Simon, H.A., and Reder, L.M. (1997). Rejoiner: Situative versus cognitive perspectives: Form versus substance. *Educational Researcher*, **26**, 18–21.

[9]   Askey, R., (1999). Knowing and teaching elementary mathematics. *American Educator*, **23**, 6–13.

[10]   Ball, D. (1990). Prospective elementary and secondary teachers' understanding of division. *Journal for Research in Mathematics Education*, **21(2)**, 132–144.

[11]   Ball, D. L., Lubienski, S. T., and Mewborn, D. S. (2001). Research on teaching mathematics: The unsolved problem of teachers mathematical knowledge. In V. Richardson (Ed.), *Handbook of research on teaching* (4th ed., pp. 433456). Washington, DC: American Educational Research Association.

[12]   Beaton, A.E., Mullis, I.V.S., Martin, M.O., Gonzalez, E.J., Kelly, D.L., and Smith, T.A. (1996). *Mathematics Achievement in the middle school years: IEA's Third International Mathematics and Science Study (TIMSS)*. Chestnut Hill, MA: Boston College.

[13]   Baumert, J., Kunter, M., Blum, W., Brunner, M., Voss, T., Jordan, A. Klusmann, U., Krauss, S., Neubrand, M., Tsai, Y-M. (2011). Teachers Mathematical Knowledge, Cognitive Activation in the Classroom,and Student Progress. *American Educational Research Journal*, March 2010, **47(1)**, 133–180.

[14]   Boysen, S.T. and Berntson, G.G. (1989). Numerical competence in a chimpanzee (*Pan troglodytes*). *Journal of Comparative Psychology*, **103**, 23–31.

[15]   Common Core State Standards Initiative. *Common Core State Standards for Mathematics*. Avaliable at www.corestandards.org.

[16] Conference Board of the Mathematical Sciences (2001). The Mathematical Education of Teachers. *Issues in mathematics education*, **11**.

[17] Conference Board of the Mathematical Sciences (Draft). The Mathematical Education of Teachers II. `http://www.cbmsweb.org/MET2/MET2Draft.pdf`.

[18] Cooper, G. and Sweller, J. (1987). Effects of schema acquisition and rule automation on mathematical problem-solving transfer. *Journal of Educational Psychology*, **79**, 347–362.

[19] Crosswhite, F.J. (1986). *Second international mathematics study: Detailed report for the United States.* Champaign, IL: Stipes.

[20] Crosswhite, F.J., Dossey, J., Swafford, J., McKnight, C., and Cooney, T. (1985). *Second international mathematics study. Summary report for the United States.* Champaign, IL: Stipes.

[21] Dempster, F.N. (1992) Using Tests to promote Learning: a neglected classroom resource. *Journal of Research and Development in Education*, **25(4)**, 213-217.

[22] Dewey, J. (1902/1975). The child and the curriculum. In M. Dworkin (Ed.). *Dewey on education: Selections* (pp. 91–111). New York: Teachers College Press.

[23] Fennema, E., Wolleat, P.L., Pedro, J.D., and Becker, A.D. (1981). Increasing women's participation in mathematics: An intervention study. *Journal for Research in Mathematics Education*, **12**, 3–14.

[24] Fomin, D., Genkin, S., and Itenberg, I. (1996). *Mathematical Circles (Russian Experience).* American Mathematical Society.

[25] Fuson, K.C. and Kwon, Y. (1992). Korean children's understanding of multidigit addition and subtraction. *Child Development*, **63**, 491–506.

[26] Fuson, K.C., Stigler, J.W.., and Bartsch, K. (1977). Grade placement of addition and subtraction topics in Mainland China, Japan, the Soviet Union, Taiwan, and the United States. *Journal for Research in Mathematics Education*, **Vol. 19, No. 5**, 449–456.

[27] Gelfand, I.M. and Shen, A. (1993). *Algebra.* Boston: Birkhäuser.

[28] Gaslin, W.L. (1975). A comparison of achievement and attitudes of students using conventional or calculator-based algorithms for operations on positive rational numbers in ninth-grade general mathematics. *Journal for Research in Mathematics Education*, **6**, 95–108.

[29] Geary, D.C., Bow-Thomas, C.C., Liu, F., and Siegler, R.S. (1996). Development of arithmetical competencies in Chinese and American children: Influence of age, language, and schooling. *Child Development*, **67**, 2022–2044.

[30] Geary, D.C., Bow-Thomas, C.C., and Yao, Y. (1992). Counting knowledge and skill in cognitive addition: A comparison of normal and mathematically disabled children. *Journal of Experimental Child Psychology*, **54**, 372–391.

[31] Hatfield, L. and Kieren, T. (1972). Computer-assisted problem solving in school mathematics. *Journal for Research in Mathematics Education*, **3**, 99–112.

[32] Hill, H. C., Ball, D. L., Blunk, M., Goffney, I. M., and Rowan, B. (2007). Validating the ecological assumption: The relationship of measure scores to classroom teaching and student learning. *Measurement: Interdisciplinary Research and Perspectives*, **5(23)**, 107117.

[33] Hill, H. C., and Lubienski, S. T. (2007). Teachers mathematics knowledge for teaching and school context: A study of California teachers. *Educational Policy*, **21(5)**, 747768.

[34] Hill, H. C., Rowan, B., and Ball, D. (2005). Effects of teachers mathematical knowledge for teaching on student achievement. *American Educational Research Journal*, **42(2)**, 371406.

[35]   Hill, H. C., Schilling, S. G., and Ball, D. L. (2004). Developing measures of teachers mathematics knowledge for teaching. *The Elementary School Journal*, **105(1)**, 1130.

[36]   Hirsch, E.D., Jr. (1996). *The schools we need and why we don't have them.* New York: Doubleday.

[37]   Howe, R. (2002). Marvelous Decimals. In *Harcourt Math, Teacher's Edition,* **Vol. 1**, pages PH1–PH20. Orlando et al: Harcourt School Pubishers.

[38]   Huey, E.B. (1908/1968). *The psychology and pedagogy of reading.* Cambridge, MA: MIT Press.

[39]   Jenson, G. (2004). *Arithmetic for Teachers: With Applications and Topics from Geometry.* Providence, RI: American Mathematical Society.

[40]   Ma, L. (1999). *Knowing and Teaching Elementary Mathematics: Teachers' Understanding of Fundamental Mathematics in China and the United States.* Mahwah, NJ: Lawrence Erlbaum Assoc., Pub.

[41]   Musser, G.L., Burger, W.F., and Peterson, B.E. (2000). *Mathematics for Elementary Teachers: A contemporary approach.* New York, et al: John Wiley & Sons, Inc.

[42]   National Council of Teachers of Mathematics (1989). *Curriculum and evaluation: Standards for school mathematics.* Reston, VA: National Council of Teachers of Mathematics.

[43]   National Council of Teachers of Mathematics. (2000). *Principles and standards for school mathematics.* Reston, VA: National Council of Teachers of Mathematics.

[44]   National Council on Teacher Quality (2008). *No Common Denominator: The Preparation of Elementary Teachers in Mathematics by Americas Education Schools.*

[45]   National Mathematics Advisory Panel. (2008). *Foundations for success: The final report of the National Mathematics Advisory Panel.* Washington, DC: U.S. Department of Education.

[46]   National Research Council (2001). *Adding it up: Helping Children Learn Mathematics.* Washington, DC: National Academy Press.

[47]   Pepperberg, I.M. (2000). *The Alex Studies: Cognitive and Communicative Abilities of Grey Parrots.* Boston: Harvard University Press.

[48]   Steven, P. (1997). *How the Mind Works.* New York: W.W. Norton & Co.

[49]   Reese, C.M., Miller, K.E., Mazzeo, J., and Dossey, J.A. (1997). *NAEP 1996 Mathematics Report Card for the Nation and the States.* Washington, D.C.: U.S. Department of Education.

[50]   Rickard, T.C., Healy, A.F., and Bourne, L.E., Jr. (1994). On the cognitive structure of basic arithmetic skills: Operation, order and symbol transfer effects. *Journal of Experimental Psychology: Learning, Memory, and Cognition*, **20**, 1139–1153.

[51]   Sagher, Y. and Siadat M.V. (1997) Building Study and Work Skills in a Mathematics Classroom. (Not published, available from authors).

[52]   Sagher Y., Siadat M.V, and Hagedorn L.S. (2000) Building Study and Work Skills in a Mathematics Classroom. *Journal of General Education,* **49(2)**, 132-155.

[53]   Schilling, S. G., and Hill, H. C. (2007). Assessing measures of mathematical knowledge for teaching: A validity argument approach. *Measurement: Interdisciplinary Research and Perspective*, **5(2)**, 7080.

[54]   Schmidt, W., Houang, R., and Cogan, L., (2002). A Coherent Curriculum: The Case of Mathematics. *American Educator*, Summer Issue, 1–18. www.aft.org/american_educator/summer2002/curriculum.pdf.

[55]   Schmidt, W., McKnight, C., and Raizen, S. (1997). *A splintered vision: An investigation of U.S. science and mathematics education.* Boston: Kluwer.

[56]   Schmidt, W.H., McKnight, C.C., Cogan, L.S., Jakwerth, P.M., and Houang, R.T. (1999). *Facing the Consequences: Using TIMSS for a Closer Look at U.S. Mathematics and Science Education.* Dordrecht, Netherlands: Kluwer Academic Publishers.

[57]   Shulman, L. S. (1986). Those who understand: Knowledge growth in teaching. *Educational Researcher*, **15(2)**, 414.

[58]   Stevenson, H.W., Lee, S.Y., Chen, C., Stigler, J.W. Hsu, C.C., and Kitamura, S. (1990). Contexts of achievement: A study of American, Chinese and Japanese children. *Monographs of the Society for Research in Child Development*, **55** (Serial No. 221).

[59]   Stevenson, H.W., Lee, S.Y., and Stigler, J.W. (1986). Mathematics Achievement of Chinese, Japanese, and American Children. *Science*, **231**, 693–699.

[60]   Stevenson, H.W. and Bartsch, K. (1991). An analysis of Japanese and American textbooks in mathematics. In R. Leetsma and H. Walberg (Eds.), *Japanese Educational Productivity*. Ann Arbor, MI: Center for Japanese Studies.

[61]   Stevenson, H.W. and Stigler, J.W. (1992). *The Learning Gap*. New York: Summit Books.

[62]   Stigler, J.W. and Baranes, R. (1988). Culture and mathematics learning. In E. Rothkopf (Ed.), *Review of Research in Education*, **Vol. XV**. Washington, D.C.: American Education Research Association.

[63]   Stigler, J.W., Lee, S.Y., and Stevenson, H.W. (1987). Mathematics classrooms in Japan, Taiwan, and the United States. *Child Development*, **58**, 1272–1285.

[64]   Stigler, J.W., Lee, S.Y., Lucker, G.W., and Stevenson, H.W. (1982). Curriculum and achievement in mathematics: A study of elementary school children in Japan, Taiwan, and the United States. *Journal of Educational Psychology*, **74**, 315–322.

[65]   Stigler, J.W. and Perry, M. (1988). Mathematics learning in Japanese, Chinese, and American classrooms, In G. Saxe and M. Gearhart (Eds.), *Children's Mathematics*. San Francisco: Jossey-Bass.

[66]   Stigler, J.W. and Stevenson, H.W. (1991). How Asian teachers polish each lesson to perfection. *American Educator*, **14(4)**, 13–20, 43–46.

[67]   Stone, J.E. (1996). Developmentalism: An Obscure but Pervasive Restriction on Educational Improvement. *Education Policy Analysis Archives*, **Vol. 4, No. 8**, 1068–2341.

[68]   Szetela, W. and Super, D. (1987). Calculators and instruction in problem solving in grade 7. *Journal for Research in Mathematics Education*, **18**, 215–229.

[69]   VanLehn, K. (1990). *Mind bugs: The origins of procedural misconceptions.* Cambridge, MA: MIT Press.

[70]   Wu, H. (1996). The mathematician and the mathematics education reform. *Notices of the AMS, December 1996.*

[71]   Wu, H. (1999). Basic skills verus conceptual understanding, a bogus dichotomy. *American Educator*, **23**, 14–19, 50–52.

[72]   Zill, N. and West, J. (2001). Entering Kindergarten: A Portrait of American Children When They Begin School. Findings from the Condition of Education. National Center for Education Statistics, (Publication 2001-035) U.S. Department of Education, Washington, DC.

[73] Mathematics Frameworks and Curriculum Maps:

- California Framework.
  Website: **www.cde.ca.gov/be/st/ss/**.

- Common Core State Standards for Mathematics
  Website: **www.corestandards.org**.

- The Common Core Curriculum Mapping Project.
  Website: **www.commoncore.org**.

- Core Knowledge Sequence: Content Guidelines for Grades K–8.
  Website: **www.coreknowledge.org**.

- The NCTM (National Council of Teachers of Mathematics) framework.
  Website: **www.nctm.org**.

[74] School curriculums, textbooks, and materials:

- *(Hong Kong)* Chan, M.H., Leung, S.W., and Kwok P.M. (1996). *Pleasurable Learning Mathematics*, **Vol. 1–3**. Hong Kong: Chung Tai Educational Press.

- *(Japan)* Japanese Ministry of Education (1984). *New Mathematics,* **Vol. 7–11**. Japan: Tokyo Shoeseki Company, Ltd. Translated by Nagata, H., et. al. (1992), *Japanese Grade 7–11 Mathematics.* Chicago: University of Chicago Mathematics Project.

- *(Russia)* Moro, M.I., Bantova, M.A., and Beltyukova, G.V. (1980). *Matematika: Ucheb-nik dlya 1–10 klassa (ninth edition)*, **Vol. 1–10**. Moscow: Prosveshchenie. Translated by Silverman, R., et. al. (1992), *Russian Grade 1–10 Mathematics.* Chicago: University of Chicago Mathematics Project.

- *(Singapore)* Hong, K.T., (1999). *Primary Mathematics 1–6 (second and third editions)* Singapore: Federal Publications.

- *(Singapore)* Meng S.K. and Yoong W.K., (1997). *New Elementary Mathematics, Syllabus D*, **Vol. 1–2**. Singapore: SNP Pan Pacific Publications.

- *(Singapore/United States)* Rosenbaum Foundation (2002). *Primary Mathematics Teacher's Guide 1A and 1B.* Chicago: Rosenbaum Foundation.

- *(United States)* Fish, D. (1858). Robinson's Progressive Pratical Arithmetic. New York: Ivison, Blakeman, Taylor and Company.

- *(United States)* Foerster, P. (1999). Algebra I: Expressions, Equations, and Applications (classic edition). Menlo Park, California, et al: Addison-Wesley Publishing.

- *(United States)* French, J. (1882). Harper's Second Book in Arithmetic. New York, et al: American Book Company.

Index